ROUTLEDGE LIBRARY EDITIONS: ENVIRONMENTAL AND NATURAL RESOURCE ECONOMICS

Volume 17

T0293122

THE WELFARE ECONOMICS OF ALTERNATIVE RENEWABLE RESOURCE STRATEGIES

THE WELFARE ECONOMICS OF ALTERNATIVE RENEWABLE RESOURCE STRATEGIES

Forested Wetlands and Agricultural Production

ROBERT N. STAVINS

Routledge
Taylor & Francis Group

LONDON AND NEW YORK

First published in 1990 by Garland Publishing, Inc.

This edition first published in 2018
by Routledge
2 Park Square, Milton Park, Abingdon, Oxon OX14 4RN

and by Routledge
711 Third Avenue, New York, NY 10017

Routledge is an imprint of the Taylor & Francis Group, an informa business

British Library Cataloguing in Publication Data
A catalogue record for this book is available from the British Library

ISBN: 978-1-138-08283-0 (Set)
ISBN: 978-1-315-14775-8 (Set) (ebk)
ISBN: 978-1-138-08363-9 (Volume 17) (hbk)
ISBN: 978-1-138-08367-7 (Volume 17) (pbk)
ISBN: 978-1-315-11215-2 (Volume 17) (ebk)

Publisher's Note
The publisher has gone to great lengths to ensure the quality of this reprint but points out that some imperfections in the original copies may be apparent.

Disclaimer
The publisher has made every effort to trace copyright holders and would welcome correspondence from those they have been unable to trace.

THE WELFARE ECONOMICS OF ALTERNATIVE RENEWABLE RESOURCE STRATEGIES

Forested Wetlands and Agricultural Production

ROBERT N. STAVINS

Garland Publishing, Inc.
NEW YORK & LONDON 1990

Library of Congress Cataloging-in-Publication Data

Stavins, R. N. (Robert N.),
The welfare economics of alternative renewable resource strategies :
forested wetlands and agricultural production / Robert N. Stavins.
p. cm. — (The Environment)
Originally presented as the author's thesis.
Includes bibliographical references.
ISBN 0-8240-0440-X (alk. paper)
1. Renewable natural resources—United States—Management. 2.
Wetlands—United States—Management. 3. Wetland conservation—
United States. 4. Agriculture—Economic aspects—United States. 5.
Welfare economics. I. Title. II. Series: Environment (New York, N.Y.)
HC103.7.S73 1990   333.75—dc20
                     90-3324

PRINTED IN THE UNITED STATES OF AMERICA

P R E F A C E

to

The Welfare Economics of Alternative Renewable Resource Strategies: Forested Wetlands and Agricultural Production

Robert N. Stavins
Assistant Professor of Public Policy
John F. Kennedy School of Government, Harvard University

(March 8, 1990)

For over 200 years, wetlands have been drained, cleared, filled, and exploited for whatever resources could be extracted from them. But in their natural state, wetlands also produce significant benefits for society: filtering and purifying water; providing essential habitat for flora and fauna; regulating flows; storing water; and buffering the effects of storms.

Despite the fact that wetlands are vital elements in ecosystems, they are disappearing rapidly. Approximately 215 million acres of wetlands existed in the 48 contiguous states at the time of European settlement, but by the mid-1970's, less than half of the original wetland acreage remained. During a recent 20-year interval, wetland losses averaged 458,000 acres annually -- an area about half the size of Rhode Island. Losses in specific regions have been even more dramatic. Originally, there were 26 million acres of wetlands in the Mississippi Delta; only 5 million remain. The prairie potholes in the Upper Midwest have shrunk from 20 million to 7 million acres. Florida's Everglades covered 2.3 million acres at the turn of the century; less than half survives. And the wetlands of California's Central Valley have been reduced from 4 million to 300,000 acres.

v

If wetlands are valuable in their natural state, why are they nevertheless being so rapidly depleted? The answer is that although wetlands serve society in multiple ways, the nature of wetland benefits are such that their owners typically cannot capture those benefits for use or sale. Flood protection benefits accrue to others downstream; fish and wildlife that breed and inhabit wetlands migrate; and benefits associated with improved water quality and sediment trapping cannot be commercially exploited. Hence, for the owner of a wetland to benefit from this resource, it is often necessary to develop it. Since most wetlands are privately owned, these areas are extremely vulnerable.

A number of Federal programs are intended to protect wetlands, but Federal policies tend to push and pull wetlands in opposing directions. Some Federal programs, such as flood-control and drainage projects of the U.S. Army Corps of Engineers and the Soil Conservation Service, have been suspected of encouraging wetland conversion by reducing the cost and risk while increasing the revenue of wetland development. Simultaneously, other Federal programs, such as Section 404 of the Clean Water Act, control or manage wetland use through regulation and mitigation to offset the effects of development projects.

Shortly after his inauguration in 1989, President George Bush enunciated a policy goal of "no net loss of wetlands," but a national wetland protection policy has yet to be established to set priorities and reconcile conflicting programs. By offering funds for activities that protect wetlands with one hand and for harmful developments with the other, agencies work at cross-purposes, and Federal activities wind up being inconsistent and financially wasteful.

The research described in this work seeks to address several important policy questions associated with the ongoing depletion of forested wetlands. First, in the context of Environmental Impact Statements (EIS's), should the estimated areas of impact of Federal flood-control and drainage projects on wetlands be limited to (minimal) construction impacts, or should they include impacts which occur when such projects cause private landowners to drain and clear their wetland holdings? In more general terms, should "secondary" (economically induced) impacts of projects be considered as part of the EIS process? From a legal standpoint, the answer is clearly yes, but during the past fifteen years, in preparing their EIS's, Federal agencies typically have *not* included areas of secondary impacts, such as wetland areas cleared and drained by private landowners. The research documented in the present study makes it clear that Federal flood-control and drainage projects do indeed directly induce private landowners to convert their wetland holdings to dry croplands.[1]

By changing relative economic returns, public infrastructure investments can induce major changes in private land use, often creating significant externalities in the process. The study indicates that over 30% of the depletion of forested wetlands in the Mississippi Valley can be attributed to private decisions induced (unintentionally) by Federal water projects, despite articulated Federal policy to preserve wetlands. To carry out this analysis, a model is developed that aggregates individual land-use decisions using an assumed parametric distribution of unobserved land quality. This allows estimation of the model with a panel of counties over time. Estimated parameters are then used in dynamic, historical simulations to quantify the importance of prices, costs, Federal flood-control and drainage projects, and other factors in explaining the observed loss of wetlands.

---

[1]See: Stavins, Robert N. and Adam B. Jaffe. "Unintended Impacts of Public Investments on Private Decisions: The Depletion of Forested Wetlands." *American Economic Review*, volume 80, number 3, June 1990.

A second crucial question is whether wetland depletion and conversion to agricultural cropland has been excessive. Answering this question requires a dynamic analysis of resource exploitation in the presence of negative environmental consequences. In this study, a model of socially optimal wetland use is developed, the structure and parameters of which bear a well-defined relationship to those emerging from the private-market model of wetland exploitation. This relationship provides a basis for internalizing environmental externalities and for identifying the optimal resource-exploitation strategy. The empirical analysis again focuses on the area of severest wetland losses in the U.S., the Lower Mississippi Alluvial Plain.

At the very least, the findings presented here suggest that the land-use impacts of development projects should be candidly assessed through the process established under the National Environmental Policy Act (NEPA).[2] Whether environmental impacts together with other costs of Federal projects will be found to outweigh project benefits is a question which must be addressed on a case-by-case basis, but it is essential that "environmental impact areas" be correctly defined to include areas where drainage and clearing are induced, not simply the relatively small areas where project construction occurs. Furthermore, so-called secondary (economically induced) impacts of Federal projects of all kinds should be assessed through the existing NEPA process.

A more general implication of the analysis is that the Federal government should begin to consider ways of narrowing the gap between the actual allocation of land between forested wetlands and agricultural cropland and what appears to be the socially desirable

---

[2]See: Stavins, Robert N. "Alternative Renewable Resource Strategies: A Simulation of Optimal Use." *Journal of Environmental Economics and Management* 18(1990), in press.

configuration, whether the chosen methods of narrowing this gap involve modifications of existing programs and policies or enactment of entirely new ones. The policy tools available to the government include: changes in the way Federal flood-control and drainage projects are planned, authorized, and financed; Federal acquisition, easement, and oversight programs; provision for preferential property tax assessments; tax credits; conversion penalties (taxes); and cross-compliance legislation linked to receipt of Federal commodity program payments. In general, a central goal of new policies ought to be eliminating unwarranted public subsidies and internalizing environmental externalities.

The methodology developed here may be applied to a variety of problems in the natural resources field, and other fields of economics, as well. One timely use of this approach would be to analyze the factors causing massive losses of tropical rain forests in areas such as the Amazon basin. Other potential uses of the approach include examination of the impacts of access-road construction on Federal timber management practices, and analysis of the effects of Federal and state highway construction on urban development. Moving beyond land-use issues, the methodology could be applied elsewhere in the natural resources field to estimate socially optimal resource exploitation involving impacts on the environment. Most generally, the approach developed in this study may be used to analyze a large class of problems in economics, for which theoretical models describe individual or firm-level behavior but for which data are available only in an aggregated form.

CONTENTS

xii

TABLES

FIGURES

ACKNOWLEDGEMENTS

I am indebted to Joseph Kalt, Adam Jaffe, and Zvi Griliches, the members of my dissertation committee, for their insights, comments, advice, and encouragement. Also, I have benefitted greatly from discussions with Partha Dasgupta, Christopher Cavanagh, Peter Timmer, Robert Pindyck, Hendrik Houthakker, Mark Watson, Jon Goldstein, Larry Goulder, and Marie Lynn Miranda. The research was supported by grants from Resources for the Future, the U.S. Department of the Interior, the Environmental Defense Fund, and the U.S. Fish & Wildlife Service.

Thanks are due to participants in seminars given at several institutions: the Departments of Economics at Harvard University, the University of Michigan, and Northwestern University; the John F. Kennedy School of Government at Harvard; the School of Natural Resources at Michigan; the Food Research Institute at Stanford University; the Rand Corporation; and Resources for the Future.

I also wish to thank James T. B. Tripp of the Environmental Defense Fund's New York office for having exposed me four years ago to his contagious enthusiasm for protecting the nation's wetland resources. It was an EDF sponsored study which led to the collection of much of the data upon which this research has drawn. I am indebted to the EDF staff members and Harvard students with whom I worked on those earlier studies (Stavins 1986, 1987a, 1987b), which are antecedent to the present analysis.

It was some seven years ago that Thomas Graff and Zach Willey of EDF's California office and Phil LeVeen of the Public Interest Economics Foundation in Berkeley first introduced me to the world of natural resource and environmental policy issues; for that, I remain grateful today. Also, a continuing intellectual debt is owed to Kenneth Robinson, Bud Stanton, and Olan Forker, all of the Department of Agricultural Economics at Cornell University, for having convinced me of the importance of institutional analysis and concomitant familiarity with empirical data.

My greatest debt is owed to my wife, Joanna, who provided remarkable emotional support during the more difficult periods of thesis gestation and continuing motivation at all other times. I am also grateful to present and past fellow graduate students for their advice and encouragement; in particular, I wish to thank Ken Kuttner, Michael Mandel, Eric Mankin, and David Yates. Lastly, the emotional support of my mother and the memory of my father have provided a source of inspiration.

Nature never gives anything to anyone; everything is sold.
It is only in the abstraction of ideals that choice comes without consequences.

Ralph Waldo Emerson

CHAPTER I

INTRODUCTION: ALTERNATIVE RENEWABLE RESOURCE STRATEGIES

Forested wetlands are among the earth's most productive ecosystems, and their continuing depletion constitutes the world's most pressing land use problem. In their natural state, wetlands provide a variety of valuable ecological services, including improved water quality, erosion control, floodwater storage, provision of hardwood timber, fish and wildlife habitat, and recreational opportunities. Through development, these wetlands provide sites for agriculture, mining, oil and gas extraction, and urbanization.

Since the time of European settlement, nearly 60% of America's original endowment of 215 million acres of inland wetlands -- forested bottomlands, marshes, bogs, swamps, and tundra -- has been converted to other uses. This depletion of wetland resources has been particularly rapid during the past thirty years. What factors have caused this relatively rapid rate of depletion, and how does it compare with what would have been socially optimal? What wetland-use patterns can be expected to emerge from now through the end of the century, and how do these patterns compare with those which would be optimal from a socioeconomic perspective?

Answering these questions requires a dynamic analysis of natural resource exploitation in the presence of negative environmental consequences. In the past, an important obstacle to such analyses has been the classic aggregation problem. Typically, only by resorting to representative-firm assumptions have theoretically consistent models of rational individual behavior been used to develop econometrically estimatable models of natural resource supply. Given the heterogeneity which exists across individual endowments of many natural resources, such representative-firm models are particularly problematic.

In this study, the representative firm approach is avoided by integrating a model of unobserved heterogeneity among firms with a model of rational individual firm-level behavior. A conceptual bridge is thus formed between theoretical models of optimal behavior and statistical models of actual market performance. The methodology establishes an econometric link between dynamic optimization models of natural resource use and economic assessments of environmental externalities.

The analysis proceeds in two stages. First, a method is developed for aggregating theoretical, firm-level, natural resource supply functions (necessary conditions from dynamic optimization procedures) into a model which may be econometrically estimated with aggregate data by taking explicit account of unobserved heterogeneity among firms; this eliminates the representative-firm assumption. Second, a generic approach is developed for estimating the socially optimal time-path of the exploitation rate of a renewable or nonrenewable natural resource, based upon observations of market behavior and information about the economic value of environmental externalities.

2

The generic methodology is developed in the context of an analysis of alternative renewable resource strategies for wetlands -- forest product production versus agricultural crop production. This empirical analysis allows for two additional, specific objectives of the research. First, important policy questions concerning the causes of forested wetland losses in the United States are addressed. Second, an approach is thereby developed for analyzing worldwide forest depletion due to urbanization and agricultural development.

Although the methodology is applied in this study to an analysis of alternative renewable resource strategies for wetlands, the approach has wide applicability in the natural resource field. Problems which may be analyzed include: a renewable resource with stock externalities, for example, whaling; a renewable resource with crowding externalities, as in a typical commercial fishery; and a nonrenewable resource with flow externalities, such as off-shore oil recovery with a risk of accidental spills.

A Generic Overview of the Analysis

Since the seminal work of Hotelling (1931), a substantial literature has developed for examining the optimal use of natural resources through the construction of dynamic optimization models, typically solved by applications of the calculus of variations, or more recently, optimal control theory.[1]   A parallel line of research has

---

[1]Important examples of this literature include: Solow 1974; and Dasgupta and Heal 1979. A survey of the literature on nonrenewable resource models was provided by Peterson and Fisher (1977), and the most comprehensive treatment of renewable resource models remains that of Clark (1979).

featured dynamic optimization models of individual firms carrying out resource extraction under competitive or other market conditions.[2] The solutions (necessary conditions for optimality) of both social-optimum and market models may provide useful indications of the direction of impact of a change in a given variable on the optimal extraction (or price) path.[3] Due to the relative simplicity of these models or the lack of requisite data, however, they have rarely been exploited for the purpose of examining the magnitude of impacts under alternative policy scenarios.

The economic literature on environmental externalities developed in the post-war period, including the formulation of a variety of methodologies for the evaluation of environmental externalities.[4] Despite the fact that a very large number of empirical studies have been conducted of the value of various environmental externalities, including those associated with the production of natural resources, the results of these studies have not been fully utilized in the sense of merging their empirical results with theoretically-based natural resource models.[5]

---

[2]Examples include: Gordon 1967; Cummings 1969; and Stiglitz 1976. An overview of this literature, as it applies to nonrenewable resources, is found in Bohi and Toman 1984.

[3]Pindyck's work on optimal exploration (1978) and the role of uncertainty (1984) are examples.

[4]Important sources on the theory of environmental externalities and alternative methods for the evaluation of such externalities are, respectively: Baumol and Oates 1975; and Freeman 1979. A survey is provided by Fisher and Peterson 1976. The state of the art in the two areas is summarized by: Maler 1985; Fisher and Krutilla 1985; and Freeman 1985.

[5]Theoretical models which provide for environmental impacts within the context of optimal control models of natural resource use include: Keeler, Spence, and Zeckhauser 1972; Forster 1973; Cropper 1976; Smith

The classic aggregation problem poses an important obstacle to the development of comprehensive models of natural resource supply in the presence of environmental consequences. Theoretically consistent models of rational individual behavior have been used to develop econometrically estimatable models of natural resource supply only by resorting to representative-firm assumptions.[6] Bohi and Toman described the failure in the literature "to bridge the gap between a theory of individual decisions and data that reflect numerous interdependent influences" (1984, p. 143).

In the present study, a step is taken toward filling this void by modelling both the individual decision process and the heterogeneity which characterizes the production sets of individual decision-makers, all in the context of a dynamic optimization model of natural resource supply in the presence of environmental externalities. In this way, a framework is developed for the identification of socially optimal natural resource exploitation in the presence of negative environmental impacts.

The overall approach is as follows. First, the expected time path of resource extraction is identified through the solution of the appropriate dynamic optimization problem. The result is a supply function for the resource, the parameters of which are estimated econometrically from market data.

The appropriate social optimization problem is also specified and solved (where the social optimum is defined as being what the market would achieve in the absence of environmental externalities). Under

---

1977; and Kamien and Schwartz 1982.

[6]Examples include: Cox and Wright 1976; and Kamien and Schwartz 1977.

certain conditions, there is a well-defined relationship between the market supply function and the "socially optimal supply function." It is therefore possible to use the econometrically estimated parameters, combined with information about the value of environmental externalities, to solve for the fitted values of the social optimum supply function, these fitted values providing the estimated socially optimal time-path of resource exploitation. Simulations of social optima may utilize additional information from the econometric analysis by taking into account not only the point estimates of parameters but their associated probability distributions as well; in other words, stochastic (Monte Carlo) simulations can be carried out.

Forested Wetlands, Agricultural Production, and the Role of Federal Flood-Control Projects

The largest remaining wetland habitat in the lower 48 states is the 5.2 million acre bottomland hardwood forest[7] of the Lower Mississippi Alluvial Plain. The Plain extends 600 miles from the confluence of the Mississippi and Ohio Rivers at Cairo, Illinois to the Gulf of Mexico, and encompasses a total area of 26 million acres in seven states (Figure 1).

In addition to being the most important wetland resource in the U.S., the Lower Mississippi Alluvial Plain is also one of the most seriously threatened. Originally, the Plain included nearly 24 million acres of bottomland hardwood forested wetlands. By 1937, however, only

---

[7]Bottomland hardwoods occur throughout the inland floodplains of the southeastern United States. These areas vary from being permanently inundated or saturated throughout the growing season to being inundated for brief periods at a frequency as low as once in 100 years (U.S. Congress 1984).

FIGURE 1:   MAJOR ORIGINAL WETLAND AREAS OF THE UNITED STATES

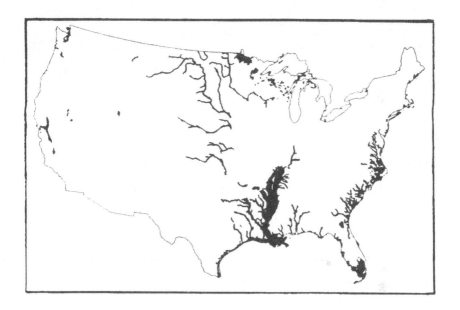

11.8 million acres (about 50%) remained. Since that time, another 6.5 million acres of hardwood forests in the Plain have been cleared, much of this land having been converted during the post-war period to agricultural row crops, primarily soybeans.[8] Today, there are less than 5.2 million acres left, approximately 20% of the original acreage.

Federal Policy Affecting Wetlands

The Lower Mississippi Alluvial Plain and other wetlands throughout the country provide habitat not only for productive forests but also for agricultural crops. Therefore, there is substantial conflict between the maintenance of wetlands in their forested state and their drainage and conversion for agricultural use. This conflict has become more visible during the past twenty years[9] with the passage of Federal laws which offer protection for wetlands, including the National Environmental Policy Act (1969) and the Clean Water Act (1972), in particular Section 404.

Other Federal policies and programs, which predate by decades the major environmental laws of the 1970's, may actually have promoted agricultural conversion of forested wetlands. These programs include the construction of Federally funded flood-protection and drainage

---

[8]This change in cropland acreages in the Lower Mississippi Alluvial Plain is dramatically illustrated in Appendices 1 and 2.

[9]In the late nineteenth and early twentieth centuries, "most interest in wetlands centered on their potential for conversion to 'useful' purposes, mainly agriculture" (Heimlich and Langner 1986, p. 4). Between 1906 and 1982, six surveys were carried out to assess, among other things, the agricultural potential of remaining wetlands across the country: Wright 1907; Gray 1924; American Society of Agricultural Engineers 1946; Shaw and Fredine 1956; U.S. Department of Agriculture 1962; Dideriksen, Hidelbaugh, and Schmude 1977; U.S. Department of Agriculture 1977; Frayer 1983; and U.S. Department of Agriculture and Iowa State University Statistical Laboratory 1984.

projects of the U.S. Army Corps of Engineers and the Soil Conservation

Service (SCS). Since these projects reduce the frequency, extent, and

duration of flooding, it is reasonable to hypothesize that they induce

conversion of forested wetlands to agricultural uses, conversion which

would not be economically feasible without flood protection and drainage

provision. Federal policies may thus affect wetlands in diametrically

opposite ways. While some Federal policies appear to encourage wetland

conversion by increasing the expected net revenue and/or reducing the

risk of wetland development, other Federal programs have the explicit

purpose of controlling or managing wetland usage through regulation or

acquisition.[10]

A question which has arisen in the context of environmental impact

statements and elsewhere is whether the estimated impact areas of

Federal projects on wetlands should be limited to (minimal) direct

construction impacts or whether they should include "indirect impacts"

arising from the clearing of wetlands by private landowners within

hydrologically affected areas. During the past twenty years, Federal

---

[10]In 1985, as a foundation for developing greater consistency in Federal
wetland policy, Congress directed the Secretary of the Interior to carry
out a study of the impact of Federal programs and policies on wetlands
throughout the nation. The Secretary's report to the Congress will be
in two volumes, the first of which is expected to be sent to the
Congress later this year and focuses on two important wetland regions --
the Lower Mississippi Alluvial Plain and the Prairie Pothole Region of
the Upper Midwest. Volume II will cover all other major wetland
regions. In order to prepare Volume I of its report to the Congress,
the U.S. Department of the Interior sponsored two studies of wetland
depletion in the Lower Mississippi Alluvial Plain. Of these, one
focused on the role played by Federal flood-control and drainage
projects (Stavins 1986, 1987a, 1987b) and was the antecedent to the
research reported in this thesis. The other focused on agricultural
commodity programs and tax code provisions; it was carried out by Kramer
and Shabman (1986), and is discussed later in the text. Three analyses
of wetland depletion in the prairie pothole region were also conducted
(see below).

agencies typically have adopted the position that their projects do not induce private clearing and drainage of forested wetlands for agricultural use. Hence, in environmental impact statements and elsewhere, these agencies typically have not included as environmental impacts of projects any clearing and drainage within hydrologically defined project areas.

Federal Flood Control/Drainage Projects and Wetland Conversion

The Mississippi River drains more than 40% of the surface area of the coterminus United States. Hence, the lower portions of the Alluvial Plain are particularly susceptible to flooding and saturation. Nearly sixty years ago, in an attempt to mitigate the effects of this continuous pattern of flooding and poor drainage in the Lower Mississippi Alluvial Plain, the Federal government became directly involved in the development of flood-control projects in the region with the passage of the Flood Control Act of 1928, enacted in response to the great flood of 1927. This legislation initiated the Army Corps of Engineers' comprehensive flood-control responsibilities in the Plain. Sixteen years later, the Corps became actively involved in the construction of drainage projects as well, under the authority of the Flood Control Act of 1944. Thus, in the post-war period, flood-control and drainage projects became the major peacetime function of the Corps of Engineers (Young and Haveman 1985). Although the first Corps projects in the region were initiated during the 1930's (Appendix 3 and

Figure 2), project construction did not reach peak levels until the 1960's.[11]

The Soil Conservation Service of the U.S. Department of Agriculture became directly involved in the development of flood-control and drainage projects in the Mississippi Alluvial Valley (MAV) when the "Small Watershed Program" was authorized by Congress in 1954. The first of these projects to be constructed in the Alluvial Plain were initiated in 1956 (Appendix 4 and Figure 3), but construction did not reach significant levels until the mid-1960's.[12]

It is hypothesized that Federal flood-control and drainage projects have played an important role in the historical pattern of forested wetland depletion in the following manner: (1) Federal projects reduce the probability of flooding (and increase the possibility of drainage) of wetlands; (2) hence, the suitability of the land for agricultural production increases; (3) therefore, the expected present value of the land for agricultural use increases relative to the land's expected present value for use in its forested state; and (4) individual landowners then decide to convert their forested wetlands to agricultural croplands.[13]

_____

[11]There are four major types of flood-control and drainage projects constructed and maintained by the Corps of Engineers: levees, floodways, channelization projects, and tributary basin modifications. These projects are associated with navigation, flood control, drainage, shore and beach restoration, erosion control, hydropower, water supply, and recreation.

[12]Soil Conservation Service projects are designed to protect, manage, improve, and develop water and land resources within watersheds up to 250,000 acres in size. Structural approaches include dams, channel modifications, and levees.

[13]Once a landowner has decided that conversion of forested wetlands to agricultural uses is physically possible and economically feasible, a series of clearing activities are typically undertaken. These vary, of

U.S. ARMY CORPS PROJECTS AUTHORIZED
1929 — 1984

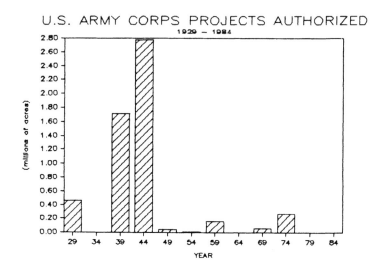

US ARMY CORPS PROJECT CONSTRUCTION
1929 — 1984

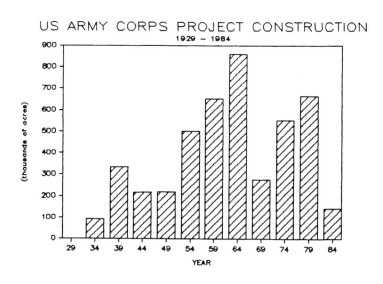

FIGURE 3:

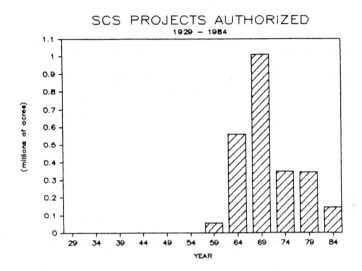

SCS PROJECTS AUTHORIZED
1929 – 1984

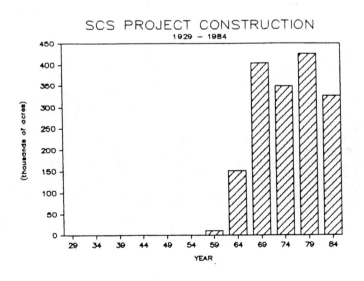

SCS PROJECT CONSTRUCTION
1929 – 1984

An Alternative View from the Corps of Engineers

Although there is substantial support for such a hypothetical
linkage between Federal projects and wetland conversion (Mattson 1975;
MacDonald, Frayer, and Clauser 1979; Shulstad, May, and Herrington 1979;
Galloway 1980; Shabman 1980; and Turner and Craig 1980), unanimous
agreement does not exist. In particular, the U.S. Army Corps of
Engineers and the Soil Conservation Service have maintained that their
projects are not responsible for wetland clearing. They assert that the
primary impact of their projects is one of increasing crop yields on
already-existing farms.

In some cases, the Corps has theorized that the causality of land
conversion runs not from flood protection to clearing, but the opposite,
from wetland clearing by landowners to flood protection by the Corps.
The reasoning here is that landowners convert their wetlands to
agricultural cropland, despite the threat of flooding and poor

---

course, depending on local conditions, but in general, eight activities
are involved: felling of trees, removal of shallow roots, windrowing,
burning, removal of remaining wood, drainage work, rough leveling, and
land breaking.

In the first step, bulldozers are used for the removal of trees. A
special blade mounted on the bulldozer enables the operator to cut off
relatively large trees below ground level, so that stumps can be left in
the ground to rot. The felled trees are pushed into windrows and
eventually burned. Shallow roots are pulled up with the use of a root
rake, ordinarily pulled behind a bulldozer. Small pieces of wood which
are missed by the mechanical equipment are picked up in a "chunking"
operation, often by hand. Drainage of fields is carried out by farmers
through ditching enterprises, which may be quite extensive. Fields are
rough-levelled with land-planes, pulled by bulldozers, and lastly,
fields are disked, using either bulldozers or tractors, depending on the
size of disk utilized. According to the Corps of Engineers, extensive
usage of mechanical land clearing equipment during "recent times" has
made it possible for a single operator to clear up to 18 acres of
forested wetland per day (1981a).

14

drainage. Then, in response to the request of farmers for help, the Corps develops and constructs projects to protect the already-developed farmlands.

In other contexts, the Corps has acknowledged that empirical research has indicated that "Corps flood-control projects and the small watershed (SCS) projects have had an effect on the extent of hardwood clearing," but the Corps has still maintained that "the magnitude of this effect cannot be determined accurately given the existing data" (1981a, p. 9-10). The Corps' explanation for the massive amount of wetland conversion which took place in the MAV during the 1960's and 1970's has focused on the role played by rising agricultural prices.

Previous Analyses of Forested Wetland Conversion[14]

There have been two principal categories of previous research -- empirical analyses and theoretical models. The empirical studies fall into two groups -- quantitative documentations of the substitution of agricultural land for forested wetlands in the Plain, and examinations of the presumed causes of this land-use change.

The relationship between changes in forested wetlands and changes in agricultural croplands in the Mississippi Valley has been documented (Turner and Craig 1980; Frey and Dill 1971; MacDonald, Frayer, and Clauser 1979; Tiner 1984; and U.S. Department of Agriculture 1984); and the causes of this cropland-forest substitution have been examined (Davis 1972; Sternitzke 1976; Mattson 1975; Shulstad and May 1979;

------

[14]This brief review of previous research is not intended to be exhaustive. A comprehensive review of previous studies of wetland conversion in the Lower Mississippi Alluvial Plain is provided in Appendix 5.

MacDonald, Frayer, and Clauser 1979; Galloway 1980; U.S. Army Corps of Engineers 1981a). Most recently, two farm-level simulation models have been used to estimate the impacts of various Federal policies on wetland conversion decisions (Heimlich and Langner 1986; Kramer and Shabman 1986).[15]

Only two theoretical models of wetland conversion have appeared in the literature.[16] Brown (1972) presents an economic formulation of the problem of "rational investment behavior in the face of floods," indicating that flood-control programs may provide incentives for landowners to reallocate their chosen uses of the land. Shabman (1980) allowed for the possibility that positive returns to wetland conversion may be a function of flood-control and drainage projects, thereby suggesting that such projects may provide an incentive for landowners to undertake the conversion of their lands.

Although these two theoretical models provide useful insights into the ways in which flood-control projects may affect landowner decisions, neither model permits parameters to be estimated with empirical data. Hence, their theoretical implications remain hypotheses, waiting to be tested.

---

[15]The recent research effort by the U.S. Department of the Interior, described earlier, included an examination of the conversion of wetlands to cropland in the Prairie Pothole region of the Upper Midwest (McColloch and Wissman 1986; Leitch and Nelson 1986; Nomsen, Higgins, Browers, and Smith 1986).

[16]A theoretical model of optimal conversion of tropical forestland to agricultural use is provided by Ehui, Hertel, and Preckel (1987). Their dynamic optimization model does not allow for farmland abandonment (reforestation) and focuses on the ecological relationship between forest depletion and agricultural yields. As a social optimization model, no provision is made (or intended) for empirical parameter estimation.

Preview of the Thesis

The econometric model developed here is based upon a dynamic
optimization model of individual, rational economic behavior (Figure 4).
A set of necessary conditions are identified under which individual
landowners may be expected to seek to convert their forested wetlands to
agricultural production or to abandon their agricultural croplands and
allow them to return to forest.

Heterogeneity across land parcels (in terms of agricultural
feasibility) constitutes the basis for aggregation of the individual
necessary conditions into a county-level model of land use. The
introduction of a partial adjustment framework provides the final step
to an econometrically estimatable model.

Particular focus is given to the role played by flood-control and
drainage projects of the U.S. Army Corps of Engineers and the Soil
Conservation Service. The model postulates that such projects may
affect land use in two major ways: first, by directly affecting the
feasibility of agricultural production (and by directly affecting the
costs of converting forested wetlands to agricultural use); and second,
by non-random selection of land parcels which receive flood protection,
i.e. by affecting the parameters of the distribution which characterizes
the underlying heterogeneity.

In an econometric analysis of land use in thirty-six counties of
the Lower Mississippi Alluvial Plain during the period 1935-1984,
various economic, climatic, and hydrologic factors are examined which
may have affected conversion and abandonment decisions, including the

17

FIGURE 4:   CONCEPTUAL FLOW CHART OF THE METHODOLOGY

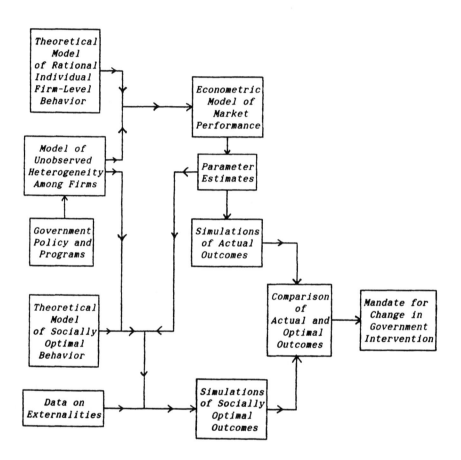

role played by Federal flood-control and drainage projects. The contributions of various factors to the actual pattern of land use are assessed through comparisons of factual and counterfactual, historical simulations.

The final stage of the research involves an examination of the socially optimal use of wetland resources, through the internalization of environmental externalities. Combining estimates of relevant environmental values, drawing on a database recently assembled by the U.S. Fish and Wildlife Service, with the econometrically estimated private-market parameters, counterfactual simulations are carried out of socially optimal past and future patterns of wetland use.

The immediately following section of this chapter highlights the major substantive and methodological conclusions of the thesis. Then, in Chapter II, a theoretical model of privately optimal resource use is developed in the context of alternative strategies for forested wetlands and agricultural production. Chapter III presents an econometric analysis, based upon the theoretical model of privately optimal land use. In Chapter IV, a welfare analysis of forested wetland depletion is carried out through the internalization of relevant environmental externalities. Finally, Chapter V summarizes the study and develops its major conclusions.

Major Conclusions of the Study

The statistical analysis described in this thesis leads to several conclusions. First, construction of Federal flood-control and drainage projects caused a higher rate of conversion of forested wetlands to agricultural croplands than would have occurred in the absence of such

projects. Second, Federal projects had this impact because they
rendered unsuitable land suitable and because, on average, land which
was already most suitable for agriculture was protected by the projects.
Third, substantial wetland conversion would have occurred as a result of
favorable economic returns to agriculture (relative to forestry), even
if no Federal flood-control and drainage projects had been undertaken.

Sensitivity analyses of the relative impacts of economic,
hydrologic, and climatic factors lead to an additional set of findings.
If there had been no Federal flood-control and drainage projects
constructed in the 36-county study area after the year 1934,
approximately 1.15 million fewer acres of forested wetlands would have
been converted, about 31% of total depletion. Long-term (steady state)
depletion due to Federal projects (constructed through the year 1984) is
estimated to amount to more than 1.23 million acres, about 32% of
estimated long-term depletion.

Of the factors considered in the econometric model, flood
protection and drainage provision afforded by Federal projects had the
largest impact on net changes in forested acreage. The joint effect of
natural topography and the mainline levee system was of secondary
importance, amounting to 846 thousand acres of depletion (23% of total
depletion) through 1984. Net forestry revenues and conversion costs
exerted substantial restraints on wetland clearing.

Turning to questions regarding the socially optimal allocation of
wetlands between forestry and agricultural uses, the study presents a
spectrum of results for a relatively broad range of environmental
externality levels. The simulations indicate that zero-level net
depletion would have been optimal in the study area over the 1935-1984

20

period if annual environmental benefits had been approximately $115 per acre, and that maintenance of the current forest-cropland wetland allocation will be optimal (for the next fifteen years) if externality levels are on the order of $175 per acre. For average environmental benefits per acre less than that amount, some continued conversion is optimal; and for benefit levels in excess of that amount, various degrees of farmland abandonment are socially optimal.

It is useful to place these last quantitative results in some perspective by comparing them with the private valuation of land in the study area. The figures just cited indicate that only if environmental values were more than twice as great as market (agricultural) values of land would zero-level net depletion have been optimal. Furthermore, assuming symmetric distributions of wetland benefits, the average annual environmental value which would have stopped a typical acre from being converted was about $55, within the range of normal annual net returns to conversion. This confirms that social optimization calls for wetland conversion to be avoided when the value of externalities is in excess of the private returns to conversion.

In terms of policy implications, the evidence presented in this study suggests, first of all, that Congress, the responsible Federal agencies, and the courts should view with skepticism environmental assessments of Federal flood-control and drainage projects which claim no responsibility for induced wetland clearing. Second, within the context of Section 404 of the Clean Water Act, pursuant to which the Corps is responsible for the regulation of wetland conversion, the study indicates that the Corps and other agencies should not evaluate permit applications for projects located in wetland areas as though wetland conversion were unrelated to project construction.

The study clearly indicates that there is a substantial divergence between actual and optimal wetland conversion, particulary in situations where environmental externalities include water quality impacts. Since wetland conversion to agricultural use increases soil erosion and chemical pollution of receiving waters, a third policy implication is that responsible Federal agencies and the Congress should consider linking expenditures of Federal funds to construct and maintain projects with adoption of efficient and enforceable programs to abate consequent water pollution.

A fourth and final policy implication of the analysis is that the Congress ought to consider various methods of narrowing the gap between the actual allocation of land between forested wetlands and agricultural cropland and what appears to be the socially desirable (optimal) configuration, whether the chosen methods of narrowing this gap involve modifications of existing programs and policies or enactment of entirely new ones. In other words, two important policy goals, from an economic perspective, are the elimination of public subsidies and the internalization of environmental externalities. Among the policy initiatives which the Congress may therefore wish to consider are: changes in the way Federal flood-control and drainage projects are planned, authorized, and financed; increased funding of Federal wetland acquisition, easement, and oversight programs; provision for preferential property tax assessments; tax credits; conversion penalties (taxes); and cross-compliance legislation linked to Federal commodity program payments.

22

Finally, from a broader perspective, this study leads to a set of methodological implications. First, a technique is developed for aggregating theoretical, firm-level, natural resource supply functions into models which can be econometrically estimated, by taking explicit account of underlying heterogeneity. Second, a generic approach is thereby developed for estimating the socially optimal time-path of the exploitation rate of a renewable natural resource, based upon observations of revealed-preference, market-based behavior, in combination with information about the economic value of environmental externalities. This methodology is applicable to a host of other policy problems associated with the use of natural resources in the presence of environmental externalities.

CHAPTER II

THEORY OF PRIVATELY OPTIMAL RESOURCE USE:
MARKET ALLOCATIONS OF FORESTED WETLANDS AND AGRICULTURAL PRODUCTION

In this chapter, a theoretical, microeconomic model of actual
(market-based) alternative uses of wetlands is developed, based upon the
notion of rational decision-making by individual landowners. The first
step is the construction of a dynamic optimization model of forestry and
agricultural production at the individual, landowner level. The model
is solved via control theoretic techniques, yielding necessary
conditions for conversion of forests to agricultural production and for
abandonment of cropland. An explicit model of the heterogeneity of land
allows for the aggregation of the respective necessary conditions, so
that a comprehensive and econometrically estimatable model of land use
is specified.[17]

---

[17]Although the economic literature on alternative land-use allocations
provides little, if any, precedent for the approach taken in this study,
there is an extensive literature on technological diffusion which does
provide some guidance. That literature's methodologies, first developed
by Griliches (1957), are somewhat limited in the current context for two
reasons: first, most diffusion-type models collapse time-series data
into estimated diffusion-slope coefficients, problematic for analyzing
the temporal relationship among construction of flood-control projects,
price changes, and land conversion decisions; and second, typical
diffusion models do not allow for "de-diffusion" (abandonment of
farmland), a significant element in the forested wetland problem.

A Dynamic Optimization Model of Forestry and Agricultural Production

Landowners observe a variety of economic, hydrologic, and climatic factors relevant to decisions regarding the use of their lands for forestry or for agricultural production.[18] Current and past values of variables presumably constitute the basis for the formation of expectations regarding future values of respective variables. In particular, landowners observe agricultural prices and production costs, typical agricultural yields for the area, typical timber returns, and the suitability of individual land parcels for agriculture. A prime factor determining the suitability of land for agricultural production (in the relevant geographic area of this study, the Lower Mississippi Alluvial Plain) is its wetness, that is, the degree of (natural and artificial) protection from flooding and poor drainage.

A landowner's decision is viewed here as the result of an attempt on his or her[19] part to maximize the expected long-term economic return

---

Nevertheless, it should be noted that the approach which is developed here, involving the concept of a "threshold level" of agricultural feasibility, owes much to previous work reported in the technological diffusion literature, particularly that of David (1966) and Pomfret (1976). Later relevant contributions include: David (1969), Jones (1977), Sargen (1979), Sahal (1981), and Whatley (1983). The literature is surveyed by Davies (1979), and Stoneman (1983).

[18]In the present empirical context, it is reasonable to focus on these two alternative land uses and to exclude consideration of potential municipal uses of drained wetlands. For further discussion of this issue, see Appendix 6. For a description of demographic and other characteristics of landowners in the study area, see Kramer and Shabman 1986; and see Appendix 7 of the present study for the size distribution of farms in 1935 and 1982.

[19]To avoid cumbersome repetition of both genders of the relevant personal pronouns, "he" is used throughout the remainder of this thesis as a shorthand for "he or she," and "his" is used to represent "his or

to the set of productive activities which may be carried out on the
land. Hence, a parcel of land may be viewed as a marketable asset,
valued for its usefulness as a factor in the production of a time stream
of goods and services. With no loss of generality, explicit
consideration of the possibility of selling land parcels may be excluded
from (kept implicit within) the optimization problem.[20]

A landowner faces a decision of whether to keep land in its current
(forested or agricultural) state, to convert forested land to
agricultural production, or to abandon agricultural land and allow it to
return to forest. Focusing for illustrative purposes on the conversion
decision, it is reasonable to expect that if it appears likely to a
landowner, on the basis of available information, that converting a
parcel of forest land to cropland will be "profitable," then the
landowner will seek to carry out the conversion; otherwise not. Thus,
conversion and other land-use decisions are functions of the relative
expected economic returns from alternative uses of the land.[21]

---

her." The choice of the male pronoun reflects the reality that the vast
majority of the relevant group of landowners and land-use decision
makers in the study area during the time period under consideration were
indeed male (Kramer and Shabman 1986).

[20]See Appendix 8.

[21]A substantial literature in economics suggests the possibility of an
alternative approach to this question. Classical and neoclassical
theories of land markets, including Ricardo's notion of rent accruing to
a unique fixed factor, Von Thunen's analysis of the location of
agricultural production (translated in Hall 1966), the bid-rent function
approach (Randall and Castle 1985), and location theory (Takayama and
Judge 1971), provide theoretical bases for viewing land-use decisions as
functions of the rents returned by alternative uses, where the price of
a specific parcel of land (if markets are efficient) is equal to the sum
of the discounted values of the streams of rents from various uses of
that land parcel over time. The present study essentially examines the
impact of alternative expected rent streams on land-use decisions, but
an alternative approach would be to focus directly on the real estate
market. The latter approach has been utilized to analyze the

A risk-neutral[22] landowner faced with the decision of how to utilize his land, given the alternatives of forestry and agriculture, may be expected to seek to maximize the present discounted value of the stream of expected future returns to his land:[23]

---

transition of land from agricultural to urban uses, both theoretically (Arnott and Lewis 1979) and econometrically (Chicoine 1981). Approaching the forest-farmland transition from this same perspective is a promising area for future research, although the available land price data are limited.

[22]Evidence exists that farmers are to some degree risk averse in their investment decisions (Young 1979), but it has also been shown that farmers' behavior is likewise consistent with simpler expected-profit maximization (Gardner and Chavas 1979; Pope 1981). Landowners face two major sources of uncertainty -- prices and weather conditions. The result of providing for risk-averse behavior in the objective functional would be the inclusion in subsequently derived necessary (first-order) conditions of both means (expected values) and variances (and covariances) of relevant (stochastic) variables. Due to the lack of sufficient data, however, only expected values are utilized in the empirical analysis. Thus, risk neutrality and independence of relevant factors are assumed. Landowners are assumed to substitute expected values, conditional on available information, for unknown values. Because flood protection projects may reduce the variance of returns (in addition to increasing average returns), the assumption of risk neutrality may lead to the underestimation of the impact of Federal projects.

[23]In the dynamic optimization problem described by equations 1 through 4, the landowner chooses a rate of conversion, g_{ijt}, and a rate of abandonment, v_{ijt}, for a homogeneous parcel, j, of land in county i at time t. Upper case letters in equation 1 represent variables which are stocks or present values, while lower case letters refer to variables which are annual flows (either in physical units or dollars). The specification of this objective function may be more intuitive when one notes that the term which represents the (discounted present value of) expected future net revenue from agricultural production, $A_{it}q_{ijt} - AC_{it}$, is equal to the price of farmland in a competitive market.

$$\max_{\{g_{ijt}v_{ijt}\}} \int_0^\infty \left[\left[A_{it}q_{ijt} - AC_{it} \right] \left[g_{ijt} - v_{ijt} \right] - C_{it}g_{ijt} + f_{it}S_{ijt} \right.$$

$$\left. + W_{it}g_{ijt} - D_{it}v_{ijt} \right] e^{-r_t t} dt \qquad (1)$$

subject to:
$$\dot{S}_{ijt} = v_{ijt} - g_{ijt} \qquad (2)$$

$$0 \le g_{ijt} \le \bar{g}_{ijt} \qquad (3)$$

$$0 \le v_{ijt} \le \bar{v}_{ijt} \qquad (4)$$

where A_{it} = weighted average of gross revenue per acre from four major

agricultural crops, expressed as the discounted present

value of an infinite stream[24] of future revenues in county i

at time t;[25]

---

[24]A continuous-time, rather than a discrete-time model is employed, despite the fact that a discrete-time formulation would take less liberty with reality, considering the fact that agricultural crops are produced on a seasonal basis. The continuous-time approach is favored here because of its notational simplicity and because it allows for easy interpretation of the dynamic optimization model's solution in the context of the relevant literature of renewable natural resource economics. Note, however, that the problem could be reformulated and solved via the discrete-time analog of the Pontryagin maximum principle (see Clark 1979, pp. 250-252). The necessary conditions which emerge from such a discrete-time formulation of the problem are parallel to those which emerge here, and the final econometric specification which results is, in fact, identical to the one developed in this study.

[25]Instead of writing the agricultural revenue term in the objective functional as the present value of future revenues times the amount of annual conversion, agricultural revenue could be represented in a manner

28

q_{ijt} = index of feasibility of agricultural production, including effects of soil quality (nutrients and texture)[26] and soil moisture in county i on land parcel j at time t;

g_{ijt} = acres of land converted from forested to agricultural use in county i on land parcel j at time t;

v_{ijt} = acres of cropland abandoned (gradually returned to a forested condition) in county i on parcel j at time t;

AC_{it} = weighted average of costs of production per acre (on harvested land) of four major agricultural crops, expressed as the discounted present value of an infinite future stream, in county i at time t;

C_{it} = average cost of conversion per acre (indexed by weather conditions)[27] in county i at time t;

---

analogous to that used for the forestry revenue term, i.e., annual agricultural revenue times the stock of farmland. While such a specification might be more in keeping with the way one thinks of the land conversion decision, the two specifications are in fact equivalent and lead to identical sets of necessary conditions. There are two advantages of the approach utilized here: first, the specification of equation 1 is consistent with typical renewable (and nonrenewable) natural resource models, and the solution hence reveals implications of the methodology for that literature; and second, the solution of the dynamic optimization problem is greatly simplified, because there is only one stock (state) variable, instead of two.

[26]In a further generalization of the model, conversion costs, in addition to agricultural yields, are later allowed to be heterogeneous across land parcels within counties, so that the conversion cost term in equation 1 is replaced by

$$\alpha_1 C_{it} \cdot q_{ijt} \cdot g_{it}$$

where α_1 is a parameter which indexes the relative effect of heterogeneity on conversion costs, compared with the effect on agricultural yields. For purposes of clarity, these and several other complications are introduced only after the basic model is fully developed.

[27]Precipitation and consequent soil moisture are later allowed to influence conversion costs; the conversion cost term in equation 1 is then replaced by

f_{it} = average annual net income from forestry per acre, a weighted

average of net revenues (stumpage values) from sawlogs and

pulpwood, in county i at time t;[28]

S_{ijt} = stock (acres) of forests in county i on parcel j at time t;

r_t = real interest rate at time t;

W_{it} = windfall of net revenue per acre from a one-time clearcut of

forest (prior to conversion) in county i at time t;

D_{it} = expected present discounted value of loss of income (for

each acre of land abandoned in county i at time t), due to

the gradual regrowth of forest (harvesting does not occur

until the year t+R, where R is the exogenously determined

rotation length).[29] So,

$$C_{it} \cdot \exp\{\alpha_2 \text{PHDI}_{it}\} \cdot g_{it}$$

where α_2 is an estimated parameter and PHDI_{it} is the Palmer Hydrological Drought Index.

[28]The annual forestry revenue term, $f_{it} \cdot S_{ijt}$, in the objective functional of the dynamic optimization problem implicitly posits the existence of an uneven aged stand of trees (with a uniform distribution of ages) which is selectively cut at each time, t. A more sophisticated model would provide for individual parcels which are essentially even-aged stands and which are clearcut at intervals of R years. In that case, the objective functional would provide for the existence of an even-aged stand (the value of which would be a function of its age) which is cut once every R years. The model might also allow for the heterogeneity of stands within counties at each point in time; one possibility is to assume that the ages of stands (each of which is even-aged) are uniformly distributed within counties. For purposes of simplicity, the abstraction of selective cutting is utilized at this stage of the analysis.

[29]Although, in the case of forested wetlands in the Lower Mississippi Alluvial Plain, there is some justification for considering the rotation length to be exogenous to landowners' decisions, an improvement in the model would be to allow for endogeneity of the rotation length. Analogously, another improvement would be to allow for endogeneity of the crop mix (as a function of relative agricultural prices and production costs).

$$D_{it} = \int_{t}^{t+R} f_{i\tau} e^{-r(\tau-t)} d\tau = F_{it} \cdot \left[1 - e^{-rR} \right] \tag{5}$$

where F_{it} is the present discounted value of an infinite future stream of annual net forest income, i.e. $F_{it} \cdot r = f_{it}$. Thus, if $R = 0$, $D_{it} = 0$ (i.e., if regrowth is instantaneous, there is no loss of revenue due to harvest delay); and if $R = \infty$, $D_{it} = F_{it}$ (if the regrowth period is infinitely long, there is a complete loss of all forest revenue);

$\bar{g}_{ijt}$ = maximum feasible rate of conversion, defined such that

$$\int_{t}^{t+\Delta} \left[\bar{g}_{ij\tau} \right] d\tau = S_{ijt} \tag{6}$$

for arbitrarily small but non-zero interval, Δ, over which $\bar{g}_{ij\tau}$ is constant;

$\bar{v}_{ijt}$ = maximum feasible rate of abandonment, defined such that

$$\int_{t}^{t+\Delta} \left[\bar{v}_{ij\tau} \right] d\tau = T_{ijt} - S_{ijt} = AG_{ijt} \tag{7}$$

for arbitrarily small but non-zero interval, Δ, over which $\bar{v}_{ij\tau}$ is constant.

AG_{ijt} = acreage of agricultural land in county i, parcel j, at time t; and

T_{ijt} = total acreage of county i, parcel j, (available for conversion,[30] in the flood plain) at time t.

---

[30]Some land in the thirty-six counties was withdrawn from availability to the private market during the study period as a result of designation of protected status by Federal and state authorities, including the U.S.

Solving the Optimization Problem:
Necessary Conditions for Land Conversion and Abandonment

In order to solve this dynamic optimization problem, the relevant Hamiltonian equation is set up,[31] with λ_{ijt} as a costate variable:

$$H_{ijt} = \left[\left[A_{it}q_{ijt} - AC_{it}\right]\left[g_{ijt} - v_{ijt}\right] - C_{it}g_{ijt} + f_{it}s_{ijt}\right.$$

$$\left. + W_{it}g_{ijt} - D_{it}v_{ijt}\right]\cdot e^{-r_t t} + \lambda_{ijt}\cdot\left[v_{ijt} - g_{ijt}\right]\cdot e^{-r_t t} \quad (8)$$

According to the maximum principle (Pontryagin et al. 1962), necessary conditions for the maximization of equation 1 subject to constraints 2 through 4, include:[32]

Fish and Wildlife Service, the U.S. Forest Service, and state fish and game agencies.

[31]This specification implies that all prices (and costs) are exogenously determined in broader national or international markets. In the present application, such assumptions are reasonable. Note also that the specification implies that there are no costs of adjustment associated with the abandonment of agricultural land and its subsequent return to a forested state. If tree-farming were prevalent in the area, which it is not, the specification would need to be modified accordingly.

[32]Given the fact that the constrained dynamic optimization problem specified by equations 1 through 4 is a linear variational problem, it will not be surprising that a bang-bang solution emerges. That is, it is optimal at any time t for an individual landowner either to convert his parcel j at the maximum feasible rate (only, of course, if the land is in a forested state), to abandon at the maximum feasible rate (only if the land is in cropland), or to do nothing at all.

$$\max_{\{g_{ijt}, v_{ijt}\}} \quad H_{ijt}\left[\cdot\right] \quad \text{for all } t \tag{9}$$

Thus, we have the following complementary slackness conditions:

$$g_{ijt}^* = \bar{g}_{ijt} \quad \text{if} \quad \frac{\partial H(\cdot)}{\partial g_{ijt}} > 0 \quad ; \quad g_{ijt}^* = 0 \quad \text{otherwise} \tag{10}$$

$$v_{ijt}^* = \bar{v}_{ijt} \quad \text{if} \quad \frac{\partial H(\cdot)}{\partial v_{ijt}} > 0 \quad ; \quad v_{ijt}^* = 0 \quad \text{otherwise} \tag{11}$$

Another necessary condition for the constrained maximization of (1) is that the partial derivative of the Hamiltonian with respect to the state variable, S_{ijt}, be equal to minus one times the derivative with respect to time of the (discounted) costate variable, λ_{ijt}:[33]

$$\frac{\partial H(\cdot)}{\partial S_{ijt}} = -\frac{d}{dt}\left[\lambda_{ijt} \cdot e^{-rt}\right] \tag{12}$$

$$f_{it} = r\lambda_{ijt} - \dot{\lambda}_{ijt} \tag{13}$$

This, in turn, yields:[34]

---

[33]One other necessary condition for the maximization of equation 1 subject to the specified constraints is the transversality condition:

$$\lim_{t \to \infty} \lambda_{ijt} \cdot e^{-rt} = 0$$

[34]Note that equation 13 is an elaboration of the so-called Hotelling rule for nonrenewable resources. If there were no in-situ value of the (wetland) resource (if standing timber had no value), as in a typical

$$\lambda_{ijt} = \frac{f_{it}}{r} + \frac{\dot{\lambda}_{ijt}}{r} \qquad (14)$$

Evaluation of the partial derivatives in the first set of necessary conditions yields:

$$g^*_{ijt} = \bar{g}_{ijt} \quad \text{if} \quad \left[A_{it}q_{ijt} - AC_{it} - C_{it} + W_{it} - \lambda_{ijt}\right] > 0 \qquad (15)$$

$$v^*_{ijt} = \bar{v}_{ijt} \quad \text{if} \quad \left[- A_{it}q_{ijt} + AC_{it} - D_{it} + \lambda_{ijt}\right] > 0 \qquad (16)$$

Substituting the expression for the costate variable from equation 14 into equation 15,

$$g^*_{ijt} = \bar{g}_{ijt} \quad \text{if} \quad \left[A_{it}q_{ijt} - AC_{it} - C_{it} + W_{it} - \frac{f_{it}}{r}\right] > \frac{\dot{\lambda}_{ijt}}{r} \qquad (17)$$

In order to identify necessary conditions for *target* allocations of land between forest and agricultural uses, the steady state solution is

_____

nonrenewable resource model, then equation 13 says that the shadow price of the resource should increase at the rate of interest. Combining this with an evaluation of the partial derivative from equation 10 indicates that the "net price" of wetlands (being valued only for agricultural production) should increase at the rate of interest. Once the positive in-situ value of the resource (for forestry and other uses) is considered, however, a wedge is driven between the two parts of the simple Hotelling rule.

of interest.[35] The previous equation leads to the following necessary

condition for optimality in the steady state:

$$g_{ijt}^* = \bar{g}_{ijt} \quad \text{if} \quad \left[A_{it}q_{ijt} - AC_{it} - C_{it} - \left[F_{it} - W_{it} \right] \right] > 0 \qquad (18)$$

Next, net forest revenue, FN_{it}, is defined so that

$$g_{ijt}^* = \bar{g}_{ijt} \quad \text{if} \quad \left[A_{it}q_{ijt} - AC_{it} - C_{it} - FN_{it} \right] > 0$$

$$(19)$$

$$g_{ijt}^* = 0 \quad \text{otherwise.}$$

Returning to the conditions for abandonment of farmland, the

expression for the costate variable from equation 14 is substituted into

equation 16, which yields:

$$v_{ijt}^* = \bar{v}_{ijt} \quad \text{if} \quad \left[- A_{it}q_{ijt} + AC_{it} - D_{it} + F_{it} \right] > \frac{-\lambda_{ijt}}{r} \qquad (20)$$

Defining the delayed net forest revenue as $\tilde{F}_{it} = F_{it} - D_{it}$, the steady

state necessary condition for abandonment is:

---

[35]As an alternative to identifying the steady state (target) necessary
condition in the context of a dynamic optimization model, it is possible
to utilize a static optimization approach. This is done in Appendix 9,
with the result that the same set of necessary conditions is found.

$$v^*_{ijt} = \bar{v}_{ijt} \quad \text{if} \quad \left[\tilde{F}_{it} - A_{it} \cdot q_{ijt} + AC_{it}\right] > 0$$

(21)

$$v^*_{ijt} = 0 \quad \text{otherwise.}$$

Having established the basic necessary conditions for conversion of forested land to agricultural use and abandonment of farmland, the respective present values are next denoted as follows, for the purpose of convenience of notation:

$$X_{ijt} = A_{it} \cdot q_{ijt} - AC_{it} - C_{it} - FN_{it}$$

(22)

$$Y_{ijt} = \tilde{F}_{it} - A_{it} \cdot q_{ijt} + AC_{it}$$

(23)

Thus, the model predicts that conversion or abandonment will occur under the following conditions:

Conversion occurs if $\quad X_{ijt} > 0$ and parcel is forested (24)

Abandonment occurs if $\quad Y_{ijt} > 0$ and parcel is cropland (25)

Clearly, abandonment and conversion are mutually exclusive activities for any given parcel of land.[36] Letting the time interval Δ in equations 6 and 7 be equal to unity (a single time period), the continuous-time model yields the following result for a discrete-time situation: when conversion occurs, $g^*_{ijt} = S_{ijt}$; and when abandonment

---

[36]See Appendix 10.

36

occurs, $v^*_{ijt} = AG_{ijt}$. In other words, for each homogeneous parcel j, it is always optimal either to convert the entire parcel from forested condition to agricultural use (only, of course, if it is in a forested state), to abandon the entire parcel (only if it is agricultural cropland), or to do nothing.

Modelling the Unobserved Heterogeneity of Land[37]

As it stands, the model implies that all land in a county is either converted to agricultural use, left alone, or abandoned. The fact that such "0-1 behavior" is not observed at the county level is presumably due to the heterogeneity of land parcels. As a means of modelling such heterogeneity, development of the model continues with an examination of the distribution of the unobserved variable, q_{ijt}, the agricultural feasibility index. Because the lognormal distribution has several desirable characteristics for the modelling of unobserved heterogeneity of soil quality, it is postulated that q_{ijt} is distributed lognormally.[38]

---

[37]Although the methodology developed in this study for modelling unobserved, underlying heterogeneity (and econometrically estimating relevant distributional parameters) has not previously been used in the natural resources literature, it is similar in some respects to an approach originally developed by Gotz and McCall (1980, 1984) for the purpose of modelling decisions by (heterogeneous) Air Force officers to take early retirement. The fundamental insight in the work of Gotz and McCall is that differences in an unobserved variable (characterizing population heterogeneity) cause individuals to respond differently to identical changes in the economic climate. More recent applications include those of Pakes (1986) and Rust (1987).

[38]Among these desirable characteristics is the fact that the distribution is anchored at the origin. Although the heterogeneity under consideration is described at this point as being associated with soil quality (and hence agricultural yields), this will be generalized below to include heterogeneous conversion costs. Two alternative distributions, the normal and the uniform, were also considered; and

A first approximation of this heterogeneity and the way in which it interacts with (but, for the time being, is not affected by) flood-control projects is as follows:

$$\log(q_{ijt}) \sim N(\mu, \sigma_i^2) \quad \text{with probability } d_{it}$$

$$ \tag{26}$$

$$q_{ijt} = 0 \qquad \text{with probability } (1 - d_{it})$$

where d_{it} is the probability that agricultural production is feasible. This probability is, in turn, a logistic function[39] of the natural lay of the land and artificial flood-protection projects:

$$d_{it} = \left[\cfrac{1}{1 + \left[\cfrac{1}{e^{\pi(z)}} \right]} \right] \tag{27}$$

$$\pi(z) = DRY_i + \beta_1 \cdot PROJ_{it} \tag{28}$$

where DRY_i is a measure of the percentage of county i which is naturally protected from periodic flooding, $PROJ_{it}$ is an index of the share of county i at time t which has been artificially protected from flooding

---

complete specifications of the final econometric model were developed for those distributions as well, as is discussed later.

[39]The logistic specification is used to constrain d_{it} to values between zero and unity, because the empirical measures of U.S. Army Corps of Engineers and Soil Conservation Service project impact areas and natural flood protection are only indexes of protection.

(by Corps of Engineers and Soil Conservation Service projects),[40] and β_1 is a parameter which indicates the impact of artificial flood protection relative to the impact of natural flood protection.

In this relatively simple, first approximation, Federal flood-control and drainage projects have the effect of rendering agricultural production feasible; and on the feasible land, the index of feasibility, q_{ijt}, is distributed lognormally and unchanging over time, i.e. linked exclusively to soil texture and soil nutrients. This approach assumes that selection by the Corps and SCS of specific land parcels for protection is independent of potential yields; the distribution of potential yields is identical to the distribution of actual yields.

A more general approach is to allow for the possibility that decisions to protect land from flooding are not made independently of the land's relative potential for agricultural production. Thus, the yield distribution is affected by flood protection. In terms of the basic model, the underlying heterogeneity is itself affected by the presence of flood-control projects. In this more general approach, the parameters of the lognormal distribution, μ and σ, are themselves

---

[40]These two variables are defined as follows:

$DRY_i = 1 - FLRISK_i$, where the latter variable is a measure of the share of county i which is subject to some risk of periodic flooding, in the absence of artificial flood-control projects; and

$PROJ_{it} = ACCU_{it} + SCCU_{it}$, the sum of the shares of county i protected at time t by U.S. Army Corps of Engineers and Soil Conservation Service projects, respectively.

functions of $PROJ_{it}$:[41]

$$\log(q_{ijt}) \sim N\left[\mu(1 + \beta_2 PROJ_{it}), \left[\sigma_i(1 + \beta_3 PROJ_{it})\right]^2\right] \quad \text{with prob. } d_{it}$$

(29)

$$q_{ijt} = 0 \qquad \text{with probability } (1 - d_{it})$$

Whereas in the simpler model the impact of Federal projects on land-use decisions is captured by the parameter β_1 (and its multiplicative effect with other parameters in the non-linear model), in the more general model, there are three project-impact parameters, β_1, β_2, and β_3.

Aggregation of Necessary Conditions for Forested Wetland Conversion

Having posited the basic nature of the heterogeneity of land, it is now possible to utilize this distributional model in order to aggregate the individual-landowner necessary conditions which were previously developed. Equation 24, above, indicates that there is an incentive to convert forested wetlands to agricultural cropland if $X_{ijt} > 0$. Hence, there is a threshold value of q_{ijt}, denoted q_{it}^x, above which the incentive for conversion manifests itself:

---

[41]In the current application, individual county variances (or means) are not estimated. Note, however, that the σ_i parameters (i = 1 to 36 counties) are indeed identified in the model of which equation 26 is a part and could therefore, in principle, be estimated, given sufficient data. The same is true of a set of μ_i parameters.

$$q_{it}^x = \left[\frac{C_{it} + FN_{it} + AC_{it}}{A_{it}} \right] \qquad (30)$$

If conversion cost, in addition to agricultural feasibility, is allowed to be heterogeneous across land parcels (within counties) and flood-control projects are believed to affect conversion costs as well agricultural feasibility (yields), then the conversion cost term in equation 1 is replaced by the term $\alpha_1 \cdot q_{ijt} C_{it} g_{it}$, where α_1 is a parameter which captures the relative effect of heterogeneity on conversion costs, compared with the effect on agricultural yields. Under these circumstances, and allowing for the parametric effect of weather (soil moisture) on conversion costs, q_{it}^x becomes:

$$q_{it}^x = \left[\frac{FN_{it} + AC_{it}}{A_{it} - \alpha_1 C_{it} \cdot \exp\{\alpha_2 PHDI_{it}\}} \right] \qquad (31)$$

In either case, there is an incentive to convert parcel j (in county i at time t) from a forested condition to agricultural cropland if $q_{ijt} > q_{it}^x$. Therefore, the privately optimal (and hence, the desired or target) stock of converted land, expressed as a fraction of all land available for conversion, is:

$$\left[\frac{AG}{T} \right]_{it}^* = \left[1 - \left[\frac{S}{T} \right]_{it}^* \right] = d_{it} \cdot \left[\int_{q_{it}^x}^{\infty} \left[f_i\{s\} \right] ds \right] \qquad (32)$$

41

where $f_i\{\cdot\}$ is the lognormal density function, and where, for the time being, the simpler model of heterogeneity (equation 26) is utilized. Therefore,

$$\left[\frac{AG}{T}\right]^{*}_{it} = d_{it} \cdot \left[1 - F_i\left[q^x_{it}\right]\right] \tag{33}$$

where $F_i\left[\cdot\right]$ is the lognormal cumulative distribution function, and

$$\left[\frac{AG}{T}\right]^{*}_{it} = d_{it} \cdot \left[1 - F\left[\left[\log\left[q^x_{it}\right] - \mu\right]/\sigma_i\right]\right] \tag{34}$$

where $F[\cdot]$ is the cumulative, standard normal distribution function.

Next, it is posited that conversion follows a partial adjustment process.[42] Thus

---

[42]The partial adjustment process is assumed to be due to a combination of factors, including liquidity constraints associated with the cost of conversion, the effect of a non-degenerate age distribution of trees in standing forests, and (empirical observations of) decision-making inertia. A desirable alternative to the ad hoc partial adjustment model would be modification of the objective function (equation 1) to allow for these various factors. Whereas liquidity constraints could be modelled with a quadratic or other non-linear cost of adjustment (conversion) function, $C(g_{ijt})$; a substantially more complex integrand would result if provision were made for the effect of the non-degenerate age distribution of trees; and it is unclear how the objective function could be modified to provide for the effects of decision-making inertia. Furthermore, the problem of empirical observations of lags in abandonment behavior would remain. Although the partial-adjustment approach may be troubling on a theoretical level, emphasis is given in this study to the task of modelling unobserved heterogeneity, at the cost of maintaining a relatively simple dynamic optimization problem.

$$\left[\frac{AG}{T}\right]_{it} - \left[\frac{AG}{T}\right]_{i,t-1} = \gamma_c \cdot \left[\left[\frac{AG}{T}\right]^*_{it} - \left[\frac{AG}{T}\right]_{i,t-1}\right] + \varepsilon^c_{it} \qquad (35)$$

where γ_c is the rate of partial adjustment, and ε^c_{it} is an error term which is composed of a county-specific (time-invariant) component, λ_i, and a component, ϕ^c_{it}, which has mean zero, so that $\varepsilon^c_{it} = \lambda_i + \phi^c_{it}$. Next, the percentage change in the forested area of county i during the period t-1 to t due to conversion, $FORCH^c_{it}$, is defined as follows:

$$\left[\frac{AG}{T}\right]_{it} - \left[\frac{AG}{T}\right]_{i,t-1} = \left[\frac{S}{T}\right]_{i,t-1} - \left[\frac{S}{T}\right]_{it} = (-1) \cdot FORCH^c_{it} \qquad (36)$$

So, by substituting equations 34 and 36 into equation 35,

$$FORCH^c_{it}(-1) = \gamma_c\left[d_{it}\left[1 - F\left[\left[\log\left[q^x_{it}\right] - \mu\right]/\sigma_i\right]\right] - \left[\frac{AG}{T}\right]_{i,t-1}\right] + \varepsilon^c_{it} \qquad (37)$$

or, equivalently,

$$FORCH^c_{it}(-1) = \gamma_c\left[d_{it}\left[1 - F\left[\left[\log\left[q^x_{it}\right] - \mu\right]/\sigma_i\right]\right] + \left[\frac{S}{T}\right]_{i,t-1} - 1\right] + \varepsilon^c_{it} \qquad (38)$$

Allowing for the more general description of heterogeneity, embodied above in equation 29, the final conversion relationship is:

$$\text{FORCH}^c_{it} \cdot (-1) = \gamma_c \left| d_{it} \cdot \left[1 - \mathbf{F} \left[\left[\log \left[q^X_{it} \right] - \mu(1 + \beta_2 \text{PROJ}_{it}) \right] \right. \right. \right.$$

(39)

$$\left. \left. \left. / \sigma_i (1 + \beta_3 \text{PROJ}_{it}) \right] \right] + \left[\frac{S}{T} \right]_{i,t-1} - 1 \right| + \epsilon^c_{it}$$

where d_{it} is a function of PROJ_{it} and FLRISK_i, as defined previously in equations 27 and 28.

The above equation represents the final specification for one-half of the model, namely situations in which conversion of forests to cropland occur. The other half of the complete model is developed next, that part allowing for situations in which farmland is abandoned and permitted to return gradually to a forested state.

Aggregation of Necessary Conditions for Farmland Abandonment

Equation 25, above, indicated that there is an economic incentive to abandon farmland and allow it to return to forest if $Y_{ijt} > 0$. There exists a threshold value of q_{ijt}, denoted q^Y_{it}, below which the incentive for abandonment manifests itself:[43]

---

[43]Note that allowing conversion costs, as well as agricultural feasibility, to be heterogeneous across land parcels (and allowing flood-control projects to affect conversion costs as well as agricultural yields) has no effect on the abandonment part of the model, since conversion costs are irrelevant to the abandonment decision.

$$q_{it}^{y} = \left[\frac{\tilde{F}_{it} + AC_{it}}{A_{it}}\right] \qquad (40)$$

Thus, there is an incentive to abandon farmland if $q_{ijt} < q_{it}^{y}$, and the privately optimal (*target*) stock of forested land is equal to the sum of the target stock of abandoned farmland plus the target stock of unconverted forest:

$$\left[\frac{S}{T}\right]_{it}^{*} = d_{it} \cdot \left[\int_{0}^{q_{it}^{y}} \left[f_{i}(s)\right] ds\right] + \left[1 - d_{it}\right] \qquad (41)$$

where $f_{i}\{\cdot\}$ is the lognormal density function, and where the simpler model of heterogeneity (equation 26) is utilized for ease of exposition. Therefore,

$$\left[\frac{S}{T}\right]_{it}^{*} = d_{it} \cdot \left[F_{i}\left[q_{it}^{y}\right]\right] + \left[1 - d_{it}\right] \qquad (42)$$

where $F_{i}[\cdot]$ is the cumulative, lognormal distribution function, and

$$\left[\frac{S}{T}\right]_{it}^{*} = d_{it} \cdot \left[F\left[\left[\log\left[q_{it}^{y}\right] - \mu\right]/\sigma_{i}\right]\right] + \left[1 - d_{it}\right] \qquad (43)$$

where $F[\cdot]$ is the cumulative, standard normal distribution function.

As with the conversion process, a partial adjustment mechanism is

45

employed, but one allowing for a different rate of adjustment, γ_a, in the abandonment case:[44]

$$\left[\frac{S}{T}\right]_{it} - \left[\frac{S}{T}\right]_{i,t-1} = \gamma_a \cdot \left[\left[\frac{S}{T}\right]_{it}^{*} - \left[\frac{S}{T}\right]_{i,t-1}\right] + \varepsilon_{it}^{a} \qquad (44)$$

where ε_{it}^{a} is an error term which is composed of a county-specific component, λ_i, and a component, ϕ_{it}^{a}, which has mean zero.[45] The percentage change in the forested area of county i during the time period t-1 to t due to abandonment, $FORCH_{it}^{a}$, is defined as:

$$FORCH_{it}^{a} = \left[\frac{S}{T}\right]_{it} - \left[\frac{S}{T}\right]_{i,t-1} \qquad (45)$$

Now, by substituting equations 43 and 45 into equation 44,

---

[44]The partial adjustment process (in the case of abandonment) is posited on the basis of empirical observations of decision-making inertia in which farmers appear to resist economic incentives to abandon farmland and allow it to return to a forested state.

[45]It may be argued that the county-specific component of the error term of the abandonment relationship ought to be distinguished from the county-specific component of the error term of the previously defined conversion relationship. Doing so would result in a final model with two fixed effects, one holding when forested land is converted and one holding when farmland is abandoned. While such an approach would be theoretically desirable, the available data (with few cases of abandonment) will not allow for such separate fixed effects to be estimated. Instead, by assuming at this stage that the county-specific component of the error term is the same for conversion and abandonment, the combination of the two parts of the model (later in the chapter) leads to the specification of a conventional fixed-effects model, the parameters of which can be estimated. Thus, some amount of generality is sacrificed in the interest of practicality.

$$\text{FORCH}_{it}^{a} = \gamma_{a} \left[d_{it} \left[F \left[\left[\log \left[q_{it}^{y} \right] - \mu \right] / \sigma_{i} \right] \right] + \left[1 - d_{it} \right] - \left[\frac{S}{T} \right]_{i,t-1} \right] + \varepsilon_{it}^{a} \quad (46)$$

Again allowing for the more general description of heterogeneity, from equation 29, the final abandonment relationship is:

$$\text{FORCH}_{it}^{a} = \gamma_{a} \left[d_{it} \cdot \left[F \left[\left[\log \left[q_{it}^{y} \right] - \mu(1 + \beta_{2}\text{PROJ}_{it}) \right] \right. \right. \right.$$

$$(47)$$

$$\left. \left. \left. / \sigma_{i}(1 + \beta_{3}\text{PROJ}_{it}) \right] \right] + \left[1 - d_{it} \right] - \left[\frac{S}{T} \right]_{i,t-1} \right] + \varepsilon_{it}^{a}$$

where d_{it} is a function of PROJ_{it} and FLRISK_{it}, as defined in equations 27 and 28. Having specified aggregated equations for forest conversion and agricultural abandonment, the next step is to combine these relationships into a complete model of wetland allocation.

A Comprehensive Econometric Model
of Forested Wetland Conversion and Agricultural Abandonment

By assuming that conversion and abandonment do not occur simultaneously in any given county (but allowing for the fact that at any time, some counties may be experiencing losses of forests while other counties are experiencing gains), it is possible to combine the conversion and abandonment relationships into an econometrically estimatable model. First, let the right-hand side of the conversion relationship, equation 39, be denoted by $G\{W_{it}\}$ and the right-hand side of the abandonment relationship, equation 47, be denoted by $V\{Z_{it}\}$:

$$FORCH^c_{it} = G\{W_{it}\} + \varepsilon^c_{it} \tag{48}$$

$$FORCH^a_{it} = V\{Z_{it}\} + \varepsilon^a_{it} \tag{49}$$

The net observed change in forested acreage from time t-1 to time t is:

$$FORCH_{it} = FORCH^c_{it} + FORCH^a_{it} \tag{50}$$

where, by definition, $-1 \leq FORCH^c_{it} < 0$ and $0 < FORCH^a_{it} \leq +1$. Given the assumption of mutual exclusivity of conversion and abandonment, the econometric model now takes the following form:[46]

$$FORCH_{it} = G\{W_{it}\} \cdot D^c_{it} + V\{Z_{it}\} \cdot D^a_{it} + \varepsilon_{it} \tag{51}$$

where D^c_{it} = 1 if the fitted value of $FORCH^c_{it}$ (in equation 39), from a first-stage estimation of equation 51, is less than zero; 0 otherwise;

   D^a_{it} = 1 if the fitted value of $FORCH^a_{it}$ (in equation 47), from a

---

[46]Although the functional form is not constrained to yield fitted values between + 1 and - 1, actual fitted values in the current application are well within these limits (between + 0.04 and - 0.04).

first-stage estimation of equation 51, is greater than zero;
0 otherwise; and

$$\varepsilon_{it} = \varepsilon_{it}^c + \varepsilon_{it}^a = \lambda_i + \phi_{it}^c + \phi_{it}^a = \lambda_i + \phi_{it}.$$

By treating the county-specific components of the error term, λ_i, as a set of fixed-effect parameters to be estimated, equation 51 becomes a single-equation, fixed-effects model. The complete, final econometric model of forested wetland conversion and agricultural cropland abandonment is summarized in Table 1.[47]

---

[47]The complete specifications for models where the heterogeneity of land is distributed normally and uniformly (instead of lognormally) are provided in Appendices 11 and 12, respectively.

$$FORCH_{it} = FORCH^c_{it} \cdot D^c_{it} + FORCH^a_{it} \cdot D^a_{it} + \lambda_i + \phi_{it}$$

$$FORCH^c_{it} \cdot (-1) = \gamma_c \left[d_{it} \cdot \left[1 - F \left[\left[\log\left[q^x_{it} \right] - \mu(1 + \beta_2 PROJ_{it}) \right] \right. \right. \right.$$

$$\left. \left. \left. /\sigma_i(1 + \beta_3 PROJ_{it}) \right] \right] + \left[\frac{S}{T} \right]_{i,t-1} - 1 \right]$$

$$FORCH^a_{it} = \gamma_a \left[d_{it} \cdot \left[F \left[\left[\log\left[q^y_{it} \right] - \mu(1 + \beta_2 PROJ_{it}) \right] \right. \right. \right.$$

$$\left. \left. \left. /\sigma_i(1 + \beta_3 PROJ_{it}) \right] \right] + \left[1 - d_{it} \right] - \left[\frac{S}{T} \right]_{i,t-1} \right]$$

$$d_{it} = \left[\frac{1}{1 + \left[\frac{1}{e^{\pi(z)}} \right]} \right] \qquad \text{where } \pi(z) = DRY_i + \beta_1 PROJ_{it}$$

$$q^x_{it} = \left[\frac{FN_{it} + AC_{it}}{A_{it} - \alpha_1 C_{it} \cdot \exp(\alpha_2 PHDI_{it})} \right] \qquad q^y_{it} = \left[\frac{\tilde{F}_{it} + AC_{it}}{A_{it}} \right]$$

CHAPTER III

ECONOMETRIC ANALYSIS OF FORESTED WETLAND CONVERSION AND FARMLAND ABANDONMENT

This chapter is divided into three major sections. First, results
are provided from econometrically estimating six alternative
specifications of the previously specified model of wetland conversion
and farmland abandonment. Second, the six estimated models are assessed
by comparing their accuracy in simulating actual changes in forested
wetland acreages in the Alluvial Plain during the sample time period,
and on this basis, one of the specifications is selected for use in the
remainder of the analysis. Third, the historic effects of major
economic, hydrologic, and climatic factors on forested wetland
conversion and farmland abandonment in the Alluvial Plain are assessed
through a series of factual and counterfactual simulations.

Parameter Estimation of Alternative Specifications

Using data for 36 counties in Arkansas, Louisiana, and Mississippi,[48] during the period 1935-1984,[49] the parameters of the model embodied in equations 27, 28, 31, 39, 40, 47, and 51 (Table 1) were estimated econometrically. Panel data were incorporated into the estimation process by stacking the data for 36 counties for each of ten (five-year[50]) time periods (a total of 50 years, 1935-1984), making a

---

[48]See Appendix 13 for a list of the 36 counties and parishes in the study area.

[49]The nature and sources of data employed and the construction of the requisite variable series are described in Appendix 6. For further detail, see Stavins 1986. The quinquennial allocation of land between forest and cropland is provided in Appendix 14.

[50]Limitations on the availability of data on the model's dependent variable (forested acreage) necessitated the use of a quinquennial as opposed to an annual model. Because of this, a simple approach (with, static, relatively myopic expectations) is used, one in which five-year averages of actual values of price (and cost) variables are substituted directly for respective expected values. This is in contrast with the approach more typical with annual-data agricultural-supply models, in which farmers' production decisions are modelled as being dependent upon the contemporaneous support price and the (one-year) lagged market price, an approach which has intuitive appeal and empirical reliability for many annual crops (Nerlove and Bachman 1960). With regard to the issue of inclusion in the model of government supported crop prices, it should be noted that soybeans, the most important crop grown on converted land, have no deficiency payment program and, at any rate, loan rates on soybeans have historically remained below market prices, a situation which is unlikely to change (Heimlich and Langner 1986). Nevertheless, it is possible that Federal commodity programs for soybeans and other crops have affected conversion/abandonment decisions through their role in reducing producer risk. An alternative to combining market and support prices would be to utilize futures' market prices, as these may be assumed to incorporate available information efficiently, and there is empirical evidence supporting their usage in agricultural supply functions (Gardner 1976). Such price series are not available for the four crops for the entire period of the analysis.

total of 360 observations.[51] Thus, a single-equation model is employed
with an additive term to allow for fixed, county effects:[52] $\sum \lambda_i \cdot D_i$,
where the λ_i are a set of fixed-effect parameters and the D_i are a set
of county dummy variables. The parameters and standard errors of this

---

[51]One other potential improvement in the model would be to utilize more
sophisticated modelling of individuals' price-expectation mechanisms,
such as: rational expectations; a weighted-average of current and past
prices; or adaptive expectations. Whereas the first two possibilities
would require only minor changes in the calculation of the "price"
variables, the adaptive expectations approach, involving all previous
prices (through a lagged dependent variable), would require a change of
specification at the individual level of the model. If the adaptive
expectations mechanism is introduced at the individual level, the
revised necessary conditions for conversion and abandonment can not be
aggregated, because an expression for the threshold level of q is not
identified. On the other hand, if the adaptive expectations mechanism
is applied at the level of the aggregated model (to all prices), the
final model which is derived is the same as that developed here, with
the exception that the error term follows a first-order moving average
process. Note that the partial adjustment mechanism posited earlier may
account for non-static price expectations, as well as for the factors
previously described.

[52]An alternative approach to incorporating panel data (without fixed
effects) would be to specify separate cross-sectional equations for each
of the ten (five-year) time periods. In that case, the single-equation
model would become a system of ten equations with cross-equation
constraints on parameters. Because the error term for a single county
would then be expected to be correlated across time, Zellner's (1962,
1963) seemingly unrelated regression (SUR) method might appear
attractive, but in the presence of a lagged dependent variable (in
combination with error terms which are correlated across time),
Zellner's SUR procedure ceases to be consistent.

Instead, an instrumental-variables approach, such as three-stage least
squares (THSLS) or the full information maximum likelihood (FIML)
method, would be appropriate. The structure and dimensions of the
multi-equation, panel-data model present problems, however, with regard
to the choice of instruments, since each cross-sectional equation is
based upon only 36 observations, while there are obviously a larger
number of excluded exogenous variables. What is needed, then, is a
THSLS estimator which allows for different sets of instruments to be
used for each equation, such as that described by Amemiya (1977).
Unfortunately, available econometric estimation programs (including
TSP, SAS, and LIMDEP) utilize a THSLS estimator which is less general in
its choice of instruments (Jorgenson and Laffont 1974). In particular,
the same set of instruments must be used in all equations.

single-equation model were estimated with nonlinear least squares[53] (Berndt, Hall, Hall, and Hausman 1974).

Possibilities of Heteroscedasticity and Serial Correlation

Despite the fact that the fixed-effects approach has presumably removed what may have been a major source of heteroscedasticity from the error term, the possibility remains that the error terms are still heteroscedastic and that the estimators are hence inefficient. In regard to hypothesis tests of the impact of Federal projects, such inefficient parameter estimates would only lead to more conservative tests than would be used if any heteroscedasticity present had been appropriately modelled (through the use of some generalized least squares estimation procedure). The parameter estimates themselves remain unbiased and consistent in the presence of heteroscedasticity.

One type of heteroscedasticity, of course, is of concern, this being that type which may lead to biased and inconsistent estimates of standard errors.[54] In order to avoid such effects on the estimated standard errors, robust (White) standard errors[55] were estimated in all cases and are reported in the tables and appendices of results which follow.

---

[53]The nonlinear least squares estimates were made with TSP Version 4.1B on a VAX 8530, running VMS Version 4.5. TSP utilizes a generalized Gauss-Newton iterative method, with analytic first derivatives of the nonlinear model, to find least-squares estimates of parameters.

[54]This type of heteroscedasticity is associated with correlation between the square of exogenous variables (and their cross-products) and the error term squared.

[55]The robust standard error estimates are consistent whether the error terms are homoscedastic or heteroscedastic, and in the latter case remain consistent even when the variance of the heteroscedastic errors are correlated with the model's exogenous variables (White 1980; Chamberlain 1982).

The possibility of serially correlated error terms is more serious, since this would result in inconsistent nonlinear least squares parameter estimates, due to correlation of the error terms with a right-hand side (endogenous) variable, namely the lagged percentage of available land which is in a forested state, $(S/T)_{i,t-1}$. It was believed that a major source of correlation of error terms across time (for each county) would be a fixed effect. This source of serial correlation, at least, has been removed from the error terms by the fixed-effects specification.

Nevertheless, it is reasonable to test for the presence of any remaining serial correlation in the fixed-effect econometric estimates. First, Durbin's test for first-order autocorrelation in the presence of a lagged dependent variable was employed, with the result that the null hypothesis of no first-order autocorrelation was not rejected.[56] A test for a more general autocorrelated (AR) or moving-average (MA) error structure was suggested by Breusch (1978) and Godfrey (1978). The Breusch-Godfrey test was employed, and the previous finding of no serial correlation was confirmed.[57]

---

[56]Durbin's (1970) test involves regressing the estimated residuals from the original equation on the lagged residuals, the lagged dependent variable(s), and all other regressors from the original equation. The test for AR1 errors is then simply a t-test on the coefficient of the lagged residual in the secondary equation. In the current application, ρ was estimated to be 0.00829, with a standard error of 0.00673.

[57]In the Breusch-Godfrey test, the estimated residuals, ε_t, from the original estimation are regressed on a constant, the regressors from the original equation, and lagged values of the estimated residuals, ε_{t-i}, where i equals 1 to p. Based upon this auxiliary regression, the null hypothesis of no serial correlation of degrees 1 through p is rejected if $N \cdot R^2 > \chi_p^2$, where χ_p^2 is the critical value from a chi-square distribution with p degrees of freedom. This was done (for specification L3, below), and it was found that

$$N \cdot R^2 = (288) \cdot (0.00829) = 2.39 < \chi_p^2,$$

Econometric Results

Before turning to the specific results from alternative
specifications, it may be noted that the overall results lend support to
the basic validity of the model. Estimated parameters are all of the
expected sign, and nearly all estimates are significant at the 90%, 95%,
or 99% level. Furthermore, both parameter and standard error estimates
(Table 2) are highly robust with respect to modifications of the
specification. Thus, the basic structural model of changes in forested
acreage being a function of expectations regarding the relative economic
returns from agriculture and forestry is strongly supported by the
statistical estimation results.[58] In addition, the fixed-effects
approach is clearly superior to a totally pooled model, both for the
less general (L1) and the more general (L2) specifications, as is
indicated by the appropriate likelihood ratio tests.[59]

---

where for p=2, the critical levels of χ^2 are 4.61, 5.99, and 9.21 at the
90%, 95%, and 99% significance levels, respectively.

[58]The possibility also exists of including in the model some indication
of individuals' expectations regarding the future construction of flood-
control and drainage projects, proxied by data on project authorizations
(see Appendices 3 and 4). Given the reality of relatively constant real
costs of conversion, however, there is no incentive for landowners to
convert forested wetland parcels prior to project construction (and
consequent flood protection).

[59]For example, in the case of the less general (L1) specification, the
value of the log likelihood function for a suitably constrained (no
fixed effects) model is 751.116. Thus, the likelihood ratio, LR = $2 \cdot (L_u$
$- L_c)$ = 69.91, where L_u is the value of the likelihood function from the
unconstrained model and L_c is the value from the constrained model. The
critical values from a χ^2 distribution with 36 degrees of freedom are
50.96 (α=.05) and 58.57 (α=.01). Estimates of the fixed-effects
parameters for the L3 specification are typical and are provided in
Appendix 15. Note that the few negative estimates are all
insignificant. Comparison may be made with a (uniform distribution)
model where a single intercept was estimated -- specification U2 in

**TABLE 2: ECONOMETRIC ESTIMATION RESULTS - SPECIFICATIONS L1 THROUGH L3
           LOGNORMAL DISTRIBUTION OF HETEROGENEITY**

Parameter	Interpretation	Alternative Specifications[a]		
		L1	L2	L3
γ_a	Abandonment Partial Adjustment	0.37618 (0.190)[b]	0.32360 (0.177)	0.36717 (0.184)
γ_c	Conversion Partial Adjustment	0.44875 (0.142)	0.69352 (0.156)	0.64826 (0.154)
μ	Mean of Heterogeneity	0.74095 (0.368)	0.83464 (0.290)	1.11650 (0.364)
σ	Standard Deviation of Heterogeneity	0.38182 (0.087)	0.44438 (0.069)	0.43848 (0.067)
β_1	Project Impact on Agric. Feasibility	9.20170 (3.216)	8.83060 (2.309)	8.93700 (2.465)
β_2	Project Impact on Heterogeneity Mean	–	1.07240 (1.467)	0.77193 (0.774)
β_3	Project Impact on Heterogeneity S.D.	–	0.53757 (0.229)	0.42799 (0.183)
α_1	Relative Conversion- Cost Impact	1.58160 (0.923)	1.02070 (1.169)	–
α_2	Weather Impact on Conversion Cost	–	–	1.59720 (0.304)
logL	Log Likelihood Value	786.072	790.621	791.698
df	Degrees of Freedom	318	316	316

[a]The specifications are described in the text. Basic features are:
  L1 -- fixed effects; lognormal distribution of heterogeneity
  L2 -- projects affect heterogeneity; fixed effects; lognormal
        distribution of heterogeneity
  L3 -- projects affect heterogeneity; fixed effects; lognormal
        distribution of heterogeneity

[b]Robust standard error estimates appear below coefficients.

The econometric results from estimating the basic model (where the underlying heterogeneity is distributed lognormally) are provided in Table 2 and Appendix 17.[60] In Table 2 are found the results for three specifications, two of which (L2 and L3) allow for flood-control and drainage projects to affect the heterogeneity (of protected land) as well as to affect agricultural feasibility directly.[61] Results for four less general specifications, in which the Corps and SCS are assumed to randomly select land for protection,[62] are found in Appendix 17.

In the three specifications in Table 2, the estimated partial adjustment coefficients on conversion, γ_c, indicate that about 60% of the targeted decrease in forested acreage (increase in agricultural cropland) is achieved in the initial five-year period. On the other hand, the estimates of γ_a indicate that about 36% of the targeted abandonment occurs in the initial period.[63]

Appendix 16.

[60]Econometric results from the estimation of specifications where the distribution of heterogeneity is assumed to be normal are provided in Appendix 18. Econometric results from specifications with uniformly distributed heterogeneity are found in Appendix 16. Note that estimates of the critical parameters of the model, including γ_a, γ_c, and β_1, are robust with respect to assumptions regarding the functional form of the underlying distribution. On the other hand, the estimates of the distributional parameters, μ, σ, ω, and θ, vary depending upon the type of distribution which is employed.

[61]See equation 29, above.

[62]See equation 26, above.

[63]As a test of the partial adjustment model, it is useful to examine whether the results are inconsistent with an instantaneous adjustment. In other words, are γ_c and γ_a significantly different from unity? The appropriate Wald tests indicate that neither γ_c nor γ_a is equal to 1.0. The calculated Wald statistics are 5.23 and 11.75, respectively; and the critical values from a χ^2 distribution with 1 degree of freedom are 3.84 ($\alpha=.05$) and 6.63 ($\alpha=.01$). For the joint test of $\gamma_c = \gamma_a = 1.0$, the calculated Wald statistic is 12.06; and the critical values from a χ^2 distribution with 2 degrees of freedom are 5.99 ($\alpha=.05$) and 9.21

The distribution of heterogeneity is seen to be non-degenerate: both the mean, μ, and the standard deviation, σ, of the lognormal distribution of heterogeneity (agricultural feasibility) are significant. Likewise, two of the three categories of impact of Federal flood-control and drainage projects on conversion and abandonment are significant: direct impact on agricultural feasibility, β_1;[64] and impact on the dispersion (standard deviation) of the underlying distribution of heterogeneity, β_3. The impact on the mean of the heterogeneity, β_2, is positive but not significant. The average direct impact of artificial flood protection on agricultural feasibility, β_1, is approximately nine times that of average "natural flood protection" (see equation 28).

It was not possible, due to limitations of the data, to estimate the equation with both a parameter for the effect of conversion costs relative to other benefits and costs, α_1, and a parameter for the effect of weather on conversion costs, α_2, although the parameters of such a specification are identified. The specification with α_1 (L2) appears to be inferior to the specification with α_2 (L3), and, in any event, the estimate of α_1 is not significantly different from 1.0. The impact of weather on conversion costs, α_2, is very significant, and the L3 specification appears to be the best of the three examined.[65]

$(\alpha=.01)$.

[64]That is, rendering feasible, land which previously was not feasible for agricultural production.

[65]These findings are confirmed by the estimation results from the simpler lognormal specifications, reported in Appendix 17, and by the normal and uniform distribution estimates, reported in Appendices 18 and 16, respectively.

Testing for Distinct Corps and SCS Effects

The protected acreages of U.S. Army Corps Of Engineers and Soil Conservation Service flood-control and drainage projects were aggregated in the single variable, $PROJ_{it}$. Thus, the β_1 parameter estimates represent the joint impact of the two types of projects. To test the hypothesis that the direct impacts of Corps and SCS projects were indeed the same, separate parameters were estimated for the direct effects of Corps and SCS projects.

In a lognormal model (specification L7 in Appendix 17) which is otherwise identical to specification L1, the point estimate of Corps impacts ($\hat{\beta}_4$ = 10.37) is substantially greater than that of SCS project impacts ($\hat{\beta}_5$ = 2.68). The precision of the β_5 estimate is very low, however, possibly due to collinearity of the two data series. The two estimated parameters are statistically equivalent, as indicated by the appropriate Wald test,[66] although the Corps parameter estimate is much more precise. The conclusion is that the effects of the Corps and SCS projects cannot be disentangled, although there is reason to be more confident about the Corps effects than the SCS effects.[67]

The difference in precision of estimates may partly be due to the much larger data set (more projects over a longer time period) upon which the Corps project impacts were estimated, compared with the SCS

---

[66]The calculated Wald statistic is 0.1957; and the critical values from a χ^2 distribution with 1 degree of freedom are 3.84 (α=.05) and 6.63 (α=.01).

[67]Given the similarity in parameter estimates but the difference in standard error estimates for Corps and SCS projects, one further test may be in order. The above model was re-estimated, constraining the SCS coefficient to be zero. The result was that the Corps coefficient estimate increased and its estimated standard error decreased, confirming the fact that a much higher degree of confidence should be attributed to the estimated impacts of Corps projects.

project impacts. Given this possibility plus the fact that the parameter estimates are statistically equivalent, the most reasonable approach is to keep the SCS projects in the model, but in the aggregated form of $PROJ_{it}$.

Selection of the Final Model

The models with the lognormal distribution of heterogeneity were judged, on theoretical grounds, to be superior to the models based upon normal or uniform distributions.[68] Empirical analysis confirmed this. Those lognormal models which allow for more general impacts of projects on conversion and abandonment (L2 and L3) appear preferable on theoretical and empirical grounds to the less general lognormal models (L1, L4, L5, L6).[69]

In order to examine more rigorously the selection of a final model, historical, dynamic simulations were carried out with the six alternative lognormal specifications to examine how well each model

---

[68]See previous discussion in section titled, "Modelling the Unobserved Heterogeneity of Land."

[69]Despite the fact that the estimates of β_2 in specifications L2 and L3 are not significant, it is wise to retain this aspect of the equation in the final specification because excluding it would bias the simulations (calculations of fitted values), although such exclusion of an insignificant variable, of course, would not bias the estimates of the remaining parameters. Moreover, there is no reason to favor the less general models, in which $\beta_2 = \beta_3 = 0$. The appropriate Wald test rejects such a null hypothesis -- the calculated Wald statistic is 9.42; and the critical values from a χ^2 distribution with 2 degrees of freedom are 5.99 ($\alpha = .05$) and 9.21 ($\alpha = .01$). Thus, the more general specifications (L2 and L3) are left as is for the purpose of examining goodness-of-fit statistics, below.

simulates the actual pattern of changes in forested acreage across the 36 counties during the period 1935-1984.[70]

A frequently utilized measure of dynamic performance is the root-mean-squared (RMS) error, but this measure suffers from the limitation that its magnitude is not standardized. To correct for this, Theil's inequality coefficient (Theil 1961) was employed:

$$
U = \left[\frac{\left[(1/T) \cdot \sum_{t=1}^{T} \left[Y_t^s - Y_t^a \right]^2 \right]^{1/2}}{\left[(1/T) \cdot \sum_{t=1}^{T} \left[Y_t^s \right]^2 \right]^{1/2} + \left[(1/T) \cdot \sum_{t=1}^{T} \left[Y_t^a \right]^2 \right]^{1/2}} \right] \tag{52}
$$

where Y_t^a = actual value of dependent variable for observation t;

Y_t^s = simulated value of dependent variable for observation t; and

T = total number of observations.

The numerator in equation 52 is the RMS error, and the scaling of the denominator insures that U has limits of 0 and 1, where $U = 0$ indicates a perfect dynamic fit. In keeping with the ordering of typical goodness-of-fit measures, the final comparative statistic, GF, is set equal to $1 - U$, so that a perfect fit is 1.0.

The composite range[71] of GF for the seven lognormal-based models is

[70]In all of the factual and counterfactual simulations reported in this study, the dummy variables, D_{it}^c and D_{it}^a, were generated on the basis of the signs of the fitted values of equation 39, the conversion relationship, because of the greater confidence attributed to the estimation of this part of the overall model.

[71]The ranking of GF for simulations of the model's dependent variable, $FORCH_{it}$, is similar but not identical to the ranking of GF for simulations of the quantity of forested land, S_{it} (Table 3). Therefore, a composite statistic is used, which is a simple average of the two

.8127 to .8113 (Table 3), and the more general models in which projects affect the underlying heterogeneity as well as feasibility are clearly favored. Consistent with prior expectations, the L3 specification is found to be the best in terms of the accuracy of its simulated values. Thus, this model is found to be superior both on theoretical and empirical grounds, and is therefore employed in the following stages of the analysis.

Implications of the Statistical Analysis

The principal implications which emerge from this phase of the analysis are as follows:

(1) construction of Federal flood-control and drainage projects caused a higher rate of conversion of forested wetlands to agricultural croplands than would have occurred in the absence of such projects;

(2) Federal projects affected the rate of conversion because they rendered unsuitable land suitable and because land which was already most suitable for agriculture was protected by the projects; and

(3) substantial wetland conversion would have occurred as a result of favorable economic returns to agriculture (relative to forestry), even if no Federal flood-control and drainage projects had been undertaken.

Thus, a preliminary answer is provided to one of the major questions addressed in this study. Federal flood-protection and
_____

goodness-of-fit statistics.

TABLE 3: GOODNESS OF FIT OF FACTUAL, HISTORICAL SIMULATIONS BASED UPON ALTERNATIVE ECONOMETRIC SPECIFICATIONS

Alternative Specifications[a]	Goodness-of-Fit Statistics[b]		
	Differences[c]	Levels[d]	Average[e]
L1	.67192 (6)	.95069 (3)	.81131 (6)
L2	.67425 (2)	.95049 (4)	.81237 (2)
L3	.67470 (1)	.95074 (1)	.81272 (1)
L4	.67350 (3)	.95073 (2)	.81212 (3)
L5	.67298 (5)	.95022 (5)	.81160 (4)
L6	.67301 (4)	.94996 (6)	.81149 (5)

[a]The alternative specifications are described in the text and in the tables and appendices of econometric estimates.

[b]The goodness-of-fit statistics reported here are equal to one minus Theil's U-statistic, and are therefore bounded by 0 and 1. Theil's U-statistic is defined in the text. Rankings are in parentheses.

[c]Based upon simulations of the dependent variable, $FORCH_{it}$.

[d]Based upon simulations of the quantity of forested land, S_{it}.

[e]A simple average of the two goodness-of-fit statistics.

drainage projects had a positive and systematic impact on the rate of

conversion of forested wetlands to agricultural cropland in the study

area during the period 1935-1984. But Federal projects were not the

only factors causing wetland conversion (and farmland abandonment) to

occur. Thus, important questions remain: given that Federal projects

encouraged the conversion of forested wetlands to agricultural uses,

what was the magnitude of this impact? When compared with other factors

which encouraged conversion, such as relatively high agricultural prices

or extended periods of unusually dry weather, were the effects of

Federal projects of substantial importance? Or were the Federal

project impacts insignificant in comparison with the effects of other

economic, hydrologic, and climatic factors?

The Effects of Major Economic, Hydrologic, and Climatic Factors on Forested Wetland Conversion and Farmland Abandonment

In order to estimate the quantitative impacts of various economic,

hydrologic, and climatic factors on the depletion of forested wetlands

and abandonment of farmland, a series of dynamic[72] factual and

counterfactual simulations[73] were carried out, using the econometrically

estimated parameter values.[74]

---

[72]The simulations must be dynamic because of the presence of the lagged
term, $(S/T)_{i,t-1}$, in equations 39 and 47.

[73]Just as the econometric estimation of the market model involves a two-
stage procedure for establishing the appropriate values of the dummy
variables for conversion and abandonment (see equation 51), so, too, the
simulations (both factual and counterfactual) involve a two-stage
approach for the establishment of the dummy variable values.

[74]In a dynamic, non-linear model, such as that utilized here,
simulations must be carried out to determine the impacts of variables,
since the impacts of exogenous variables depend on the size of the
variation of the respective variables, the level of other exogenous

Dynamic Simulation Methodology

To estimate the impact of a particular variable, such as the cost of conversion, three steps are involved. First, in the "factual simulation," the extent of conversion or abandonment is simulated using the econometrically estimated parameters and the actual, historical values of all variables. Second, in a "counterfactual simulation," the extent of conversion/abandonment is simulated using some counterfactual value of the cost of conversion (such as zero), while maintaining all other variables at their actual levels. Third, the difference between these simulated levels of changes in forested wetland acreage represents the impact of the given variable, conversion cost, on wetland depletion or farmland abandonment. This same approach is used below to estimate the quantitative impact on wetland changes of each of the basic variables in the econometric model, including Federal flood-control and drainage projects.

The Impact of Federal Flood-Control and Drainage Projects on the Conversion of Forested Wetlands and the Abandonment of Agricultural Cropland

The quinquennial (five-year) impacts of Federal projects on forested wetland depletion and farmland abandonment were estimated by taking the difference between the factual simulation and a related counterfactual simulation where the project levels were held at zero for all years. The actual depletion of forested wetlands in the 36-county sample area over the 50-year study period totalled approximately 3.64 million acres, while the historically simulated depletion is 3.68

---

variables, and the starting values of endogenous variables.

million acres.[75] The counterfactual simulation indicates that if no

projects had been built in the study area during the 1935-1984 period,

net depletion would have amounted to only about 2.53 million acres by

the year 1984.[76] Therefore, depletion due exclusively to the

construction and maintenance of Federal projects amounted to

approximately 1.15 million acres (Table 4). In other words, taking into

account all factors which affected individual landowners' decisions to

convert wetlands and abandon farmland, the statistical evidence

indicates that if there had been no Federal flood-control and drainage

projects constructed in the 36-county study area within the Lower

Mississippi Alluvial Plain after the year 1934, about 1.15 million fewer

acres of forested wetlands would have been converted. This impact

accounts for about 31% of all wetlands lost during the period.[77]

    Given the partial adjustment nature of the model, these figures are

not representative of the total, long-term impacts of projects, but only

---

[75]The six alternative lognormal specifications yield factual simulations
of total depletion ranging from 3.68 (L3) to 3.70 million acres (L6),
overall departures from actual depletion ranging from 1.1% to 1.8%
(Appendix 19). The total forested area in 1935, the first year of the
analysis, was approximately 6.275 million acres, while actual remaining
wetland forest amounted to about 2.638 million acres in 1984, the final
year of the study. Simulated 1984 forested areas range from 2.639 to
2.662 million acres (Appendix 20).

[76]The factually and counterfactually simulated quinquennial changes in
forested wetland acreage are provided in Appendix 21. The simulated
quinquennial levels of forested wetland acreage are found in Appendix
22.

[77]As is indicated in Appendix 23, the net impact of Federal projects on
wetland depletion is primarily due to the direct impact of projects on
agricultural feasibility (β_1). The impact of projects on the mean of
the heterogeneity distribution contributed only slightly to wetland
depletion, while project impacts on the variance of the distribution
actually discouraged wetland conversion, albeit by a relatively small
amount. Overall, if the indirect effects of projects on the underlying
distribution had been ignored, the net impact of Federal projects on
forested wetland depletion would have been overestimated.

TABLE 4: QUINQUENNIAL IMPACTS OF MAJOR VARIABLES ON FORESTED WETLAND DEPLETION IN THIRTY-SIX COUNTIES OF THE LOWER MISSISSIPPI ALLUVIAL PLAIN, 1935-1999[a]

Five-Yr Period	Factual Simula- tion	Impacts on Forested Wetland Acreage				
		$PROJ_{it}$	DRY_{it}	$PHDI_{it}$	C_{it}	FN_{it}
		(1,000 acres)				
1935-1939	-287	-5	-137	-105	99	101
1940-1944	-348	-13	-143	-99	97	97
1945-1949	-377	-12	-140	-89	88	97
1950-1954	-263	-13	-114	-77	75	74
1955-1959	-412	-100	-117	-67	63	76
1960-1964	-524	-145	-112	-77	71	75
1965-1969	-570	-267	-47	-35	22	32
1970-1974	-326	-225	-22	57	63	17
1975-1979	-267	-238	-8	66	70	4
1980-1984	-303	-134	-9	22	29	9
50-Year Impact	-3,677	-1,150	-846	-404	677	584
1985-1989	-106	-47	-3	8	10	3
1990-1994	-37	-17	-1	3	4	1
1995-1999	-13	-8	0	1	1	0
65-Year Impact	-3,834	-1,223	-850	-392	692	588
Long Term Impact	-3,841	-1,227	-850	-392	692	588

[a]The final model, specification L3, is utilized throughout.

of their impact through the year 1984. Factual and counterfactual simulations were therefore carried out through the year 1999, with the result that during the extended 65-year period the overall impact of Federal projects is expected to amount to 1.22 million acres of depletion, about 32% of expected total forested wetland losses (Table 4). In any event, the quinquennial impacts of projects appear to have peaked during the decade of the 1970's.

By solving the econometrically estimated equations for the (steady-state) target stock of forested wetlands,[78] it is estimated that total, long-term wetland depletion will amount to 3.84 million acres. Thus, about 96% of predicted long-term wetland depletion has already taken place.[79] Long-term (steady state) depletion due to Federal projects (constructed through the year 1984) is estimated to amount to 1.23 million acres, about 32% of estimated long-term depletion.

Relative Importance of Economic, Hydrologic, and Climatic Factors

Of the factors considered in the econometric model of forested wetland conversion and farmland abandonment (Table 1), the flood protection and drainage provision afforded by Federal projects had the

---

[78]The factually simulated long-term (steady-state) target stock of forested wetlands is approximately 2.500 million acres (Appendix 22). Total forested wetland stock in the 36 counties was 6.275 million acres in 1935, having fallen to about 2.638 million acres at the end of 1984. The factually simulated stock for the year 1999 is 2.507 million acres.

[79]Predictions of total, long-term impacts must be viewed with some caution because of the implicit assumption of constant future relative prices. Therefore, the discussion focuses on simulations of the period of analysis (1935-1984), as well as the next fifteen years (through the year 1999).

largest impact on net changes in forested acreage (Table 5).[80] The

joint effect of natural topography and the mainline levee system[81] was

of secondary importance, amounting to 846 thousand acres of depletion

(23% of total depletion) through 1984. Net forestry revenues and

conversion costs[82] exerted substantial restraints on wetland clearing

(Table 5). Had there been no costs involved for landowners in

undertaking wetland clearing, there would have been an additional 677

thousand acres of conversion (18% of total depletion) during the 50-year

study period. Similarly, if there had been no net revenues generated by

forestry activities, the model indicates that another 584 thousand acres

of forested wetlands would have been converted to agricultural uses

(about 16% of total depletion).

---

[80]Agricultural product prices are not considered in Table 5 because,
given the structure of the model, the methodology employed to develop
the table is not appropriate for assessing the role played in wetland
depletion by agricultural prices. An appropriate, alternative
methodology is utilized in the following section of the text.

[81]The "effect of natural topography" refers to the variable, DRY_i ($= 1 -$
$FLRISK_i$), a measure of the natural flood-proneness of counties (prior
to the construction of the flood-control and drainage projects of
concern). The "mainline levee system" (see Stavins 1987b) along the
Mississippi River, which was in place and providing protection virtually
from the beginning of the study period, may also have had a significant
impact on wetland depletion. Data on the area protected by the MLS are
not available. The protected area is approximately proportional to the
area affected by the great flood of 1927, but the flood data are highly
correlated with natural topography, and so multicollinearity prohibits
estimation of both the natural topography and the MLS effects in the
same equation. With the omission of the MLS proxy variable, the FLRISK
variable accounts for both phenomena. The reported impact of Federal
projects on wetland conversion refers exclusively to interior levee
development and thus underestimates the complete impact of all Federal
projects.

[82]The conversion cost term in the model is a combination of a time-
series of average conversion costs and a parameterized, complete panel
of data on soil moisture (PHDI). Thus, the impact attributed to
conversions cost is due to conversion costs indexed by soil moisture.

**TABLE 5:   DEPLETION OF FORESTED WETLANDS
DUE TO MAJOR ECONOMIC, HYDROLOGIC, AND CLIMATIC VARIABLES
LOWER MISSISSIPPI ALLUVIAL PLAIN[a]**

| Contributing Factor | Impacts on Net Change in Forested Wetland Acreage | | | |
| | 50-Year Period 1935-1984 | | 65-Year Period 1935-1999 | |
	Level[b]	Share[c]	Level	Share
Federal Flood-Control and Drainage Projects	- 1,150,000	31.3%	- 1,223,000	31.9%
Natural Topography and Mainline Levees[d]	- 846,000	23.0%	- 850,000	22.2%
Conversion Costs[e]	+ 677,000	18.4%	+ 692,000	18.0%
Net Forestry Revenue	+ 584,000	15.9%	+ 588,000	15.3%
(Total Factually Simulated Change)	- 3,677,000		- 3,834,000	

[a]The final model, specification L3, is utilized throughout.

[b]Acres, rounded to the nearest thousand acres.

[c]Percentage of total, factually simulated net change in forested acreage.

[d]The variable DRY_i (= $1-FLRISK_i$) is a measure of the natural flood-proneness of counties (prior to the construction of flood-control and drainage projects). The "mainline levee system" (see Stavins 1987) along the Mississippi River, which was in place and providing protection from the beginning of the study period, may have had a significant impact on wetland depletion. Data on the area protected by the MLS are not available. The protected area is approximately proportional to the area affected by the 1927 flood, but the flood data are highly correlated with natural topography, and so multicollinearity prohibits estimation of both natural topography and MLS effects. With the omission of the MLS proxy variable, the FLRISK variable accounts for both impacts. Therefore, the reported impact of Federal projects on wetland conversion refers exclusively to interior levee development, and thus underestimates the complete impact of all Federal projects.

[e]The conversion cost term in the model is a combination of a single time-series of average conversion costs and a parameterized, complete panel of data on soil moisture (PHDI). Thus, the impact attributed to conversion cost is due to conversion costs indexed by soil moisture.

The Impact of Agricultural Product Prices on Conversion and Abandonment

The U.S. Army Corps of Engineers has suggested that, even if no flood-control or drainage projects had been developed by the Federal government during the past fifty years, nevertheless, landowners would still have been induced to clear massive amounts of forested wetlands for agricultural purposes due to relatively high farm product prices.[83] This hypothesis needs to be addressed, but the approach utilized above for assessing the relative importance of hydrologic and climatic factors is inappropriate for the examination of the role played by agricultural product prices.[84] An alternative and complementary approach is utilized.

Once again, the difference between pairs of historical and counterfactual simulations provide estimates of the impacts of respective variables. The scenarios of interest are:

(1) the depletion which would have occurred if there had been no Federal flood-control and drainage projects constructed between 1935 and 1984 and real crop prices were at their actual, historic levels (Table 6, column 3);

---

[83]The relevant measure presumably was high real farm product prices (net of production costs) _relative_ to real forest product prices (net of costs). By focusing on agricultural product prices in the simulations, agricultural costs of production and net forestry revenues are held constant.

[84] Given the structure of the model, the methodology employed to develop the results in Table 5 is not appropriate for assessing the role played by agricultural prices. Clearly, if agricultural prices had been at a zero level (as would have been assumed for a parallel counterfactual simulation), there would have been no economic incentive to convert wetlands and much previously converted land would have reverted to a forested condition. Thus, all conversion would be ascribed to the effect of agricultural prices. But, the number of additional acres of wetlands there would be in the total absence of an agricultural sector is not the relevant issue. The question is what effect changing real agricultural prices had on conversion.

TABLE 6: FORESTED WETLAND DEPLETION
DUE TO FEDERAL FLOOD-CONTROL PROJECTS AND AGRICULTURAL PRODUCT PRICES,
LOWER MISSISSIPPI ALLUVIAL PLAIN, 1935-1984

5-Year Period	Factually Simulated Wetland Change	Counterfactual Simulations			Impacts Due to		
		No Federal Projects	Flat Ag Prices	Flat Ag Prices and No Projects	Federal Projects	Change in Ag Prices	Changing Ag Prices Given No Projects
(1)	(2)	(3)	(4)	(5)	(6)	(7)	(8)
				(1,000 acres)			
1935-39	-287	-283[a]	-288[b]	-284[c]	-5[d]	+1[e]	+1[f]
1940-44	-348	-335	-280	-267	-13	-68	-68
1945-49	-377	-365	-286	-274	-12	-91	-91
1950-54	-263	-250	-207	-195	-13	-56	-55
1955-59	-412	-313	-413	-313	-100	+1	+1
1960-64	-524	-379	-539	-395	-145	+16	+16
1965-69	-570	-303	-624	-360	-267	+54	+56
1970-74	-326	-101	-351	-128	-225	+25	+27
1975-79	-267	-29	-309	-74	-238	+42	+45
1980-84	-303	-169	-343	-215	-134	+41	+47
Total Change	-3,677	-2,527	-3,641	-2,505			
Total Net Impact					-1,150	-36	-22

[a]Projects held constant at pre-study-period (1934) level; all other variables, including agricultural product prices, at historical levels.

[b]Simulation with agricultural product prices held constant at 1934 level; all other variables, including projects, at historical levels.

[c]Simulation with agricultural product prices and projects held constant at 1934 level; all other variables at historical levels.

[d]Difference between column 3 and column 2.

[e]Difference between column 4 and column 2.

[f]Difference between column 5 and column 3.

(2)   the depletion which would have occurred if real crop prices
       were fixed at their pre-study-period (1934) levels and
       projects were at their actual, historic levels (Table 6,
       column 4); and

(3)   the depletion which would have occurred if there had been no
       Federal projects constructed during the period and real crop
       prices were fixed at their 1934 levels (Table 6, column 5).

While 1.15 million acres of conversion may be attributed to the effect
of Federal projects (Table 6, column 6), only 36 thousand acres of net
depletion appears to be due to the sole effect of changing agricultural
product prices (Table 6, column 7).

The 2.527 million acres of conversion (Table 6, column 3) which
would have occurred even in the absence of Federal projects was
presumably due to the combined effects of all other economic, climatic,
and hydrologic factors (including flood-protection provided by the
mainline levee system). Which part of this depletion can be attributed
exclusively to agricultural price effects? If there had been no Federal
projects and real crop prices were fixed at their 1934 levels, there
would have been an estimated 2.505 million acres of conversion. Thus,
in the absence of Federal projects, changing agricultural prices would
have had only a small net effect on forested wetland acreages (Table 6,
column 8).

Summary Measurements of the Role Played by Federal Projects
in Forested Wetland Depletion

Depletion due exclusively to flood-protection and drainage
provision provided by U.S. Army Corps of Engineers and Soil Conservation
Service projects amounted to 1.150 million acres (31% of simulated

depletion) during the period 1935-1984 and nearly 1.223 million acres
(32% of simulated depletion) through the year 1999. Long-term (steady
state) depletion due to Federal projects (constructed through the year
1984) is estimated to amount to 1.227 million acres, about 32% of
estimated long-term depletion (Table 7).

Through 1984, the average county proportion of project-protected
land converted to agricultural use amounted to about 69%, and the
simulations indicate that this share will rise to more than 72% by the
end of the century (Table 7). This is not to suggest, however, that
this simulated conversion is all due to flood-protection (provided by
projects). These figures are responsive only to the question, "For
every 100 acres of forested wetlands protected by projects, how many
acres on average per county are converted to agricultural use (for any
reason)?"

A more interesting question to ask is: "For every 100 acres of
forested wetlands in a county which receive flood protection and
drainage provision from Federal projects, how many acres, on average,
are therefore converted from their forested state to agricultural
cropland?" The answer to this question may be thought of as the
"average propensity to convert wetlands." As the figures in the bottom
row of Table 7 indicate, by 1984, approximately 22% of the acreage
afforded protection by Federal projects had been converted from a
forested state to agricultural use because of the protection provided by
projects, and this share is predicted to reach 23% by the end of the
century.

Having established the importance of the role played in forested
wetland depletion by flood-control and drainage projects of the U.S.

TABLE 7:   THE IMPACT OF FEDERAL FLOOD-CONTROL AND DRAINAGE PROJECTS[a]
ON FORESTED WETLAND DEPLETION IN THE LOWER MISSISSIPPI ALLUVIAL PLAIN
SUMMARY MEASUREMENTS

| | Time Period of Simulation Analysis | | |
	1935-1984	1935-1999	Long Term (Steady State)
	(1,000 acres)		
Wetland Depletion	3,637	-	-
Simulated Depletion	3,677	3,834	3,841
Depletion Due to Federal Projects	1,150	1,223	1,227
Share of Simulated Depletion Due to Federal Projects	31.3%	31.9%	31.9%
Project Acreage[b]	5,316	5,316	5,316
Average Share of Protected Land Converted per County	69.2%	72.1%	72.3%
Average Propensity to Convert[c]	21.6%	23.0%	23.1%

[a]The final model, specification L3, is utilized throughout.

[b]Total protected acreage through 1984 of U.S. Army Corps of Engineers and Soil Conservation Service projects. Assumes that no additional projects are constructed post-1984 but that all projects are maintained.

[c]Average percentage of project-protected forested wetlands converted to agricultural croplands because of project protection.

Army Corps of Engineers and the Soil Conservation Service, it remains to be seen whether the Federal government ought to be congratulated or condemned for providing this service. The critical issue may be characterized by asking whether the world had more pressing needs (during the 1935-1984 period and in the future) for agricultural cropland or for forested wetlands. In other words, did (and does) the world need soybeans more than water quality? Addressing such questions requires a welfare analysis of the optimal use of wetlands, and it is to this that we turn in the next chapter.

CHAPTER IV

WELFARE ANALYSIS OF FORESTED WETLAND DEPLETION

This chapter provides for the internalization of environmental externalities associated with the conversion of forested wetlands to agricultural uses, so that the socially optimal time-path of resource use (wetland conversion) can be identified. First, a model of socially optimal wetland use is developed, the structure and parameters of that model bearing a well-defined relationship to the previously estimated econometric model of private-market wetland usage. Then, an historical welfare analysis is carried out, in which the simulated optimal use of wetlands is contrasted with the actual (and the factually simulated) use of wetlands during the period 1935-1984. Following this, a parallel analysis of alternative wetland strategies is carried out from the present through the end of the century.

A Model of Socially Optimal Wetland Use

Having developed previously the econometric model of actual, market-based wetland use, it is not difficult to generate the model of socially optimal land use through suitable modifications of the private-market model. In accordance with the first basic theorem of welfare

economics, "socially optimal" land use is defined here as being the

land-use allocation which would be achieved by a well-functioning, free

market economy in the absence of externalities.[85]

A Dynamic Social Optimization Model
of Forestry and Agricultural Production

There are two possible approaches to transforming the previously

specified (private, market-based) dynamic optimization model into a

model of socially optimal use of wetlands. Both approaches involve the

internalization of environmental externalities.[86] First, one may view

the relevant externalities as environmental benefits of forested

wetlands,[87] benefits which are ordinarily ignored in market

---

[85]This definition of social optimality is virtually tautological, as it
is essentially a restatement of the second theorem of welfare economics,
based upon the usual convexity and continuity assumptions regarding
consumers' preferences and firms' production sets. An explicit
statement of the way in which a market for externalities produces a
Pareto efficient allocation is provided by Varian (1984), pp. 261-262.
Strictly speaking, the simulated environmental-cost-internalized time-
paths of quinquennial changes in forested acreage are not necessarily
optimal paths; rather, they represent paths which would be taken if
Pigouvian taxes were utilized in order to encourage movement toward
optimal steady-state levels of forests and cropland. This is because
the partial adjustment parameters are not necessarily the same in the
market model and the true social optimum model.

[86]In addition to the effects of environmental externalities, another
potential source of divergence between actual and socially optimal
conversion of forested wetlands is associated with the public goods
nature of flood-control projects: in the absence of other
externalities, the market may be expected to under-provide such
projects. This effect is opposite in direction to that of environmental
externalities, which are the focus of the analysis here.

[87]Environmental benefits of forested wetlands, to be discussed later,
include improved water quality, erosion control, floodwater storage,
groundwater recharge, fish and wildlife habitat, and recreational
opportunities. One ecological service of forested wetlands which is *not*
an externality to the land-use decision, of course, is the production of
hardwood timber, for which relatively well-developed markets exist
throughout the Lower Mississippi Alluvial Plain.

transactions. Thus, the social optimization problem may be posited by
substituting the following term for the $f_{it}s_{ijt}$ term in equation 1:

$$(f_{it} + e_{it}) \cdot s_{ijt} \qquad (53)$$

where e_{it} = average annual environmental benefit per acre from forested
wetlands in county i at time t.[88] From this perspective, socially
optimal use of the land is achieved if landowners, when deciding how to
utilize their wetlands, take into account all benefits of forested
wetlands, not only their wetlands' financial benefits due to timber
production.

The other, parallel approach is to view the externalities as
environmental costs associated with the conversion of forested wetlands
to agricultural cropland. In this case, the social optimization problem
is posited by substituting the following term for the AC_{it} term in
equation 1:

$$(AC_{it} + E_{it}) \qquad (54)$$

where E_{it} = average environmental cost per acre due to conversion of
forested wetlands to cropland, expressed as the discounted present value
of an infinite future stream, in county i at time t.[89] From this second

---

[88]A more general specification of environmental values would allow for
downward-sloping demand for environmental amenities. Thus, we
substitute the function, $e_{it} = e[s_{ijt}/T_{ijt}]$, for the set of e_{it} values
in equation 53.

[89]Consistent with the notation used for other benefits and costs,

$$e_{it} = r \cdot E_{it}.$$

perspective, socially optimal use of the land is achieved if landowners, when deciding how to utilize their wetlands, take into account the environmental costs of agricultural production (and wetland loss), in addition to the usual, financial costs of agricultural production.

These two perspectives on the nature of an externality are, of course, symmetric and, indeed, fundamentally equivalent. It is therefore not surprising that the two approaches to respecifying the objective functional of the dynamic optimization problem lead to the same set of necessary conditions when the problem is solved. Hence, there is no loss of generality involved in focusing on one of the approaches, namely the first approach, that expressed above in equation 53. Substitution of the term, $(f_{it} + e_{it}) \cdot S_{ijt}$, for $f_{it} S_{ijt}$ in the objective functional leads to a parallel modification of the Hamiltonian (equation 8, above), and to the following set of necessary conditions for socially optimal land use:

$$f_{it} + e_{it} = r\lambda_{ijt} - \dot{\lambda}_{ijt} \qquad (55)$$

$$g^*_{ijt} = S_{ijt} \quad \text{if} \quad \left[A_{it} \cdot q_{ijt} - AC_{it} - C_{it} - FN_{it} - E_{it} \right] > 0 \qquad (56)$$

$$v^*_{ijt} = AG_{ijt} \quad \text{if} \quad \left[\tilde{F}_{it} - A_{it} \cdot q_{ijt} + AC_{it} + E_{it} \right] > 0 \qquad (57)$$

Consistent with these necessary conditions for socially optimal conversion of forested wetlands to agricultural use and socially optimal abandonment of farmland, the respective present values are denoted as follows:

$$X_{ijt} = A_{it} \cdot q_{ijt} - AC_{it} - C_{it} - FN_{it} - E_{it} \qquad (58)$$

$$Y_{ijt} = \tilde{F}_{it} - A_{it} \cdot q_{ijt} + AC_{it} + E_{it} \qquad (59)$$

Based upon these definitions, and allowing for the parametric effect of weather on conversion costs, the threshold values of q_{ijt} for socially optimal conversion and abandonment are, respectively:

$$q_{it}^x = \left[\frac{FN_{it} + AC_{it} + E_{it}}{A_{it} - \alpha_1 C_{it} \cdot \exp\{\alpha_2 PHDI_{it}\}} \right] \qquad (60)$$

$$q_{it}^y = \left[\frac{\tilde{F}_{it} + AC_{it} + E_{it}}{A_{it}} \right] \qquad (61)$$

With these modifications of the market model, it is a simple matter to specify the complete, final model of socially optimal forested wetland conversion and agricultural cropland abandonment (Table 8).[90]

---

[90]There are a variety of ways in which the environmental aspects of the problem can be modelled more precisely. For example, instead of modelling the social welfare problem as one in which there is a given environmental value per acre for the stock of forested wetlands, a term could be included in the objective functional to represent the social cost associated with a unit of water pollution (one of many consequences of the substitution of agricultural production for forested wetlands). The problem would then include an additional (differential equation) constraint, expressing the condition that the time rate of change of the stock of pollution be equal (at all times) to a function of the rate of conversion and the stock of agricultural land minus the natural rate of pollutant decay, which itself may be modelled as a function of the stock

**TABLE 8: SIMULATION MODEL OF SOCIALLY OPTIMAL
FORESTED WETLAND CONVERSION AND AGRICULTURAL CROPLAND ABANDONMENT**

$$\text{FORCH}_{it} = \text{FORCH}^c_{it} \cdot D^c_{it} + \text{FORCH}^a_{it} \cdot D^a_{it} + \lambda_i + \phi_{it}$$

$$\text{FORCH}^c_{it} \cdot (-1) = \gamma_c \left[d_{it} \cdot \left[1 - F\left[\left[\log\left[q^x_{it} \right] - \mu(1 + \beta_2 \text{PROJ}_{it}) \right] \right. \right. \right.$$

$$\left. \left. \left. / \sigma_i (1 + \beta_3 \text{PROJ}_{it}) \right] \right] + \left[\frac{S}{T} \right]_{i,t-1} - 1 \right]$$

$$\text{FORCH}^a_{it} = \gamma_a \left[d_{it} \cdot \left[F\left[\left[\log\left[q^y_{it} \right] - \mu(1 + \beta_2 \text{PROJ}_{it}) \right] \right. \right. \right.$$

$$\left. \left. \left. / \sigma_i (1 + \beta_3 \text{PROJ}_{it}) \right] \right] + \left[1 - d_{it} \right] - \left[\frac{S}{T} \right]_{i,t-1} \right]$$

$$d_{it} = \left[\frac{1}{1 + \left[\dfrac{1}{e^{\pi(z)}} \right]} \right] \qquad \text{where } \pi(z) = \text{DRY}_i + \beta_1 \text{PROJ}_{it}$$

$$q^x_{it} = \left[\frac{\text{FN}_{it} + \text{AC}_{it} + E_{it}}{A_{it} - \alpha_1 C_{it} \cdot \exp\{\alpha_2 \text{PHDI}_{it}\}} \right] \qquad q^y_{it} = \left[\frac{\tilde{F}_{it} + \text{AC}_{it} + E_{it}}{A_{it}} \right]$$

Internalizing Environmental Externalities: Simulation of the Socially
Optimal Rates of Conversion and Abandonment

Once the parameters of the market model (Table 1) -- α_1, α_2, β_1,
β_2, β_3, γ_a, γ_c, μ, σ_i -- have been econometrically estimated, the
optimal time path of conversion/abandonment is identified through a
counterfactual, dynamic[91] simulation of the (social optimum) model
specified in Table 8.[92]

Such an approach accounts for environmental externalities, but
other externalities may also be present.[93] In particular, a major
source of divergence from the social optimum may be associated with the
presence of subsidies in the form of large-scale Federal flood-control
and drainage projects. Since, in the absence of Federal projects, the
private market, itself, may have led to the construction of some such
projects, bounds on the socially optimal rate of forested wetland
conversion may be established by comparing counterfactual simulations
with and without the Federal projects.[94]

---

of pollution.

[91]Recall that the simulations must be dynamic because of the presence of
the lagged term, $(S/T)_{i,t-1}$, in equations 39 and 47.

[92]Once again, the simulations involve a two-stage approach for
establishment of the dummy variable values.

[93]In the case of a fishery or other common property resource, the
private market harvest rate departs from the socially optimal rate not
only because of typical environmental externalities, such as
recreational value of the fishery, but also because of two more basic
consequences of the common property nature of the resource -- the stock
externality and the crowding externality (Smith 1969).

[94]An additional source of divergence from the social optimum may exist
when farm-level agricultural crop prices are insulated from the market
by Federal commodity programs. In such a case, if effective farm-level
prices are used in the econometric estimation, this type of externality
may be internalized in the counterfactual, social optimum simulation by

**Historical Welfare Analysis of Alternative Forested Wetland Uses,
1935-1984**

This part of the study provides empirically-based estimates of the
optimal allocation of wetlands between agricultural and forest uses in
the sample area during the 50-year period from 1935 through 1984.
Employing the simulation model of socially optimal forested wetland use
(Table 8), the net environmental benefits of forested wetlands are
internalized.

Environmental Benefits of Forested Wetlands

A wide variety of private and public benefits are lost when
forested wetlands are drained, cleared, and converted to agricultural
cropland. Six major categories of such wetland benefits are ordinarily
external to economic transactions: water quality effects, floodwater
storage, erosion control, groundwater recharge, fish and wildlife
habitat, and recreational opportunities.[95]

In the present application, the water quality effects of wetlands
are of particular importance. Wetlands help maintain and improve the

---

using (farm-level) agricultural product prices which reflect the social
value of respective commodities. As was discussed previously, however,
Federally supported crop prices are not employed in the present
analysis.

[95]For a comprehensive examination of wetland values, see Greeson,
Clark, and Clark 1979. Two recent studies provide surveys of the
literature on ecological values of wetlands: Tiner 1984; and U.S.
Congress (Office of Technology Assessment) 1984. Tiner provides a
useful taxonomy of wetland values, which is reproduced in Appendix 24.
The U.S. Fish and Wildlife Service is developing a computerized database
on wetland values, containing some 7,000 entries; this database is
discussed later in the context of economic valuations of wetland
externalities.

quality of waters which flow over and through them by trapping suspended sediments, removing nutrients, and processing chemical[96] and organic wastes. Because of their location between land and water, wetlands are particularly effective filters (Tiner 1984), intercepting runoff from land and helping to filter sediments, nutrients, and wastes from passing waters.[97]

Another important positive externality associated with wetlands is the role which they play in storing flood waters and retarding and reducing flood peaks. By temporarily storing storm waters and providing capacity for the transport of those waters, wetlands can substantially reduce the intensity and frequency of downstream flooding (Ogawa 1982).[98] A related wetland benefit is associated with the function wetlands play in controlling erosion. Vegetated freshwater (and saltwater) wetlands located adjacent to rivers and other open bodies of

---

[96]The impact of forested wetlands (as opposed to agricultural use) on water quality is two-fold in regard to chemical pollution: on the one hand, forested wetlands trap chemical pollutants; and, additionally, crop production results in runoff into waterways of pesticide and fertilizer residues.

[97]Dissolved nutrients, particularly nitrogen and phosphorus, are directly taken up by wetland vegetation during the growing season and by chemical absorption at the wetland soil surface (Tchobanoglous and Clup 1980). Both organic and inorganic suspended materials tend to settle out in wetland areas (Boto and Patrick 1979), and some pollutants are then converted by biochemical processes to less harmful substances; others remain buried; and others are taken up by wetland vegetation and either recycled or transported from it (Boyt, Bayley, and Zoltek 1977).

[98]The value of wetlands for flood-protection was dramatically demonstrated quite close to home. In 1976, the New England Division of the U.S. Army Corps of Engineers examined various alternatives for providing flood protection in the lower Charles River watershed near Boston, including: (i) construction of a 55,000 acre-foot reservoir; (ii) development of an extensive system of walls and dikes; and (iii) perpetual protection of 8,500 acres of wetlands. The Corps concluded that wetlands protection was the least-cost solution to the problem, and completed wetland acquisition in the Charles River basin in 1983.

water significantly reduce shoreline erosion caused by strong currents
during flooding and by waves generated by storms and boat traffic
(Allen 1979).

Most wetlands are areas of groundwater discharge and some may thus
add to locally available water supplies (Tiner 1984). Also, wetlands
supplement (recharge) groundwater through infiltration/percolation of
surface water to the saturated zone, although adjacent upland areas
often have a greater potential to recharge groundwater sources (because
of their more permeable soils).

The most important values of wetlands may be associated with their
use as habitat for fish and wildlife. The bottomland hardwood forests
of the Lower Mississippi Alluvial Plain are particularly crucial in this
regard, providing wintering habitat for millions of migratory birds,
especially mallards and wood ducks, serving as critical habitat for
numerous fin fishes, and supporting a variety of mammal species (Barton
1985). Most freshwater fishes are actually dependent upon the existence
of wetlands, either feeding in wetlands (or upon wetland-produced food),
using wetlands as nursery grounds, or spawning in the aquatic portions
of wetlands (Peters, Ahrenholz, and Rice 1979).

In addition to providing year-round habitats for many bird species,
wetlands are particularly important for migratory waterfowl. The
forested wetlands of the Mississippi Alluvial Plain constitute the
primary wintering grounds for major populations of numerous species of
migratory birds and are important breeding grounds for many other
species.[99] At least fifty fur-bearing mammals and other game species

---

[99]The Mississippi Alluvial Plain is an important breeding area for wood
ducks, herons, egrets, and white ibises. Wild turkeys also nest in the
bottomland hardwood forests. Other common bird inhabitants include

(in addition to waterfowl) depend on wetlands for food, cover, or water (Tiner 1984). Other mammals, both large and small, frequent wetlands, and numerous species of reptiles and amphibians depend upon wetland areas as their sole habitat.

In addition to the ecological services described above, wetlands directly provide utility to persons through recreational opportunities, including fishing, hunting, boating, hiking, and observation of wildlife. Waterfowl hunting and fishing are particularly important in the Lower Mississippi Alluvial Plain (U.S. Congress 1984).

Economic Valuation of Environmental Benefits of Forested Wetlands

Since the Second World War, a large literature has developed on methods of estimating the economic value of environmental externalities,[100] including hedonic price and wage methods (Freeman 1985), contingent valuation procedures (Freeman 1979), and the Hotelling-Clawson-Knetsch method (McConnell 1985). These various techniques have been applied extensively to the valuation of environmental benefits of forested and other wetlands,[101] including benefits associated with water quality, floodwater storage, erosion

---

barred owls, downy and red-bellied woodpeckers, cardinals, warblers, wood peewees, yellow-throats, and wood thrushes (Wharton and Kitchens 1982).

[100]Recent surveys of these methodologies are provided by Freeman 1985, and Fisher and Krutilla 1985.

[101]A classic wetland valuation study is that of Hammack and Brown 1974; more recent empirical analyses include those of Bardecki 1984 and Farber 1987. Surveys of previous studies are found in Shabman and Batie 1985, and Gibbons 1986.

control, groundwater recharge, fish and wildlife habitat, and
recreational opportunities (Heimlich and Langner 1986).[102]

Although the economic valuation techniques are well developed, most
studies are limited by available data and by conceptual problems
associated with the valuation methodologies (Shabman and Batie 1985).
Therefore, specific wetland value estimates should be considered only as
crude indicators of true externality values. Given this caveat, it may
be noted in passing that annual environmental benefits of wetlands have
been estimated throughout the range of $25 per acre (fish and wildlife

---

[102]In addition to the direct, user values of wetlands, it may be argued
that some wetlands have an option value for people who are willing to
pay to preserve them for future use. The original notion of option
value (Weisbrod 1964; Zeckhauser 1969; and Cicchetti and Freeman 1971),
however, requires risk aversion, and, in any event, the degree to which
the option value concept applies in the context of wetlands being
converted to agricultural use depends upon the degree to which the
consequent ecological modifications are irreversible. In their seminal
article on what has come to be known as quasi-option value, Arrow and
Fisher (1974) used the example of a virgin redwood forest, used
alternatively for wilderness recreation or clear-cut logging:
"Although this sort of transformation may be technically reversible, the
length of time required for regeneration of the forest for purposes of
wilderness recreation is so great that, given some positive rate of time
preference, it might as well be irreversible" (p. 314). While the time
required for the regeneration of forested wetlands is less than that for
virgin redwood forests, it is still significant (possibly in excess of
100 years). Although the change from forestry to crop production is
immediate, the change from cropland back to forestry involves
substantial delays. This asymmetry is by no means equivalent to an
absolute irreversibility (the limiting case of such asymmetric costs of
change). The fact remains, however, that once conversion from forest to
farmland has occurred, a window of opportunity (of 60 to 100 years - the
forested wetland rotation length) has been lost. From this perspective,
the nature of the forest-cropland decision is consistent with the notion
of (quasi-) option value as the conditional value of information (Conrad
1980, Hanemann 1982, Fisher and Krutilla 1985). It should also be
noted, however, that there is an ongoing controversy regarding the
validity of option value as a measure of benefits (Graham 1981; Cory and
Saliba 1987).

habitat in northern Louisiana) to more than $8,000 per acre (water

quality enhancement in central Georgia).[103]

Given the tremendous heterogeneity of wetland values and the

uncertainty which is involved in individual estimates, the analysis here

does not focus on a specific set of estimated values, but presents a

spectrum of results for a broad range of externality levels.

Simulating the Socially Optimal Rate of Conversion and Abandonment, 1935-1984

The estimated parameters from the econometric (market-based) model

(Table 1) -- α_1, α_2, β_1, β_2, β_3, γ_a, γ_c, μ, σ_1 -- are substituted for

the respective parameters in the social-optimum simulation model (Table

8). Initial conditions are taken as given. Combining actual, historic

values of the relevant variables with hypothetical figures for the total

---

[103]The wide range of estimates is largely due to the heterogeneity of
wetland values (a function of both physical heterogeneity of wetlands
themselves and geographic and demographic variations in the demand for
wetland services). Examples from various studies include: $27/acre per
year for Massachusetts inland recreational fishing benefits (U.S. Army
Corps of Engineers 1976); $490/acre per year for Michigan coastal
wetland waterfowl and recreational fishing benefits (Jaworski and
Raphael 1978); and $6,800/acre annually for waste assimilation in
Virginia wetlands (Gosselink, Odum, and Pope 1973).

A major effort is currently being undertaken by the National Wetlands
Inventory of the U.S. Fish and Wildlife Service to compile a database by
reviewing all available literature on the attributes, functions, and
related values of wetlands throughout the country. Approximately 7,000
records have been compiled, many focusing on the bottomland hardwood
forests of the southern United States. One possible extension of the
research reported in this study is to use refined estimates of the mean
and variance of the distribution of wetland values to carry out
stochastic simulations of the optimal use of forested wetlands. The
distribution of wetland values can conceivably be approximated by
drawing upon the National Wetlands Inventory database to summarize
estimates of the values of wetlands in the study area.

value[104] of environmental externalities, E_{it},[105] a series of counterfactual, dynamic simulations were carried out, yielding estimates of the changes which would have occurred in forested wetland acreages _if_ landowners had taken environmental consequences into account at the time of their land-use decisions.

Because subsidized (totally government funded) Federal flood-control and drainage projects cause an additional divergence of observed land-use from the socially optimal level, a set of social-optimum simulations were also carried out under the counterfactual condition that no projects existed. In the absence of Federal projects, of course, it is possible that the private market would have led to the construction of some such projects. Therefore, bounds on the socially optimal rate of forested wetland conversion and farmland abandonment are established by comparing counterfactual (social-optimum) simulations with and without Federal projects.[106]

---

[104]In each simulation, a single environmental value is used for all counties at all times, so that E_{it} = E. Another area for further research is to carry out simulations which account for differences across counties and across time in the value of environmental externalities. Also, future research might utilize the more general specification of a non-linear environmental benefit function mentioned earlier, to allow for the reality that many wetland environmental values are inversely related to the _local_ stock of wetlands.

[105]Although the simulations utilize a constant (real) level of E for all counties and time periods, the model does allow for the incorporation of different externality values across counties and across time.

[106]It is conceivable that these bounds could be narrowed (and possibly eliminated) if the implicit (marginal) subsidy inherent in Federal flood-control and drainage projects could be estimated. This estimate (in dollars per acre per year) should be subtracted from the "with-Federal-projects line" in Figure 5, having the effect of shifting it to the left. A difficulty is that it is the marginal subsidy implicit in Federal projects, not the average subsidy which is required for such calculations.

The results of the two sets of simulations are summarized in Table 9. For externality values ranging from $25 up to $1,000 per acre per year, the socially optimal, total 50-year net change in forested wetland acreage in the study area is reported, first, for the case of Federal projects having been constructed and maintained at their actual, historical level, and second, for the case of no Federal projects having been constructed during the post-1934 period.[107]

As can be seen in Figure 5, zero-level net depletion would have been optimal if environmental benefits were about $150/acre (per year). If no projects had been built, however, zero net depletion would have been optimal at an environmental externality level of only $80/acre (per year). This is not to suggest that under these two scenarios, no conversion (or abandonment) would have occurred, only that the net change at the end of the 50 years would have been nil. At an assumed externality value of $50/acre, for example, it would still have been optimal (had there been no projects) to convert substantial amounts of forested land to cropland from about 1940 through the 1960's (Appendix 25). But, after that time, lower agricultural prices combined with the environmental values of wetlands would have argued for significant abandonment of marginal farmland.

---

[107]The simulations reported in Table 9 have been scaled so that the factual simulation (value of environmental externality = 0; "with Federal projects") matches the actual net depletion which occurred during each time period. The re-scaling was carried out in terms of percentage deviations of simulated values from actual values. This is in keeping with the usual practice in such economic simulation models. Thus, the first row of figures in Table 9 are indicative of the actual total depletion which occurred (3.637 million acres) and the depletion which would have occurred had there been no projects (2.487 million acres). The difference between these, 1.150 million acres, is the previously reported depletion due to Federal projects during the 50-year period.

TABLE 9:   SIMULATED TOTAL SOCIALLY OPTIMAL CHANGES IN FORESTED WETLANDS
           FOR ALTERNATIVE VALUES OF ENVIRONMENTAL BENEFITS,
           THIRTY-SIX COUNTIES, LOWER MISSISSIPPI ALLUVIAL PLAIN, 1935-1984[a]

Value of Environmental Benefits Per Acre	Simulated Socially Optimal Changes	
	With Federal Projects[b]	No Federal Projects[c]
(dollars)	(1,000 acres)	
0	- 3,637	- 2,487
25	- 3,012	- 1,560
50	- 2,313	- 839
75	- 1,660	- 150
100	- 1,029	+ 486
125	- 474	+ 1,056
150	+ 35	+ 1,548
175	+ 527	+ 2,031
200	+ 938	+ 2,491
225	+ 1,385	+ 2,939
250	+ 1,776	+ 3,276
275	+ 2,109	+ 3,596
300	+ 2,391	+ 3,909
325	+ 2,695	+ 4,185
350	+ 3,002	+ 4,449
375	+ 3,282	+ 4,646
400	+ 3,529	+ 4,820
425	+ 3,726	+ 5,004
450	+ 3,990	+ 5,209
475	+ 4,122	+ 5,387
500	+ 4,326	+ 5,474
600	+ 4,792	+ 5,895
700	+ 5,204	+ 6,192
800	+ 5,572	+ 6,340
900	+ 5,848	+ 6,455
1,000	+ 6,052	+ 6,567

[a]The final model, specification L3, is utilized.

[b]Simulated socially optimal changes in forested wetland acreage, given
the existence of Federal flood-control and drainage projects.

[c]Simulated socially optimal changes in forested wetland acreage in the
absence of any Federal flood-control and drainage projects.

FIGURE 5: OPTIMAL FORESTED AREA CHANGES

Mississippi Alluvial Plain, 1935–1984

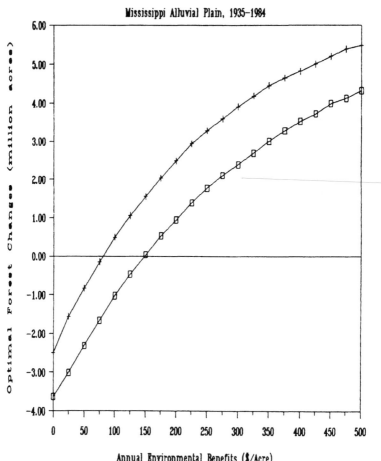

Annual Environmental Benefits ($/Acre)

□   With Fed Projects   +   No Federal Projects

Given the bounds which are established on socially optimal wetland use by the two sets of simulations[108] -- with and without Federal projects, the vertical gap in Figure 5 between the two curves may be viewed as a social-optimum confidence interval of sorts. The horizontal distance between the two curves also has an interesting interpretation. Recall that the "with-projects" curve crosses the zero-level of net change in forested wetlands at an environmental benefit value of about $150/acre, while the "without-projects" curve intersects at about $80/acre, a difference of $70/acre. This suggests that, on average, landowners were indifferent between flood-control projects and an annual payment of $70/acre (when the allocation of land between forest and farmland was that of 1935). In other words, landowners' average annual marginal valuation of projects was $70 per acre of protection. The analogous numbers for later periods, when there was less forest stock remaining, are given by the horizontal distance between the two curves at various points of total net loss of wetlands. Thus, the results confirm that the marginal valuation of project protection declined as more land was converted from forested condition to cropland and only land of inferior quality remained.[109]

---

[108]If the public-good nature of flood-control projects results in the market under-producing projects (in the absence of environmental externalities), the upper bound in Figure 5 would be somewhat lower than is indicated.

[109]A possible area for further research is to contrast information on actual project costs (measured in dollars per acre per year) with the above estimates of implicit willingness-to-pay for Federal project protection. Such a comparison could form the basis for a benefit-cost evaluation of the projects. Difficulties with doing this, however, are twofold: first, it is by no means a trivial task to determine the construction costs of U.S. Army Corps of Engineers and Soil Conservation Service flood-control and drainage projects; and second, it is the marginal, not the historical average costs which would be required.

Welfare Analysis of Alternative, Future Forested Wetland Uses,
1985-1999

The simulation model of socially optimal forested wetland use is
next employed for the purpose of developing empirically-based estimates
of the optimal allocation of wetlands between agricultural and forest
uses during the fifteen-year period from 1985 to the end of the century.
As with the preceding historical welfare analysis, the analysis for
1985-1999 does not focus on any specific set of estimated environmental
benefit values, but instead provides results for a broad range of
possible externality levels.

The simulation methodology is parallel to that used in the
historical analysis. The base-line case of a zero externality level is
based upon the assumption that all real prices (of agricultural crops,
sawlogs and pulpwood, costs of production, and conversion costs) remain
constant through the year 1999.[110] The simulations of the 1985-1999
period are based upon the further assumption that all Federal flood-
control and drainage projects constructed through the year 1984 are
maintained but that no additional projects are constructed during the
post-1984 period. Thus, the simulation results are indications of
socially optimal behavior only in the limited sense of being

---

[110]Another possible area for future research is to develop base-line
simulations of various scenarios of estimated future values of the
model's exogenous variables, in particular, agricultural prices
(Heimlich and Langner 1986). Also, the consequences of alternative
future scenarios regarding forestry prices, costs of wetland conversion,
agricultural costs of production, and even weather conditions could be
examined. See the discussion below regarding the expected impact on
wetland depletion of future changes in agricultural price levels.

conditional upon the existence of Federal projects throughout the study area.[111]

The results of the simulations are summarized in Table 10. Given the existence of large-scale flood protection and drainage provision afforded by projects of the U.S. Army Corps of Engineers and the Soil Conservation Service, conversion of forested wetlands to agricultural cropland is predicted (at 1984 real agricultural price levels) to continue (at a declining rate), amounting to an additional loss of 156 thousand acres by the turn of the century. Taking into account the value of the net environmental benefits of forested wetlands, and again given the existence of Federal projects, it is estimated that maintenance of the current forest-cropland wetland allocation will be optimal (for the next fifteen years) at annual externality levels on the order of $175 per acre (Figure 6). For average environmental benefits per acre less than that amount, some continued conversion is called for; and for benefit levels in excess of that amount, various degrees of future farmland abandonment are socially optimal.[112]

A question which has arisen is whether a future, sustained increase in agricultural prices would cause the rate of forested wetland conversion to cropland to approach the record levels attained during the 1960's and 1970's. A series of counterfactual simulations carried out with the present model suggests otherwise. As can be seen in Appendix

---

[111]Counterfactual simulations in which Federal projects are held at a zero-level, as in some of the historical simulations, are less meaningful in the context of optimal future behavior. If Federal projects are held at a zero-level, the result is that immediate abandonment of farmland is favored, even at environmental benefit levels as low as $25 per acre.

[112]Simulated quinquennial optimal changes are provided in Appendix 26.

TABLE 10: ESTIMATED FUTURE SOCIALLY OPTIMAL CHANGES
IN FORESTED WETLANDS
FOR ALTERNATIVE VALUES OF ENVIRONMENTAL BENEFITS,
THIRTY-SIX COUNTIES, LOWER MISSISSIPPI ALLUVIAL PLAIN, 1985-1999[a]

Value of Environmental Benefits Per Acre	Simulated Socially Optimal Changes in Forested Wetland Acreage Given the Existence of Federal Projects
(dollars)	(1,000 acres)
0	- 156
25	- 130
50	- 105
75	- 80
100	- 58
125	- 37
150	- 18
175	- 3
200	+ 32
225	+ 59
250	+ 104
275	+ 130
300	+ 155
325	+ 173
350	+ 188
375	+ 223
400	+ 260
425	+ 273
450	+ 300
475	+ 315
500	+ 341

[a]The final model, specification L3, is utilized.

FIGURE 6: OPTIMAL FUTURE FOREST CHANGES

Mississippi Alluvial Plain, 1985-1999

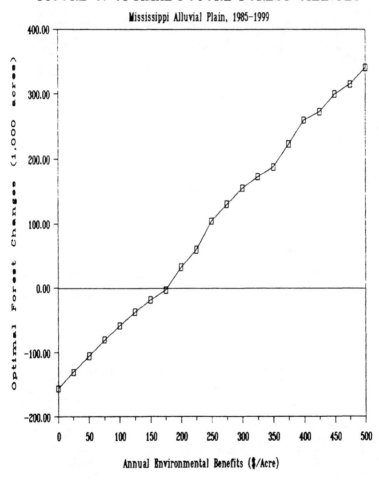

27, a doubling of the real 1984 composite agricultural price level during the 1989-1999 period would induce an additional 100 thousand acres of depletion. Thus, a doubling of prices would lead to a tripling of the overall rate of wetland conversion.

Two important caveats should be noted. First, this is a conservative assessment, considering the fact that 1984 farm prices were very low in real, historical terms. Second, if new Federal projects were to be constructed, the impact of increased agricultural product prices would be much, much greater, given the multiplicative nature of the interaction between agricultural feasibility and agricultural prices in landowner decision making.[113]

Major Findings of the Welfare Analysis of Forested Wetland Depletion

The simulations reported in this chapter suggest that if all wetlands in the study area had annual ecological (external) values[114] in the range of $80 to $150 per acre, zero-level net depletion of forested wetlands in the study area during the 1935-1984 period would have been socially optimal. Likewise, annual wetland values on the order of

---

[113]Most actual predictions of agricultural prices through the end of this century (for the four crops of interest in this study) have involved lower, not higher, real prices. Heimlich and Langner's (1986) estimates translate into composite, weighted future (1986-91) prices on the order of 70% of their 1980-84 level. While counterfactual, future simulations with such estimates would be of interest, the results, given the nature of the present model, would possibly be misleading. This is because if crop prices were to decline substantially (for soybeans, for example), there would presumably be significant substitution of other crops before land was abandoned outright. The model, however, does not allow for such effects, since the crop mix is exogenous to the system.

[114]Throughout the chapter, "wetland value" refers exclusively to external values, i.e. the total, social value of wetlands minus their private, market valuation.

$175/acre would argue for no change in the current forest/cropland
allocation of wetlands. But wetland values have been found to vary
tremendously: as reported above, from perhaps less than $25/acre
annually to as much as $10,000/acre per year. What conclusions, then,
can be drawn from the quantitative findings from the social optimum
simulations?

The answer is that, given the tremendous heterogeneity of wetland
values, these findings are only of limited significance. As suggested
previously, however, a promising area for further research is to exploit
the present model with better estimates of the ecological values of
wetlands. This can be done by: (a) estimating wetland values (E_{it})
which vary across time (quinquennially) and across space (i.e., from one
county to another); (b) taking into account the heterogeneity of wetland
values within counties;[115] and (c) utilizing a non-linear environmental
benefit function.

Accepting the limited significance of the quantitative findings
reported above, it is still of interest to place these results into some
perspective by comparing them with the private valuation of land in the
study area. First, note again that a range of $80 to $150 annual
ecological value per acre would have justified the optimality of zero-
level net depletion of forested wetlands in the study area during the
1935-1984 period. Such a range of annual benefits may be thought of

---

[115]A first approximation might be to allow for a **relative** probability
density function of wetland values which is the same as that of
agricultural revenues. This is not as unreasonable as one might think,
since wetland ecological values are distributed in a highly skewed
manner, with many areas of relatively low value per acre (fisheries
habitat) and a small number of areas with extremely high value per acre
(water quality protection). Such a first approximation may be
undertaken simply by shifting E_{it} in equations 60 and 61 from the
numerator to the denominator.

instead as an average present value on the order of $2,000 per acre.[116] Such an ecological value of wetlands is more than twice the current market value of wetlands in the study area (whether forested or cropped) -- typical land prices in the area are in the range of $500 to $900 per acre.[117] Thus, abstracting for the moment from the (wetland valuation) heterogeneity issue described above, the study indicates that only if the environmental values of the land were more than twice as great as their market (agricultural) value would zero-level net depletion really have been optimal.

The $2,000 figure is not indicative of the average environmental value per acre required to stop conversion, but is simply the value which would have led (if internalized) to zero net depletion historically. Assuming symmetric distributions of wetland values (for ease of calculation), the indication is that the average environmental value which would have stopped a typical acre from being converted was about $1,100 (the externality value which would have argued for half as much conversion as there actually was). This translates into an annual ecological benefit level of $55, which is within the range of typical annual net (private) returns to conversion.[118] This is as we would expect, since social optimization would call for wetland conversion to be avoided whenever the marginal value of externalities is in excess of the private returns to conversion.

---

[116]Assuming a real annual discount rate of 5%.

[117]Personal communication with Charles Baxter, U.S. Fish and Wildlife Service, Vicksburg, Mississippi, April 1988.

[118]Gross agricultural revenue minus agricultural production costs minus net forest revenue foregone minus costs of conversion.

In any event, recognizing again that wetlands are not all alike, it is surely the case that the environmental values of substantial areas of wetlands are greater than $2,000 per acre ($115/acre per year). This is validated by the evidence, cited above, of annual wetland benefits in excess of this amount (particularly for water quality protection), and by the revealed preferences of private groups such as the Nature Conservancy and public entities such as the U.S. Fish and Wildlife Service in their purchases (for purposes of protection) of specific wetland habitats.

CHAPTER V

SUMMARY AND CONCLUSIONS

This study has examined the causes of rapid depletion of forested
wetland resources in the United States during the past fifty years, and
has compared historical rates of depletion with what would have optimal
from a socioeconomic perspective. Likely future wetland-use patterns
were also examined and contrasted with those which would have been
socially optimal.

Examining these issues required a dynamic analysis of natural
resource exploitation in the presence of negative environmental
consequences. In the past, an important obstacle to such analyses has
been the classic aggregation problem. Typically, only by resorting to
representative-firm assumptions have theoretically consistent models of
rational individual behavior been used to develop econometrically
estimatable models of natural resource supply. Given the heterogeneity
which exists across individual endowments of many natural resources,
such representative-firm models are particularly problematic.

In this study, the representative-firm approach was avoided by
integrating a model of unobserved heterogeneity among firms with a model

104

of rational individual behavior. A conceptual bridge was thus formed
between theoretical models of optimal behavior and statistical models of
market performance. The methodology established an econometric link
between dynamic optimization models of resource use and economic
assessments of environmental externalities.

The analysis proceeded in several stages. The expected time path
of forested wetland resource exploitation was first identified by
solving the relevant dynamic optimization problem. The resulting
theoretical, firm-level, resource supply functions were then aggregated
into a model which could be econometrically estimated with aggregate
market data by taking explicit account of unobserved heterogeneity among
firms; this avoided the representative-firm assumption. The empirical
analysis drew upon panel data for 36 counties in the Lower Mississippi
Alluvial Plain during the period 1935-1984. The principal causes of
forested wetland depletion were identified, including the role played by
Federal government flood-control and drainage projects.

The respective social optimization problem of wetland use was also
solved, and it was found that under specific conditions there is a well-
defined relationship between the aggregate market supply function and
the "socially optimal supply function." Thus, the econometrically
estimated parameters, together with data on environmental externality
values, could be used to solve for the fitted values of the social
optimum supply function. In this way, a generic approach was developed
for estimating the optimal time-path of resource exploitation, based
upon observations of market behavior and information about the value of
environmental externalities.

The immediately following sections of this chapter provide a summary of the thesis, highlighting its major substantive conclusions. Succeeding sections consider policy implications of the analysis and review suggested areas for further research. Finally, a generic overview of the analysis is provided and a few methodological conclusions are offered.

Alternative Renewable Resource Strategies for Forested Wetlands

Forested wetlands are among the earth's most productive ecosystems, and their continuing depletion is one of the world's most serious environmental threats. In the United States, wetland depletion has been particularly rapid in the Lower Mississippi Alluvial Plain, the largest remaining, contiguous wetland habitat in the country. In their natural state, wetlands provide valuable ecological services, including improved water quality, erosion control, floodwater storage, groundwater recharge, provision of hardwood timber, fish and wildlife habitat, and recreational opportunities. Through development, these wetlands alternatively provide sites for agriculture, mining, oil and gas extraction, and urbanization.

Because of possible conflicts with explicit Federal policy (under Section 404 of the Clean Water Act) protecting wetlands from unreasonable development pressures, particular interest has focused on the role played in forested wetland clearing by two Federal government programs -- flood-control and drainage projects of the U.S. Army Corps of Engineers and the Soil Conservation Service. Previous research has not provided satisfactory evidence of the connection between Federal

106

projects and the observed conversion of forested wetlands to agricultural croplands.

In the current study, it was hypothesized that projects reduce the probability of flooding (and increase possibilities for drainage) and thereby increase the suitability of wetlands for agriculture. As a result, the expected present value of the land for agricultural use increases relative to its expected present value in its forested wetland state, and this change in the relative expected value of alternative land uses provides an incentive for landowners to convert their forested wetlands to cropland.

A Model of Privately Optimal Resource Use

To test this hypothetical linkage and to examine the broader questions being addressed, an econometric model was developed in Chapter II from a microtheoretic structure of rational behavior by individual landowners. A dynamic optimization model of forestry and agricultural production at the individual level was solved via control theoretic techniques, yielding sets of necessary conditions under which individual landowners may be expected to seek to convert their forested wetlands to agricultural production or to abandon their agricultural croplands and allow them to return to a forested state.

Heterogeneity across land parcels (in terms of agricultural feasibility) constituted the basis for aggregating the respective necessary conditions into a comprehensive, county-level model of land use. The introduction of a partial adjustment framework with fixed effects provided the final step to an econometrically estimatable model. Particular focus was given to the role played by flood-control and

107

drainage projects. The model postulated that such projects affect land use in two major ways: first, by directly affecting the feasibility of agricultural production (and by affecting the costs of converting forested wetlands to agricultural use); and second, by non-random selection of land parcels which receive flood protection, i.e. by affecting the distribution of underlying land heterogeneity.

Econometric Analysis of Forested Wetland Conversion and Farmland Abandonment

Using quinquennial panel data for thirty-six counties in Arkansas, Louisiana, and Mississippi, during the period 1935-1984, the parameters of the model were estimated econometrically in Chapter III. A number of variants on the basic specification were considered, including lognormal, normal, and uniform distributions of heterogeneity. The overall results lent support to the basic validity of the model: estimated parameters were all of the expected sign; nearly all estimates were significant at the 90%, 95%, or 99% level; and parameter and standard error estimates were highly robust with respect to modifications of the specification.

The models with lognormal distributions of heterogeneity were judged, on theoretical and empirical grounds, to be superior to the models based upon normal and uniform distributions. Final model selection was carried out by comparing the results of historical, dynamic simulations. Theil's inequality coefficient was employed to assess the respective simulations, with the result that the most general of the lognormal models was favored.

108

Parameter estimates led to several findings. First, construction

of Federal flood-control and drainage projects caused a higher rate of

conversion of forested wetlands to agricultural croplands than would

have occurred in the absence of such projects. Second, Federal projects

had this impact because they rendered unsuitable land suitable and

because, on average, land which was already most suitable for

agriculture was protected by the projects. Third, substantial wetland

conversion would have occurred as a result of favorable economic returns

to agriculture (relative to forestry), even if no Federal flood-control

and drainage projects had been undertaken.

The Effects of Major Economic, Hydrologic, and Climatic Factors

In order to estimate the relative impacts of various economic,

hydrologic, and climatic factors, a series of dynamic factual and

counterfactual simulations were carried out, using the econometrically

estimated parameter values. The quinquennial (five-year) impacts of

Federal projects on forested wetland depletion and farmland abandonment

were thus estimated by taking the difference between factual simulations

and related counterfactual simulations where project levels were held at

zero for all years. The results indicated that if there had been no

Federal flood-control and drainage projects constructed in the 36-county

study area after the year 1934, approximately 1.15 million fewer acres

of forested wetlands would have been converted, about 31% of total

depletion. Long-term (steady state) depletion due to Federal projects

(constructed through the year 1984) was estimated to amount to more than

1.23 million acres, about 32% of estimated long-term depletion.

Of the factors considered in the econometric model, flood

109

protection and drainage provision afforded by Federal projects had the largest impact on net changes in forested acreage. The joint effect of natural topography and the mainline levee system was of secondary importance, amounting to 846 thousand acres of depletion (23% of total depletion) through 1984. Net forestry revenues and conversion costs exerted substantial restraints on wetland clearing.

Through 1984, the average county proportion of project-protected land converted to agricultural use amounted to about 69%, and the simulations indicated that this share will rise to more than 72% by the end of the century. But this simulated conversion is not all due to flood-protection provided by projects. An important question to ask is: "For every 100 acres of forested wetlands in a county which receive flood protection and drainage provision from Federal projects, how many acres, on average, are therefore converted from their forested state to agricultural cropland?" The answer to this question is that, by 1984, approximately 22% percent of the acreage afforded protection by Federal projects had been converted from a forested state to agricultural use because of the protection provided by projects, and this share was predicted to reach 23% by the end of the century.

A Model of Socially Optimal Wetland Use

Chapter IV of the study provided for the internalization of environmental externalities associated with the conversion of forested wetlands to agricultural uses, so that the socially optimal time-path of resource use (wetland conversion) could be identified. First, a model of socially optimal wetland use was developed, the structure and parameters of that model bearing a well-defined relationship to the

110

estimated econometric model of private-market wetland usage. Then, an historical welfare analysis was carried out, in which the simulated optimal use of wetlands was contrasted with the actual (and the factually simulated) use of wetlands during the period 1935-1984. Finally, a parallel analysis of alternative wetland strategies was carried out from the present through the end of the century.

The model of socially optimal land use was generated through modifications of the private-market model, "socially optimal" land use being defined in this context as the land-use allocation which would be achieved by a well-functioning, free market economy in the absence of externalities. Without loss of generality, the relevant externalities were modelled as being (environmental) benefits of forested wetland stocks, benefits which are ordinarily ignored in market transactions. Appropriate respecification of the dynamic optimization model led to new sets of necessary conditions for conversion and abandonment, and thus to an aggregated model of socially optimal use of wetlands.

Simulated Socially Optimal Wetland Use, 1935-1984

Given the observed heterogeneity of wetland values and the uncertainty involved in individual estimates, the analysis did not focus on a specific set of estimated values, but instead presented a spectrum of results for a relatively broad range of externality levels.

The estimated parameters from the econometric (market-based) model were substituted for the respective parameters in the social-optimum simulation model. Combining actual, historic values of the relevant variables with hypothetical figures for the total value of environmental externalities, a series of counterfactual, dynamic simulations were

111

carried out, yielding estimates of the changes which would have occurred

in forested wetland acreages if landowners had taken environmental

consequences into account at the time of their land-use decisions.

Because subsidized (totally government funded) Federal flood-

control and drainage projects caused an additional divergence of

observed land-use from the socially optimal level, a set of social-

optimum simulations were also carried out under the counterfactual

condition that no projects existed. In the absence of Federal funding,

of course, the private market may have led to the construction of some

such projects. Therefore, bounds on the socially optimal rate of

forested wetland conversion and farmland abandonment were established by

comparing counterfactual (social-optimum) simulations with and without

Federal projects. The results of the two sets of simulations indicated

that zero-level net depletion would have been optimal in the area if

annual environmental benefits had been on the order of $150 per acre.

If no projects had been built, however, zero net depletion would have

been optimal at an annual environmental externality level of only

$80/acre.

Welfare Analysis of Alternative Future Wetland Uses, 1985-1999

The simulation model of optimal forested wetland use was also

employed for the purpose of developing empirically-based estimates of

the optimal allocation of wetlands between agricultural and forest uses

during the fifteen-year period from 1985 to the end of the century. As

with the historical welfare analysis, the analysis for 1985-1999 did not

focus on a specific set of estimated environmental benefit values, but

instead provided results for a range of possible externality levels.

112

The simulation methodology was similar to that used in the historical analysis, and it was assumed that real prices (of agricultural crops, sawlogs and pulpwood, costs of production, and conversion costs) would remain constant through the year 1999, and that all Federal flood-control and drainage projects constructed through the year 1984 would be maintained but that no additional projects would be constructed. Therefore, these final simulation results were indications of socially optimal behavior only in the limited sense of being conditional upon the existence of Federal projects throughout the study area.

The baseline simulation indicated that, given the existence of large-scale flood protection and drainage provided by Federal projects, conversion of forested wetlands to agricultural cropland should be expected (at 1984 real agricultural price levels) to continue (at a declining rate), amounting to an additional loss of 156 thousand acres by the turn of the century. Taking into account the value of the net environmental benefits of forested wetlands, and again given the existence of Federal projects, it was estimated that maintenance of the current forest-cropland wetland allocation would be optimal (for the next fifteen years) at externality levels on the order of $175 per acre. For average environmental benefits per acre less than that amount, some continued conversion would be optimal; and for benefit levels in excess of that amount, various degrees of farmland abandonment would be socially optimal.

Placing the Findings of the Welfare Analysis in Perspective

What conclusions can be drawn from the quantitative findings of the welfare analysis, given the observed heterogeneity of wetland ecological values? The answer is that the numerical results are only of limited direct significance. It was still useful, however, to place the results into perspective by comparing them with the private valuation of land in the study area. Abstracting from the wetland-valuation heterogeneity issue, the study indicated that only if environmental values were more than twice as great as market (agricultural) values of land would zero-level net depletion really have been optimal. Furthermore, assuming symmetric distributions of wetland values, the average annual environmental value which would have stopped a typical acre from being converted was about $55, within the range of normal annual net returns to conversion. This confirms that social optimization calls for wetland conversion to be avoided when the value of externalities is in excess of the private returns to conversion.

Policy Implications of the Study

The statistical analysis described in this study provides strong evidence of the significant impact which flood-control and drainage projects of the U.S. Army Corps of Engineers and the Soil Conservation Service have had on the conversion of forested wetlands to agricultural uses. What then does the study imply regarding future Federal water policy? The findings indicate, first of all, that Congress, the responsible Federal agencies, and the courts should view with skepticism

114

environmental assessments[119] of Federal flood-control and drainage projects which claim no responsibility for induced wetland clearing.

Federal subsidies in the form of flood-control and drainage projects have played and continue to play an important role in providing incentives for private, individual decisions to convert forested wetlands to agricultural cropland. Whether environmental impacts together with other costs of Federal projects will be found to outweigh project benefits is a question which must be addressed on a case-by-case basis; the implication of this study, however, is that the correct environmental impact area must include the hydrologically affected area where drainage and clearing are induced, not simply the (relatively small) area of project construction activities.

Second, within the context of Section 404 of the Clean Water Act, pursuant to which the Corps is responsible for the regulation of wetland conversion, the study indicates that the Corps and other agencies should not evaluate permit applications for projects located in wetland areas as though wetland conversion were unrelated to project construction. Although the welfare analysis presented here is by no means exact, it is clear that there is a substantial divergence between the actual rate of forested wetland conversion and that which is optimal in a socioeconomic sense.

The divergence between actual and optimal wetland conversion is particulary great in situations where environmental externalities include water quality impacts. Since wetland conversion to agricultural use increases soil erosion and chemical pollution of receiving waters, a

---

[119]Carried out under authority of the National Environmental Policy Act of 1969.

third policy implication is that responsible Federal agencies and the

Congress should consider linking expenditures of Federal funds to

construct and maintain projects with adoption of efficient and

enforceable programs to abate consequent water pollution.

More generally, a fourth implication of the analysis is that the

Congress ought to consider various methods of narrowing the gap between

the actual allocation of land between forested wetlands and agricultural

cropland and what appears to be the socially desirable (optimal)

configuration, whether the chosen methods of narrowing this gap involve

modifications of existing programs and policies or enactment of entirely

new ones. The set of policy initiatives which should be considered

certainly ought to include changes in the way Federal flood-control and

drainage projects are planned, authorized, and financed. Thus, a

reasonable policy goal, from an economic perspective, would be the

development of some means for the elimination of public subsidies and

the internalization of environmental externalities.[120]

Among the other policy initiatives which the Congress should

consider are: funding of Federal acquisition, easement, and oversight

programs;[121] provision for preferential property tax assessments;[122] tax

---

[120]This may already be coming to pass. The Water Resources Development
Act of 1986 provides for increased cost-sharing of project financing and
for emphasis of the principle that project beneficiaries should bear the
costs, including any environmental costs, of generating benefits. It is
too early to say, however, whether the laudable goals of the Act will be
implemented through subsequent legislation and regulation.

[121]One such Federal program already in existence is the acquisition of
wetland habitats by the U.S. Fish and Wildlife Service from revenues
from the sale of mandatory Federal "Duck Stamps" to holders of state
hunting licenses (authorized by the Migratory Bird Conservation Act of
1934). One interesting proposal is that a "Sport Fishing Conservation
Stamp" be created along the same lines as the Duck Stamp program. A
recent analysis of state fishing license demand indicates that a $5
sport-fishing stamp program will generate up to $100 million annually

credits;[123] conversion penalties (taxes); and cross-compliance

legislation linked to receipt of Federal commodity program payments.[124]

In this last regard, the so-called "swampbusting provisions" of the most

recent Farm Act[125] constitute a move in the right direction, although it

is not yet clear whether USDA's interpretation and execution of the law

will be consistent with its intent.[126]

Suggestions for Further Research[127]

There are three possible avenues for further research:

improvements to the current model; additional applications of the model;

and extensions of the methodology to other policy problems.

---

for wetlands acquisition (Wolf 1988).

[122]Potential uses of taxation and other methods of protecting wetlands are examined by Kusler 1983.

[123]The elimination of favorable tax treatment of wetland conversion is also desirable. To a large degree, this has already been accomplished by the Tax Reform Act of 1986, whereby certain tax code provisions which previously provided an incentive for wetland conversion were eliminated.

[124]Recent studies (such as Kramer and Shabman 1986) have analyzed the wetland-conversion incentives provided by various agricultural programs and subsidies, including: price and income support programs; subsidized loans; crop insurance; disaster aid; and technical assistance.

[125]Title XII-C of Public Law 99-198, the Food Security Act of 1985, provides that a farm operator is ineligible for price-support payments, farm storage facility loans, crop insurance, disaster payments, and insured or guaranteed loans for any year in which annual crops were produced on converted wetlands.

[126]The U.S. Department of Agriculture, charged with administering the Food Security Act, has maintained that wetland conversion due to stream channelization and other Army Corps of Engineers projects is not subject to the swampbuster provisions (Heimlich and Langner 1986).

[127]Only a few selected, suggested improvements in the private market and social optimum models are highlighted in this section; these and other potential improvements have been discussed (in footnotes) throughout the study.

Improvements in the Current Model

Improvements to the present model can be thought of as applying to the underlying theoretical model, the econometric estimation method, or the simulation model. One improvement in the underlying theoretical model would be to respecify the landowner's decision problem as one involving a discrete-time (non-continuous), stochastic optimization process. Furthermore, the objective function of the dynamic optimization model could be improved by providing for even-aged forest management and for an endogenous rotation length, and also by treating the agricultural crop mix as endogenous to landowner decision-making.

In terms of econometric estimation methods, it would be desirable to use a systems method of estimation allowing for a fully general error-term structure,[128] such as three-stage least squares (THSLS). As was explained previously, this was not done in the current study because of limitations (regarding choice of instruments) in available econometric estimation programs.

The simulation model could be improved by incorporating distinct environmental externality estimates temporally and across counties, and by providing for a non-linear environmental benefit function. One final area of possible improvement to the current model is to utilize

---

[128]As is explained in detail in Chapter III, the fixed-effects specification in the single-equation framework was employed to remove a major component of serial correlation in the error term. Additionally, the method of Breusch (1978) and Godfrey (1978) was used to test for remaining first or second order serial correlation (both AR and MA).

stochastic simulations instead of the simple, deterministic point-
estimates which are employed in the study.[129]

Additional Applications of the Model

In order to help evaluate alternative policies to deal with the
wetland depletion problems examined in this study, the efficacy of
specific policy instruments can be analyzed quantitatively with the
model, as long as the policy instruments can be expressed in terms of
their effects on project-impact areas, annual revenues or costs of
agriculture or forestry, or conversion costs. The policies and programs
which may thereby be analyzed include: the elimination of Federal
subsidies for construction and maintenance of flood-control and drainage
projects; wetland easements; preferential property tax assessments; tax
credits; and cross-compliance agricultural policies.[130]

Another possible application of the model is to contrast
information on actual Federal project construction costs (measured in
dollars per acre per year) with estimates from the factual and
counterfactual simulations of implicit willingness-to-pay for Federal

---

[129]Uncertainty could be taken into account when carrying out
simulations. In the case of uncertainty associated with parameter
estimates, this may be done with stochastic (Monte Carlo) simulations.
An additional source of simulation error, however, is associated with
the fact that future values of exogenous variables and all environmental
externality values are themselves estimates. The discussion in Chapter
IV examined ways in which a probability distribution of environmental
values could be approximated. But, since explicit probability
distributions of crop price and other forecasted time series are not
available, the Monte Carlo approach would be problematic in any event.
An alternative approach is the bootstrapping of confidence intervals
(Prescott and Stengos 1987).

[130]The impact of cross-compliance agricultural policies can be examined
with the model if the model is augmented to include consideration of
effective support-price levels.

project protection. Such a comparison could form the basis for a benefit-cost evaluation of projects.

Extensions of the Methodology to Other Policy Problems

The methodology developed in this study may be applied to a variety of problems in the natural resources field, and other fields of economics, as well. For example, one obvious use of this approach would be to analyze the factors causing massive losses of tropical rain forests in areas such as the Amazon basin. Similarly, a valuable historical analysis would examine upland forest depletion and later farmland abandonment in the 19th and 20th centuries in areas such as New England and the Middle Atlantic states. Were these patterns of change symptomatic of rational responses to relative price changes? Were such dramatic land-use reallocations socially optimal?

Other related, potential uses of the approach include the examination of the impacts of public road construction in rural areas on timber management practices, and the analysis of the effects of Federal and state highway construction on urban development.

Moving beyond land-use questions, the generic methodology has wide applicability in the natural resources field. Problems which may be analyzed include: a renewable resource with stock externalities, for example, whaling; a renewable resource with crowding externalities, as in a typical commercial fishery; and a nonrenewable resource with flow externalities, such as off-shore oil recovery with a risk of accidental spills.

120

A Methodological Overview of the Analysis

Two broad objectives were achieved in the research described in
this study. First, a method was developed for aggregating a
theoretical, firm-level, natural resource supply function into a model
which could be econometrically estimated, by taking explicit account of
underlying heterogeneity and thus eliminating the common but problematic
representative-firm assumption. Second, a generic approach was
developed for estimating the socially optimal time-path of the
exploitation rate of a renewable natural resource, based upon
observations of revealed-preference, market-based behavior, in
combination with information about the economic value of environmental
externalities. A conceptual bridge was thus formed between a
statistical model of actual market performance and a theoretical model
of socially optimal behavior.

The generic methodology was developed in the context of an analysis
of alternative renewable resource strategies for forested wetlands.
Thus, two additional objectives were accomplished: important policy
questions concerning the causes and consequences of forested wetland
losses in the United States were addressed; and an approach was thereby
developed for analyzing a host of other policy problems associated with
the use of natural resources in the presence of environmental
externalities.

APPENDICES

APPENDIX 1:

Cropland Acreage Changes, 1949-69

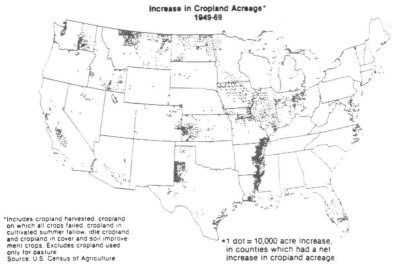

Increase in Cropland Acreage*
1949-69

*Includes cropland harvested, cropland
on which all crops failed, cropland in
cultivated summer fallow, idle cropland,
and cropland in cover and soil improvement crops. Excludes cropland used
only for pasture.
Source: U.S. Census of Agriculture

•1 dot = 10,000 acre increase,
in counties which had a net
increase in cropland acreage.

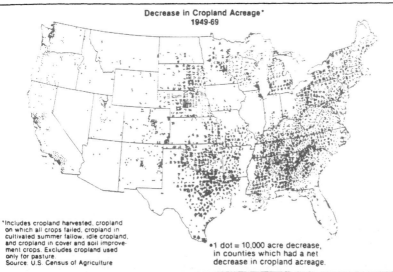

Decrease in Cropland Acreage*
1949-69

*Includes cropland harvested, cropland
on which all crops failed, cropland in
cultivated summer fallow, idle cropland,
and cropland in cover and soil improvement crops. Excludes cropland used
only for pasture.
Source: U.S. Census of Agriculture

•1 dot = 10,000 acre decrease,
in counties which had a net
decrease in cropland acreage.

SOURCE: U.S. Department of Agriculture, Economic Research Service. Cropland
Use and Supply: Outlook and Situation Report. CUS-2. Washington,
D.C., September 1985, p. 15.

123

Cropland Acreage Changes, 1969-82

Increase in Cropland Acreage*
1969-82

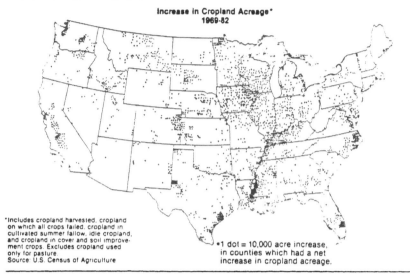

*Includes cropland harvested, cropland
on which all crops failed, cropland in
cultivated summer fallow, idle cropland,
and cropland in cover and soil improvement crops. Excludes cropland used
only for pasture.
Source: U.S. Census of Agriculture

•1 dot = 10,000 acre increase,
in counties which had a net
increase in cropland acreage.

Decrease in Cropland Acreage*
1969-82

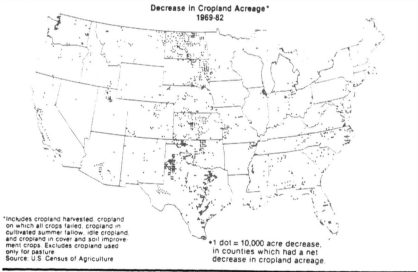

*Includes cropland harvested, cropland
on which all crops failed, cropland in
cultivated summer fallow, idle cropland,
and cropland in cover and soil improvement crops. Excludes cropland used
only for pasture.
Source: U.S. Census of Agriculture

•1 dot = 10,000 acre decrease,
in counties which had a net
decrease in cropland acreage.

SOURCE: U.S. Department of Agriculture, Economic Research Service, September
1985, p. 17.

Year	Projects Authorized	Projects Initiated	Projects Completed	Project Construction
		(acres)[a]		
1929[b]	213,071	0	0	0
1934	0	0	0	0
1939	1,044,939	65,117	21,710	50,648
1944	1,995,046	1,109,477	43,407	93,703
1949	10,000	614,969	0	122,477
1954	0	394,000	16,000	343,571
1959	150,000	284,400	971,229	512,316
1964	0	170,000	690,229	742,618
1969	59,470	52,813	817,406	187,573
1974	5,000	732,280	0	414,044
1979	0	54,470	824,262	534,451
1984	0	0	93,283	112,325
TOTAL	3,477,526	3,477,526	3,477,526[c]	3,113,726

[a]Acreages refer to areas hydrologically affected by projects.

[b]Five-year intervals refer to quinquennial periods ending in the indicated year.

[c]Acreages of "projects completed" overestimate true values, due to the inclusion in the original data of some projects which only were nearing completion.

125

APPENDIX 4:   SOIL CONSERVATION SERVICE
FLOOD CONTROL AND DRAINAGE PROJECTS
THIRTY-SIX INTERIOR COUNTIES
LOWER MISSISSIPPI ALLUVIAL PLAIN
1959 - 1984

Year	Projects Authorized	Projects Initiated	Projects Completed	Project Construction
		(acres)[a]		
1959	13,564	0	0	0
1964	862,782	675,254	0	168,785
1969	828,464	538,198	203,171	558,090
1974	394,333	397,079	539,652	471,578
1979	556,842	798,379	478,489	500,580
1984	223,700	662,929	341,367	503,202
TOTAL	2,879,685[b]	3,071,839	1,562,679	2,202,235

[a]Acreages refer to areas hydrologically affected by projects.

[b]Project authorization acreages omit additions to authorized acreages
through amendments to initial authorizations, and thus underestimate
true values.

This appendix on previous investigations of forested wetland
conversion in the Mississippi Alluvial Plain is divided into two major
sections: empirical studies and theoretical models.

Empirical Studies

The empirical studies themselves fall into two groups --
quantitative documentation of the substitution of agricultural land for
forested wetlands in the Plain, and examinations of the presumed causes
of this land-use change.

Quantitative Documentation of Cropland-Forest Substitution

Turner and Craig (1980) documented instances of conversion of
forested wetlands to agricultural use as early as the late eighteenth
century, and Harrison, in his massive (1961) history of the development
of agriculture in the Mississippi Delta, documented continuing patterns
of such conversion.[1]

In an important study, Frey and Dill (1971) used aerial photographs
from 1950 and 1969 to identify shifts in land-use. They found that
some 4 million acres of forested wetlands in the Lower Mississippi
Alluvial Plain were converted to agricultural use during the two
decades they examined. Murphy (1975) utilized forest surveys and
reported that 1.4 million acres of Louisiana wetlands were converted to

---

[1]Historical documentation of changing land-use patterns may provide
important lessons: Weller and Stegman (1977) described how the wetland
hardwood ecosystems of Missouri were long ago totally depleted as a
result of conversion to agricultural production.

agricultural use during the ten-year period, 1964-1974. He noted that most of the clearing was for soybean production.

MacDonald, Frayer, and Clauser (1979) were among the first to report the striking (negative) correlation which exists between changes in forested wetland acreages and changes in agricultural acreages in the Alluvial Plain. In an analysis for the U.S. Fish and Wildlife Service, Tiner examined depletion of forested wetlands in the MAV from 1937 to the present and concluded that "these forested wetlands have been cleared and drained for crop production" (1984, p.48).

Lastly, the U.S. Department of Agriculture (Economic Research Service, September 1985), in a recent examination of cropland use and supply, cited the conversion of forest land as the major source of newly developed agricultural crop land in the Lower Mississippi Alluvial Plain. Their graphic image of the location of new crop land throughout the United States over the period 1949-1969 provides, in effect, a rather accurate outline of the range of the Mississippi Alluvial Plain (Appendix 1, upper box).[2]

Examinations of the Causes of the Cropland-Forest Substitution

A number of empirical investigations of the causes of cropland-forest substitution in the Alluvial Plain have noted the importance of agricultural crop prices, particularly soybeans, as an important determinant of the relative profitability of agricultural production versus timber production. Davis (1972) examined the economic potential

---

[2]Appendix 2 provides a similar figure for the period 1969-1982. In the later period, the conversion was less drastic, and its location had shifted slightly southward. This slow migration of the center of conversion activity from the north (Missouri) to the south has been continuous for up to 100 years.

for converting woodlands and pastures to cropland in the MAV. Using a

budgeting approach, he estimated the minimum crop prices at which

conversion would be economically feasible.

Sternitzke (1976) likewise observed the importance of soybean

prices as a force behind wetland conversion, but noted further that the

profitability of agricultural production was also affected by local

hydrologic conditions, which were partly determined by flood-control and

drainage projects of the Federal government.

Seven other major empirical studies have been undertaken of the

causes of the observed cropland-forest substitution in the Lower

Mississippi Alluvial Plain -- one by the University of Arkansas, and two

each by the U.S. Fish and Wildlife Service, the Economic Research

Service of USDA, and the U.S. Army Corps of Engineers.

(1) Economic Research Service Study of Small Watershed Projects

In 1975, the Economic Research Service (ERS) of the U.S. Department

of Agriculture released its examination of the effect of some 60 Small

Watershed Program (PL 566) projects on major uses of land in the

southeast, the Lower Mississippi Alluvial Plain, and the Missouri River

tributaries region (Mattson 1975). In this study, Mattson used aerial

photographs from the period 1955-1970 to compare areas where projects

had been installed with areas where projects were planned but had not

yet been developed.[3] Within the MAV, he found that "cropland expansion

---

[3]The land usage in affected areas of ten installed projects was compared
with that of ten uninstalled projects. Eight distinct land uses were
identified on the aerial photos for two dates: cropland, grassland,
idle-transitional, forest, urban, rural-urban, reservoirs, and
miscellaneous.

on protected bottomlands of installed projects was well ahead of the rate of planned projects," (p. 13) and concluded as follows:

> The combination of the major flood-control and
> drainage works, principally by the Corps of
> Engineers, with complementary development of small
> watershed projects, will probably continue to make
> possible the rapid expansion of intensive cropping,
> displacing lower intensive forest uses (Mattson
> 1975, p.29).

(2) Shulstad, May, and Herrington: Economic Feasibility of Conversion

Shulstad and May (1979) examined the private economic feasibility of wetland conversion by comparing the discounted stream of net returns from agriculture with the discounted stream of returns from commercial forestry plus conversion costs. They concluded that within a wide range of scenarios, positive economic returns to conversion existed. This indicated that conversion tended to be profitable if agricultural production was possible. What Shulstad and May did not address, however, was whether the positive economic returns they observed were partly a function of government programs and projects, such as those of the Corps and SCS.

In a later article growing out of the same research effort, Herrington and Shulstad (1982) again examined the economic feasibility of converting Mississippi Delta woodlands to pasture and cropland. They reported that "drainage was the foremost limitation to woodland conversion" (p.6), and concluded that

> Under conditions of high yield management, the
> conversion of all remaining woodland and pastureland
> in private ownership within the Mississippi Delta
> region *that is not frequently flooded* or too steep
> is economically feasible .... (p.29) [emphasis
> added]

(3) The U.S. Fish and Wildlife Service's Investigation of Bottomland Hardwood Losses in the Lower Mississippi Alluvial Plain

In a major research effort, sponsored by the U.S. Fish and Wildlife Service (USF&WS), MacDonald, Frayer, and Clauser (1979) attempted to identify the major causes of the depletion of forested wetlands in the Lower Mississippi Alluvial Plain. They found that typical net income per acre from agricultural crop production vastly exceeded average income per acre from forest use within the Alluvial Plain. Thus, they were able to posit the existence of a strong economic incentive to convert wetlands to agricultural purposes in situations where agricultural production was feasible.

In the next step of their analysis, MacDonald, Frayer, and Clauser posited that artificial flood protection and drainage projects of the U.S. Army Corps of Engineers and the Soil Conservation Service tended to affect positively the feasibility of agricultural production. They also noted, however, that agricultural prices (plus other economic variables) and climatic factors should also play important roles in wetland conversion decisions by individuals.

In the absence of a theoretical model of how these variables interact in the determination of land-use decisions, the authors chose to examine some raw statistical correlations of the variables of interest. They noted what appeared to be a positive relationship over time between rates of wetland clearing in the Plain and the number of Army Corps and SCS projects being completed.[4] By using transparent

---

[4]The variables being compared in the USF&WS study were the number of completed Corps and SCS projects (by county) and the degree of forested wetland conversion (per county). Data on the extent (size in acres of the affected areas) of projects were not available until such information was assembled by the Environmental Defense Fund as part of the study (Stavins 1986) which is the antecedent of this research.

overlays, they concluded that "significant correlations were observed between forest clearing and completed COE and PL-566 projects for the 1957-1967 and 1967-1977 time periods" (1979, p.74).[5]

The USF&WS research (MacDonald, Frayer, and Clauser 1979) was the most ambitious attempt up to that time to evaluate the causes of wetland depletion in the Lower Mississippi Alluvial Plain. It is therefore important to examine these results. First of all, the "correlations" described by MacDonald, Frayer, and Clauser (1979) were, in fact, qualitative impressions based upon visual inspection of maps and overlays. Given the lack of data on the impact areas of Corps and SCS projects, a more rigorous analysis may not have been possible. Nevertheless, the fact remains that no degree of statistical meaning can be attached to the findings.

Due to the fact that the USF&WS research team was working without a theoretically defined model of wetland conversion, no means was provided for analyzing the relative roles played by agricultural and forestry prices, natural hydrologic variations, and Federal flood-control projects, despite the fact that data were collected on all of these variables, plus others. Thus, although the MacDonald, Frayer, and Clauser study provided valuable land-use data, the analysis could not answer questions regarding the causes of wetland conversion.[6]

---

[5]The USF&WS researchers also indicated that natural hydrologic variations (extended dry periods) were positively correlated with rates of bottomland hardwood forest clearing, and that soybean prices in the post-war period seemed to be correlated with periods of intensive clearing.

[6]To the authors' credit, they clearly realized the limitations of their analysis, and therefore couched their conclusions with numerous caveats such as "Although it cannot be stated unequivocally ..." and "... although the effect can only be inferred ...."

Given these limitations of the USF&WS study, it should not be surprising that the U.S. Army Corps of Engineers subsequently indicated their lack of confidence in the study's results. Noting the observed positive correlation between acreage losses in bottomland hardwood forests and the completion of Corps and SCS projects, the Corps stated:

> These observations suggest that the Corps flood-control projects and the small watershed projects have had an effect on the extent of bottomland hardwood clearing, but the magnitude of this effect cannot be determined accurately given the existing data (U.S. Army Corps of Engineers 1981a, p.9-10).

(4) The U.S. Army Corps of Engineers' Examination of the Tensas River Basin

The Corps concluded from their own analysis of reaches of the Tensas River that agricultural prices, primarily of soybeans, were major forces behind wetland conversion: "Since 1962, the increasing worldwide demand for soybeans and the accompanying price increases have been prime factors in the draining and clearing of large parcels of formerly wooded terrain" (1981a, p.9-18). This finding is consistent with the USF&WS study's conclusions.

The same Corps study also examined the question of the impact of Corps projects on land clearing, again for various reaches of the Tensas River. The analysis found simple correlations between rates of land clearing and frequency of flooding in the range of 0.09 to 0.81. Given the fact that these correlations come from what is, in effect, a two-variable "model" of what is essentially a multivariate situation, this range of simple correlation coefficients actually may be taken as providing relatively positive evidence of a statistical association

133

between frequency of flooding and land clearing activity. The Corps, however, concluded from their analysis that:

> There is no significant relationship between flood
> frequency and rate of land clearing in the Tensas
> study area. These relationships indicate that a
> project which affects the frequency of flooding will
> not necessarily affect the rate of land clearing.
> (1981a, p. 9-15).

Even if the reported correlation coefficients were insignificant, it would be impossible to draw any firm conclusions from such evidence, given the likelihood of Type II error in the face of a simple "model" which ignored the multiplicative role of prices, agricultural yields, climate, and other relevant variables. On the other hand, considering the simplicity of the Corps of Engineers' analysis, their reported range of correlation coefficients might even be presented as evidence that flood frequency does affect land clearing.

(5) The U.S. Army Corps of Engineers' Evaluation of Water Resources Development in the Yazoo-Mississippi Delta

In 1980, the Corps of Engineers' Institute for Water Resources sponsored an empirical analysis of the consequences of Federal flood-control projects in the four million acre Yazoo-Mississippi Delta. The study (Galloway 1980)[7] utilized a geographic-analysis approach to estimate what the condition of the Delta would have been (in terms of land-use, etc.) in 1970 under various counterfactual assumptions regarding the construction of flood-control projects

The analysis was carried out in three stages. First, physical conditions of the Delta under the counterfactual scenarios were

---

[7]Colonel Gerald E. Galloway, Jr. is professor and deputy head of the Department of Geography and Computer Sciences, U.S. Military Academy, West Point, New York. He was formerly the District Engineer of the U.S. Army Corps of Engineers for the Vicksburg (Mississippi) District.

estimated through geographic analysis. Second, social and economic conditions, including land-use patterns, which would have obtained under the estimated physical conditions, were predicted through comparison with analog areas. In the third and final step, differences between the actual 1970 social and economic conditions and those predicted under the counterfactual assumptions were taken as being indicative of the impact of the respective flood-control projects.

The results of this analysis indicated that in the absence of most interior flood-control projects,[8] the total area of forested wetlands in the Yazoo-Mississippi Delta would have decreased from 1.8 million acres in 1920 to about 1.7 million acres in 1970, whereas the actual 1970 total forested wetland area was only 850 thousand acres. A complementary set of predictions was developed for the total land in agricultural usage. Galloway concluded that if interior flood-control projects had not been constructed after 1928 (but the main line levees were strengthened and maintained), the total agricultural acreage of the Delta in 1970 would have been about one-third less than what it was. Concomitantly, forested wetlands would have "remained near their original condition" (Galloway 1980, p.191).

(6) Heimlich and Langner: A Farm-Budgeting Approach

In this USDA study, Heimlich and Langner (1986) utilized a farm-budgeting approach to analyze the impact of deficiency payments, price support levels, and income tax provisions on the conversion of forested wetlands to agricultural use. They did not include an examination of the impacts of flood-protection and drainage projects.

─────────────────────────

[8]This scenario assumed that the major levees along the Mississippi River had been constructed and maintained at their true historical levels.

135

(7) Kramer and Shabman: A Farm-Level Simulation Model

The U.S. Fish and Wildlife Service recently sponsored a number of
studies of the impact of Federal programs and policies on wetlands, as
is discussed in the text of Chapter I. Two of these studies examined
wetland depletion in the Lower Mississippi Alluvial Plain. Of these,
one was the antecedent to the research reported in this thesis (Stavins
1986, 1987a); and the other was carried out by Kramer and Shabman
(1986).

The Kramer and Shabman analysis utilized a farm-level, cash-flow
model to simulate the rate of return associated with decisions to
convert bottomland hardwood areas to agricultural production under
alternative Federal policy environments, including individual
agricultural programs, conservation programs, and tax code provisions.
Simulations were conducted under alternative sets of assumptions,
reflecting differing ownership patterns, crop mixes, and soil
characteristics.

Kramer and Shabman concluded that Federal agricultural income and
price support subsidies significantly increase the expected
profitability and reduce the risk of conversion of forested wetlands to
agricultural cropland. Provisions of the U.S. tax code were also found
to provide an inducement for the conversion of wetlands to cropland.

In summary, the empirical investigations which have been conducted
to date provide valuable evidence regarding the pattern of wetland
conversion, and these studies have, in general, indicated the important

136

role played by flood protection and drainage projects in inducing

wetland conversion.[9]

Theoretical Models of Wetland Conversion

Only two formalized models of wetland conversion have appeared in

the literature. The first, that of Brown (1972), does not directly

address the conversion issue but does present a useful formulation of

the problem of "rational investment behavior in the face of floods." The

other model (Shabman 1980) focuses on the precise issue which is of

concern here, the economic causes of wetland conversion. Both models

provide valuable insights into the way in which flood-control and

drainage projects may affect individual landowner decisions; but neither

model directly allows for relevant parameters to be estimated with

empirical data.

Brown's Model of Rational Investment Behavior in the Face of Floods

Brown developed a model for evaluating the economic benefits of

flood protection, and as one step in his derivation he recognized that a

landowner's decision regarding the use of his land (for one of a set of

potential activities) is a function of the probability of flooding,

where the investment decision criterion is the expected present value of

the land (when utilized for alternative uses).[10] As it is only this

---

[9]Most recently, Tiner summarized the findings of the earlier studies, and concluded that "Federal flood-control projects and small watershed projects have accelerated wetland conversion to cropland, especially from the 1950's to the present" (1984, p.48).

[10]In his 1972 book, Brown presented a stochastic model of investment decisions in the context of possible catastrophic losses. The economic costs of flooding and the benefits of flood protection were the focus of Brown, Contini, and McGuire (1972). Lind (1967) approached the same

137

landowner-decision aspect of Brown's model which is of interest in the
present context, a description of the formal structure of the overall
model is not included here. Instead, a rather simplified description of
the relevant aspects of the analysis is provided.

Brown began with the assumption that a rational landowner will seek
to maximize the expected present discounted value of the net income from
a parcel of land. Given this, a landowner will select that activity
which has the greatest expected present value (assuming that a finite
set of mutually exclusive activities are available). In this framework,
the value of the land is identical to the expected present value of the
land when put to its highest valued use. A change in land value due to
flood protection can be calculated as the change in the expected value
of the "best" use of the land subsequent to a change in the probability
of flooding.

What is crucial in the context of land-use decision making is that
the chosen use of the land may change as a result of the change in
flooding probability. For example, as the probability of flooding
decreases, the highest valued use of the land[11] might be expected to
change from timber production to agricultural crop production, to
commercial and residential use. This happens, in this example, because
it is reasonably assumed that the value of woodlands is only slightly

---

problem from an essentially non-stochastic framework. A less technical
economic analysis of stream channelization was provided by Brown (1974).

[11]Reference is to the highest privately valued use of the land.
Assuming that negative externalities of loss of wetlands exist, if these
environmental externalities were internalized, rational individual
decision-making would instead be expected to lead to the highest
socially valued use of the land. In this case, it would of course be
less likely, ceteris paribus, that the selected land use would change
from woodland to crop production, despite a decrease in flooding
probability.

affected by flooding, while the values of cropland and residential property are affected more.

Even from this simplified version of Brown's formal model, it is clear that the relative value of wetlands for agricultural production (compared with the value of wetlands in their forested state) may be expected to increase as a result of a flood-control or drainage project, and that rational landowners then may be expected to convert their holdings of forested wetlands to agricultural cropland.

Shabman's Model of the Private Feasibility of Wetland Conversion

The model developed by Shabman (1980) is the only formal economic model of wetland conversion which has been reported in the literature. Shabman expanded upon the conceptual framework of Shulstad, May, and Herrington (1979) by positing two decision criteria for the landowner, one of economic feasibility and one of financial feasibility,[12] and by allowing for the possibility that positive returns to wetland conversion might partly be a function of Federal flood-control and drainage projects.

Shabman begins with the supposition that "for the individual farmer, bottomland conversion is justified when the market value of the

---

[12]Only Shabman's economic feasibility condition is examined, although both are necessary conditions (but neither is a sufficient condition) for a landowner to make a favorable assessment of the prospects for wetland conversion. The financial feasibility condition is a minimum cash flow condition, which states that conversion will only take place if the farming operation will earn a stream of revenues which is continuously sufficient to cover both production costs and payments on loans taken out due to the conversion decision. Given constraints of data availability and various assumptions made in the text, the econometric model developed in this study is consistent with Shabman's economic feasibility equation. These considerations also dictate that the financial feasibility condition is not explicitly considered in the econometric analysis. Alternative means of taking liquidity constraints into account in the econometric model are discussed in the text.

farm products produced is expected to exceed the farmer's costs of developing and farming these lands" (1980, p.402). Thus, a condition of private economic feasibility may be specified:

$$r \geq i_t = i_m + i_p \tag{1}$$

where r = internal rate of return to conversion;

  i_t = target interest rate established by the landowner, depending upon both the opportunity cost of capital and the landowner's attitude toward risk;

  i_m = the market interest rate; and

  i_p = a risk premium, assuming risk aversion on the part of the landowner.

Given the above formulation of the problem, a rational landowner would implicitly determine the relevant internal rate of return, r, from the following expression:

$$K = \sum_{y=1}^{Y} \left[\left[P_y Q_y - (C_y + T_y) \right] (1 + r)^{-y} + V_0 (1 + \alpha)^Y (1 + r)^{-Y} \right] \tag{2}$$

where K = investment necessary to initiate farming, i.e. cost of land acquisition and/or cost of conversion plus costs of machinery and equipment purchase;

  Y = landowner's planning horizon;

  P_y = expected crop prices;

  Q_y = expected production of crops;

  C_y = expected agricultural production costs;

T_y = expected value of foregone timber production;

V_0 = current difference in sale value between agricultural land and forested wetland; and

α = expected rate of growth of difference (V_0)

Within the context of this model of economic feasibility, Shabman hypothesized the ways in which flood-control and drainage projects might affect land-conversion decisions. Projects will increase the expected production from farming by reducing the probability of losses due to flooding and/or poor drainage. This will have the effect of increasing both the expected net returns and the market value of the farmed land. Also, flood control and drainage projects may be expected to decrease the expected costs of conversion of the land, and so K will decrease. All three of these effects will result in an increase in r, the internal rate of return, in the above equation.

Furthermore, because projects reduce the probability of output losses due to flooding, the risk premium in the first equation may also be reduced. The two sets of impacts, then, will have the overall effect of increasing the economic feasibility of conversion.[13] In a world of rational economic behavior, it is assumed that wetland conversion to agricultural use will essentially be a function of the expected economic return to conversion. Hence, Shabman was able to claim that it is reasonable to expect that Federal flood-control and drainage projects provide an incentive for individual landowners to undertake the conversion of forested wetlands.

---

[13]For a discussion of the ways in which flood-control and drainage projects may be expected to affect the financial feasibility of wetland conversion, see Shabman (1980), p.404.

As indicated previously, neither Brown's nor Shabman's analysis included empirical dimensions, and so both studies' theoretical conclusions, while quite compelling, must remain hypotheses, waiting to be tested. At the very least, however, the empirical and theoretical analyses reviewed in this appendix provide support for the series of hypotheses developed in the text of the present study:

(1) Federal flood-control and drainage projects reduce the probability of flooding and increase the possibility of drainage of wetlands;

(2) the result of these changed hydrologic conditions is that the suitability of the land for agricultural production increases;

(3) as a consequence of this, the expected present value of the land for agricultural use increases relative to the land's expected present value for use in its forested wetland state; and

(4) the decision by individual landowners to convert forested wetlands to agricultural uses is essentially a function of this relative present value; i.e. wetland conversion is a function of the expected economic return to conversion.

This chain of hypotheses describes a causal linkage through which the construction of Federal flood-control and drainage projects systematically leads to the conversion of wetlands to alternative uses.

APPENDIX 6: DATA SOURCES AND VARIABLE CONSTRUCTION[1]

This appendix provides background information on the data utilized to estimate the parameters of the econometric model of forested wetland conversion. Each of the variables of the model is briefly described, as are the major sources of data which were used. For some variables, a substantial amount of calculation was required to construct the requisite series of data; these calculations are also described.

Within the appendix, variables are divided into the following major categories: (1) land-use patterns; (2) agricultural revenue; (3) agricultural costs of production; (4) forestry net revenue; (5) artificial flood protection and drainage provision; (6) natural flood and drainage conditions; (7) weather conditions; (8) costs of conversion; and (9) other variables. Information concerning the nature and use of respective variables presented in the text in the course of model development is not repeated here.

Land-Use Patterns

In this part of the appendix, the criteria for establishing the study area and the sample time frame are discussed, and the construction of the data on forested land areas is described.

---

[1]The data utilized to estimate the parameters and standard errors of the econometric model described in the text were collected as part of a previous research effort, sponsored by the U.S. Department of the Interior and carried out on behalf of the Environmental Defense Fund. For further details regarding data sources and variable construction, see Stavins 1986.

Identification of Study Area and Sample Time Frame

The Lower Mississippi Alluvial Plain (MAV) was the exclusive focus of the study. The Alluvial Plain contains what is, by far, the largest remaining, contiguous wetland habitat in the coterminus United States, a 5.2 million acre bottomland hardwood forest.

Originally, the Mississippi Alluvial Plain included nearly 24 million acres of bottomland hardwood forested wetlands. By 1937, only 11.8 million acres remained. Since that time, another 6.5 million acres of hardwood forests in the Plain have been cleared, much of this land having been converted during the post-war period to agricultural row crops. Today, less than 5.2 million acres remain, about 20 percent of the original acreage.

The sample area is limited to portions of the Alluvial Plain within three states, Arkansas, Louisiana, and Mississippi, together accounting for approximately 90 percent of the total area of the Alluvial Plain and about 90 percent of the Corps and SCS projects constructed during the sample time period. The decision to focus on the three major states was due to the unavailability of land-use data for the three "minor" states (Kentucky, Missouri, and Tennessee) for the first half of the relevant time period. Furthermore, data on the three minor states which were available (for the second half of the time period) were judged less reliable than those for the major states, due to sampling methodology (Warren E. Frayer, p.c., June 1985).

Other limitations of the data made it necessary to restrict the econometric analysis to those counties within the 3-state area of the MAV which lie wholly within the Alluvial Plain. As a result, 36 "interior" counties, of a total of 89 counties, are considered (Appendix

144

13). These 36 counties comprise 13 million acres, about 60 percent of the total area of the Lower Mississippi Alluvial Plain within the three states.

The empirical analysis covers the time period from 1935 through 1984, with some lagged variables being considered back to 1934. This time period, determined essentially by the availability of data, includes the entire period during which Federal flood-control and drainage projects have been constructed in the Alluvial Plain.

Forested Acreage

The U.S. Forest Service (USFS) periodically measures land-use at sample sites, using a sampling procedure based upon aerial photographs.[2] Sample locations are established at the intersection of grid lines three miles apart, and ten plots, measuring one acre each are classified on a simple forest/non-forest basis. The 0-1 observations are converted into estimates of the share of the land which is forested by county, and are regularly published by the Forest Service in its series of Survey Reports and Resource Bulletins.

These "forest inventory" data constituted the major source for county-level estimates by Frayer (1979). For use in the present study, Frayer's county-level estimates were combined with a set of updated survey-based estimates (Warren Frayer, p.c., June 1985) to yield a

---

[2]For further information regarding the Forest Service's inventory process, see MacDonald, Frayer, and Clauser 1979, p.16.

consistent set of observations of forested acreage[3] per county over a 50-year time frame.[4]

The USFS inventory data are collected approximately every ten years, with the collections taking place in different years across counties. In order to construct an internally consistent set of data on forested acreage which took the form of a usable panel of observations moving through time, a process of interpolation-by-related-series was used, in which the very close relationship between changes in forest acreage per county and changes in total agricultural acreage per county was utilized to develop sets of county estimates of forested acreage. Data were not pooled at this stage; instead, separate econometric estimates were developed for each county:

$$y_{it} = \alpha_i + \beta_i x_{it} + \varepsilon_{it} \qquad (1)$$

where y_{it} = change in USFS forest acreage estimate for county i during the time period t-1 to t;

---

[3]Total forested acreage is used in this study, not bottomland hardwood acreage. The two are very close in magnitude and highly correlated (MacDonald, Frayer, and Clauser 1979, pp. 30, 67).

[4]An additional set of data on forested acreage per county was assembled, based upon photo-interpretation work carried out by the U.S. Fish and Wildlife Service for the MacDonald, Frayer, and Clauser (1979) study. This data set was used only to verify the county-level trends found with the Forest Service inventory data, although future econometric analysis could be carried out using the photo-interpreted (PI) data. The advantage of the PI data set is that its reliability is apparently constant across all 89 counties, whereas the Forest Service data are reliable only for the 36 interior counties. On the other hand, the Forest Service data cover a 50-year period, while the PI data cover a period only half as long. Furthermore, Turner and Craig (1980), in their analysis of Louisiana's forested wetlands, found that available aerial photogrammatic data were unreliable; hence, they depended exclusively on U.S. Forest Service inventory data.

146

x_{it} = change in total agricultural acreage for county i during

the time period t-1 to t, based upon estimates from the

U.S. Department of Commerce (1924-1982) and state

sources;[5]

α_i, β_i = estimated parameters for county i; and

ε_{it} = error term with mean zero.

Then, the 36 estimated equations were used to find respective

fitted values -- changes in forested acreage for ten quinquennial

periods, ending in the years 1939, 1944, 1949, 1954, 1959, 1964, 1969,

1974, 1979, and 1984.[6] From these estimated changes, respective

estimates of forested acreage (S_{it}) for the pivotal years were

calculated.[7]

Agricultural Revenue

The variable, a_{it}, average (gross) agricultural revenue per acre in

county i during the period t-1 to t, is a weighted average, which takes

into account agricultural prices, production levels, yields, and

---

[5]Arkansas Crop and Livestock Reporting Service (various years);
Louisiana Crop and Livestock Reporting Service (various years);
Mississippi Crop and Livestock Reporting Service (various years); Nelson
and Cadwallander 1983, 1984; Nelson and Adenji 1983; Harsch 1984; Donald
Von Steen, p.c., July 1985; Bergen Nelson, p.c., July 1985; and George
Knight, p.c., July 1985.

[6]These particular years were utilized because of their close match with
Census of Agriculture data and because the terminal year of the series,
1984, was the final year for which data were available.

[7]The interpolation-by-related-series process yields essentially unbiased
predictions, although prediction error is present. This error appears
in the dependent variable of the land-conversion equation, and,
therefore does not bias the statistical estimation process, since
measurement error in the dependent variable is picked up by the error
term of the equation.

acreages. Gross revenues from four crops were combined in the calculation of weighted agricultural revenue per acre:

$$a_{it} = \left[\sum_{j=1}^{J}\left[L_{ijt}PR_{ijt}Y_{ijt}\right]\right] / \left[\sum_{j=1}^{J}L_{ijt}\right] \tag{2}$$

where L_{ijt} = average (land area) acreage of crop j harvested in county
        i during the period t-1 to t;

   PR_{ijt} = average real price of crop j in county i during the
        period t-1 to t;

   Y_{ijt} = average yield of crop j in county i during period t-1 to
        t; and

   j = 1,2,3,4 (soybeans, cotton, rice, corn).

The selected crops, soybeans, cotton, rice, and corn,[8] together account for more than 75 percent of the total acreage devoted to crop production in the three states during the relevant period. The time path of average real agricultural revenue for the entire 36-county area is shown in Appendix 32.

Agricultural Crop Acreages

Five-year-average total county harvested acreages for each of the four crops were estimated, based upon data from the U.S. Census of

---

[8]Maps of the location of production of soybeans, cotton, rice, and corn in the lower 48 states (as of 1976) are provided in Appendices 28, 29, 30, and 31, respectively.

Agriculture (1925-1982) and other sources.[9] Totals for the 36 counties
are provided in Appendix 32.

Agricultural Production Levels

Quinquennial averages of total county production of the four crops
were estimated, based on U.S. Census of Agriculture data plus other
sources.[10]

Agricultural Yield Levels

Quinquennial averages of (average annual) county yields of the four
major crops were calculated by dividing total production levels by total
harvested acreage. Summary statistics are found in Appendix 33.

Agricultural Prices

Real farm-level prices[11] for the four crops were calculated as the
average price over respective quinquennia, and separate price series
were used for each state.[12] Average prices across the three states are
found in Appendix 34.

---

[9]The additional sources are: Nelson and Cadwallader 1985; Arkansas Crop
and Livestock Reporting Service 1947-1984; Mississippi Crop and
Livestock Reporting Service 1985; Bergen Nelson, p.c., July 1985;
Fielder and Parker 1972; George Knight, p.c., July 1985; and McCandliss
1955.

[10]See previous footnote.

[11]Real prices were obtained by converting current dollars to the average
dollars of the final time period, 1980-84, through use of the Wholesale
Price Index (U.S. Council of Economic Advisers 1978, 1985).

[12]Sources for agricultural prices for Arkansas were: Arkansas Crop and
Livestock Reporting Service 1983; and Donald Von Steen, p.c., July 1985.
Sources for Louisiana were: Fielder 1982, 1984; and Louisiana Crop and
Livestock Reporting Service 1985. Sources for Mississippi were:
McCandliss 1955; Liles 1975; Harsch 1978; Mississippi Crop and Livestock
Reporting Service 1981, 1982, 1983; and George Knight, p.c., July 1985.

Effective Support Prices

Effective price support levels (a concept developed by Houck and others[13] were obtained (Randall Kramer, p.c., August 1985) for all available years. For the pre-1946 period, actual support prices were used; these are identical to effective support prices since there were no set-aside programs in the pre-1946 period. As is explained in the text, however, the effective support prices were not utilized in the final model. The five-year averages are presented in Stavins 1986.

Agricultural Costs of Production

Agricultural production costs for each crop were estimated as averages of the costs reported in state documents.[14] The costs considered were cash expenses, which include variable plus fixed expenses (general farm overhead, taxes and insurance, and interest), but not capital replacement nor allocated returns to owned inputs. Costs for each crop were weighted by acreage:

---

[13]See Houck, Abel, Ryan, Gallagher, Hoffmann and Penn 1976; Houck and Ryan 1972; Houck and Subotnik 1969; Gallagher 1978; and Gallagher and Green 1984.

[14]Sources consulted in constructing the agricultural production cost estimates included the following: May, Walden, and Welsh 1978; May and Walden 1979, 1980; May, Walden, Smith, Hale, and Stuart 1981; Dorland, Fisher, Garner, Smith, Hale and Stuart 1982; Mississippi Agricultural and Forestry Experiment Station 1982, 1983, 1984, 1985; Parvin, Anderson, Cooke, Holder, Hamill 1975; Parvin, Anderson, Cooke, Heagler, and Toney 1975; Woolf and Brugman 1973; Woolf, Vidrine, and Martinez 1976; Paxton 1977, 1978; Woolf 1979; Beasley and Woolf and 1972; Smith, May, Walden, and Halbrook 1977; Dunnuck, McPeek, and Jackson 1960; Jackson and VonSteen 1978; McElroy and Gustafson 1985; Fielder and Nelson 1982; Zacharias and McManus 1985; Parvin, Anderson, Holder, and Cooke 1976; Lavergne and Paxton 1985; Paxton and Lavergne 1983, 1984; Musick 1982; Musick and Salassi 1983; Paxton and Huffman 1979; Paxton, Huffman, and Boweher 1980; U.S. Department of Agriculture 1978, 1981; Parvin, Hamill, Cooke, Holder, Cameron 1977, 1978, 1979; Crowe 1956; Langsford and Thibodeaux 1939; and Wilson and Bryan 1938.

$$ac_{it} = \left[\sum_{j=1}^{J} \left[L_{ijt} CR_{ijt} \right] \right] / \left[\sum_{j=1}^{J} L_{ijt} \right] \qquad (3)$$

where CR_{ijt} = average real cost of production of crop j in county i
during the period t-1 to t.

Summary statistics of the final variable, ac_{it}, are in Appendix 35.

Forestry Revenue

Five sets of variables are examined here: net revenue per acre,
forest product (sawlog and pulpwood) prices, volumes, growth rates, and
yields.

Forestry Net Revenue Per Acre

Annual forestry net revenue per acre in county i during the period
t-1 to t, fn_{it}, consists of two components: the difference between the
(annualized) revenue stream generated by periodic harvesting of timber
and the (annualized) one-time revenue received from a clearcut of the
forest prior to conversion of the property to agricultural usage.[15]
Thus, real forestry net revenue per acre is a weighted average of annual
revenues from sawlogs and pulpwood minus the annuity of a windfall which
is gained from a clearcut of timber if conversion is carried out:

---

[15]The existence of a market for timber is assumed. This assumption is
acceptable for modelling purposes in the absence of a reasonable
alternative structure for modelling the effect of potential timber
revenue on landowners' decisions regarding the use of their land. As is
discussed in the text, however, many areas are not clearcut for timber
prior to clearing; in some cases, all on-site vegetation may be felled
and burned (Herrington and Shulstad 1982).

$$fn_{it} = \left[\sum_{m=1}^{M} PR_{mit} V_{mit} G_{mit} / S_{it} \right] - \sum_{m=1}^{M} \left[PR_{mit} V_{mit} / S_{it} \right] / \sum_{p=1}^{P} (1+r_t)^{-p} \qquad (4)$$

where PR_{mit} = average real net price of forest product m (sawlogs and
pulpwood) in county i during the period t-1 to t;

V_{mit} = average volume (stock) of product m in county i during
period t-1 to t;

G_{mit} = average annual growth rate of stock of m in county i
during the period t-1 to t;

P = planning horizon utilized by landowners; and

r_t = average net borrowing cost, a real, after-tax rate of
interest.

Note that $\tilde{F}$, the discounted present value of the stream of
(delayed) forest revenue which is initiated when farmland is abandoned,
is defined in the text of Chapter 2.

Sawlog and Pulpwood Prices

Real prices for each county (during each time period) were
separately estimated for sawlogs (stumpage value) and pulpwood by
calculating weighted averages of state-level hardwood and softwood
(pine) prices,[16] where weights were (percentage) sawtimber volume
distributions (between hardwoods and softwoods) in the sawlog case, and

---

[16]Sources for mixed hardwood and softwood stumpage and pulpwood prices
were: Reynolds and Pierson 1939; U.S. Department of Agriculture 1940,
1941, 1942, 1945, 1955; Arkansas Forestry Commission 1953-1983; Timber
Mart South 1981- 1984; Mississippi State Forestry Commission 1969-1980;
Louisiana Forestry Commission, 1944-1983; Sternitzke 1965; and Murphy
1975.

weights were growing stock distributions (again, between hardwoods and softwoods) for the pulpwood price calculations. In both cases, the weights varied across the three states and across time (Stavins 1986). The region-wide average nominal prices which resulted from this process are found in Appendix 36.

Sawlog and Pulpwood Volumes

The USFS forest inventory procedure described above for acreage estimates also produces estimates of sawlog and pulpwood volumes of standing timber on a county basis. Frayer (1979) drew upon these inventories to formulate sets of county-level estimates across time. These constituted the primary source of volume data for use in this study (together with update work by Frayer (p.c., June 1985)).

Working separately with sawlog and pulpwood volumes, the raw volumes were first standardized across time to account for the different measurement scales used over the period 1935-1984 (Stavins 1986). Next, the adjusted volumes were converted to units compatible with the respective price series (thousand board feet, Doyle log scale, for sawlogs, and million cords, for pulpwood). Lastly, appropriate five-year averages were calculated. The final study-area averages are found in Appendix 36.

Sawlog and Pulpwood Yields

In order to estimate annual yields of sawlogs and pulpwood per acre, the county volume measures were multiplied by appropriate annual percentage growth rates. For sawlogs, growth rates[17] of sawtimber, both

---

[17]Sources of the growth rates for Arkansas were: Wheeler 1953; Sternitzke 1960; Hedlund and Earles 1970; and U.S. Department of Agriculture 1980. Sources for Louisiana were: U.S. Department of

hardwood and softwood, were used, whereas, for pulpwood, the growth rate
of all species of the growing stock was utilized (Stavins 1986). The
growth rates varied by state and five-year interval. Division of the
annual county yields by county forested acreage produced the data series
on annual forestry yields per acre for the two categories, sawlogs and
pulpwood. Study-area averages are found in Appendix 36.

Artificial Flood Protection and Drainage Provision

Two categories of artificial flood protection and drainage projects
were considered: projects of the U.S. Army Corps of Engineers and
projects of the Soil Conservation Service.

U.S. Army Corps of Engineers Project Impacts[18]

The "protected acreage" of projects is used in this study as the
primary measure of project impact. This "protected area" is
hydrologically defined to include the area which experiences at least
some reduction in the extent and frequency of flooding as a result of
project construction. The protected area is a proxy for a more complete
multidimensional measure of area affected plus degree of effect (e.g.
change in probability of flooding).

Corps projects which had as a primary purpose flood control or
improved drainage, were authorized or constructed (in part) between 1928

Agriculture 1955; and Earles 1975. Sources for Mississippi were:
Sternitzke and Putnam 1956; U.S. Department of Agriculture 1958, 1978;
Hedlund and Earles 1969; and Thomas and McWilliams 1982.

[18]The history, basic purpose, and types of Army Corps projects in the
Alluvial Plain are described in Stavins 1986. Further information
regarding the estimation of Corps project impact areas can also be found
there.

and 1985, and had impact areas located within the study area[19] were examined. In many cases, protected area estimates were available from Corps documents; in other instances, personal communications with Corps officials provided the requisite information.[20] In addition to the total acreage protected by each project, information was collected on the dates of authorization, amendment, initiation of construction, and completion of projects.

Uniform construction rates were assumed[21] for all projects (unless information indicating otherwise was immediately available), in order to obtain estimates of annual construction from data on project initiations and completions. For projects still under construction, estimates were obtained of the share of the project completed as of the end of 1984.

Information regarding the proper allocation of protected acreage among affected counties was obtained from Corps documents, personal communications with Corps officials, and planimetry of project maps. The results of the entire process were a set of estimates of county impact areas for individual projects (Stavins 1986). These project acreages were then aggregated for each county, and the resultant annual county-level data were aggregated to quinquennial estimates. The final

---

[19]An exception is the set of Yazoo headwater reservoirs, which provide protection to some one million acres within the 89-county MAV, although the projects themselves are located outside the study area.

[20]The "raw data" collected from various Corps documents and personal communications are described in detail in Stavins 1986, which also provides a project-by-project list of sources of information.

[21]An improvement in the model would be to utilize available information on the rate of expenditure for project construction over time to estimate likely construction schedules, and then to weight distributions of protected acreage over time to reflect these schedules. The Chief of Engineer's Annual Report for each Corps district, issued every two years, represents one possible source.

variable may be thought of as an index of project impacts. Summary

statistics (further aggregated to totals for the 36-county sample area)

are found in Appendix 3 and Figure 2.

Soil Conservation Service Project Impacts[22]

As with the Army Corps projects, protected acreage is used as the

fundamental measure of SCS project impacts, where this protected area is

hydrologically defined to include the area which experiences at least

some reduction in the extent and frequency of flooding as a result of

project construction. The Soil Conservation Service provided a list of

projects within the study area which were designed primarily for flood

control and/or drainage purposes (John Peterson, p.c., June 1985; O. P.

Lee, p.c., June 1985). State SCS offices provided additional

information on the dates of authorization, initiation, and completion of

projects. Also, SCS officials provided complete information on the

impact areas of projects.[23]

To estimate annual construction levels, uniform construction rates

were assumed. For projects still under construction, estimates were

---

[22]The history, basic purpose, and types of Soil Conservation Service
projects in the Alluvial Plain are described in Stavins 1986. Further
information regarding the estimation of SCS project impact areas can
also be found there.

[23]Two measures were provided by SCS of the impact area of each project
(see Stavins 1986): "watershed acres" and "benefited acres." The first
refers to the total area within the relevant drainage basin, an area
which receives some degree of flood protection from most SCS
flood-control projects within the MAV. The second measure is
essentially an economic one and contains only that area within the
drainage basin which is judged likely to receive sufficient protection
to cause a significant increase in economic returns. Clearly, the
first measure is consistent with the measure used for the Corps
projects, and is the theoretically appropriate measure, given the nature
of the model developed in Chapter II. Hence, it is the "watershed"
acreage which is utilized in the analysis.

obtained of the share of the project completed as of the end of 1984.[24]
Information regarding the proper allocation of protected acreage among
affected counties was obtained from documents, personal communications,
and planimetry of project maps.

The results of the entire process were a set of estimates of county
impact areas for individual SCS projects (Stavins 1986). Project
acreages were aggregated within counties and across five-year intervals
to produce the required data set. The final variable may be thought of
as an index of project impacts. Summary statistics (totals for the
36-county sample area) are found in Appendix 4 and Figure 3.

Natural Flood and Drainage Conditions

A measure of the average natural hydrologic condition of sample
counties was developed from data in the National Resources Inventory
(NRI) of 1982, conducted by the Soil Conservation Service (U.S.
Department of Agriculture 1984h). The NRI databank contains hydrologic
and other information for sample parcels[25] throughout the three states
of interest -- Arkansas, Louisiana, and Mississippi. The NRI
investigators determined whether sample parcels (averaging 250 per
county) were prone to flooding currently or ever had been.[26] These

---

[24]Sources included: Max Gudmund, p.c., August 1985; Dennis Hackbard,
p.c., August 1985; and Gene Simmons, p.c., August 1985.

[25]Data on Federal lands are not included, but in the case of the three
states of interest, this does not substantially affect the results.

[26]Reference is to field #19 in the NRI data tapes. Note that field #81
also provides an estimate of the probability of flooding on sample
parcels, but that the latter estimate applies to current status only,
and thus takes into account the effect of artificial flood-control and
drainage projects (Keith Schmude, Keith Young, p.c., July 1985).

results, expressed as sets of up to 700 0-1 observations per county (in the NRI databank), were combined with other information from the databank to yield estimates of the average natural probability of flooding:

$$FLRISK_i = \left[\sum_{j=1}^{J_i} FP_{ij}EF_{ij}\right] / \left[\sum_{j=1}^{J_i} EF_{ij}\right] \tag{5}$$

where $FLRISK_i$ = average natural proclivity for flooding in county i;

FP_{ij} = flood-proneness measure for sample point j in county i, from the NRI, equal to one if the sample area was ever prone to flooding and equal to zero if the area was never prone to flooding,

EF_{ij} = the NRI expansion factor for sample point j in county i, the number of acres that the observation represents, taking into account sampling procedures and total state area; and

J_i = total number of sample points in county i (average=250).

The resultant set of $FLRISK_i$ estimates ranges from 0.0 to about 0.88. Because the model employed in the analysis utilizes this information as an indication of "natural flood protection and drainage provision," the relevant variable for the analysis is the quantity, DRY_i = 1 - $FLRISK_i$, with implicit bounds of zero and unity.

Weather Conditions

Two measures of weather conditions were considered, one being essentially local in nature, and the other taking account of regional conditions.

Palmer Hydrological Drought Index

The Palmer Hydrological Drought Index has been estimated by the National Climatic Data Center (Asheville, North Carolina) for 344 climatological regions throughout the coterminous United States on a monthly basis since 1931. The index is based upon data related to precipitation, evapotranspiration, runoff, recharge, and soil water loss, and has a built-in lag in order to reflect more accurately conditions of soil moisture, streamflow, and lake levels.[27]

Monthly drought index data for the period 1931-1984 for 16 climatic regions in the study area[28] were aggregated into quinquennial averages by county (Karl, Metcalf, Nicodemus, and Quayle 1983a, 1983b, 1983c; and Thomas R. Karl, p.c., July 1985). The resulting set of drought index data, $PHDI_{it}$, provides a complete panel of observations.

Mississippi River Discharges

The Palmer Hydrological Drought Index (PHDI) does not capture the impact on local soil moisture conditions of flood waters moving into an area from outside of the given climatological region. To allow for this

---

[27]Detailed descriptions of the Palmer Hyrdrological Drought Index and a related Drought Severity Index are found in: Karl 1983, 1985.

[28]Data from April through September only were utilized, because this time frame represents the limit of the growing season for the relevant crops. Maps of the climatic regions within Arkansas, Louisiana, and Mississippi are found in Stavins 1986.

159

effect, the flood stages of the Mississippi River north of the sample
area were examined. Quinquennial averages of daily[29] discharge rates
(in millions of cubic feet per second) at Hickman, Kentucky, were
constructed from data provided by the U.S. Army Corps of Engineers.[30] A
single time-series, $DSCHG_t$, was thus constructed. Preliminary analysis
indicated, however, that this variable did not play a discernable role
in conversion or abandonment decisions.

Cost of Converting Forested Wetlands to Agricultural Cropland

A single time-series (C_t) of the average cost of conversion of
wetlands to cropland was developed, based upon limited published data
(Herrington and Shulstad 1982) plus numerous personal communications.[31]
The data are summarized in Appendix 35. Because geographic differences
in the cost of conversion are partly a function of average soil
moisture, a panel of conversion cost estimates were developed by
allowing for the interaction of C_t and $PHDI_{it}$, as described in the text.

---

[29]Three dates for each year were used: April 15, May 15, and June 15.

[30]The data provided by the Corps' Memphis District office was for the
period 1928-1984. Some of the data was considered to be preliminary
until subsequent publication in Stages and Discharge of the Mississippi
River and Tributaries in the Memphis District (Gene A. Dodson, p.c.,
July 1985).

[31]The following persons, identified in the list of personal
communications at the end of the study, provided quantitative estimates
of historical clearing costs, based upon their professional and personal
experience: Charles Carlton, Gordon Fields, Robert Harrison, Sandy
Ingram, Randall Kramer, J. S. McKnight, and J. Scott McWilliams.

Other Variables

Other variables, included in various versions of the econometric model, may be considered within two categories:[32] annual net borrowing cost and measures of urbanization pressure on land use.

Annual Net Borrowing Cost

Those variables which represent one-time costs or benefits, namely, conversion cost and the revenue from a clearcut prior to conversion, are converted to annuities, in keeping with the structure of the model developed in Chapter II. The discount rate which is utilized for intertemporal weighting is the annual net borrowing cost, r_t, calculated as follows:

$$r_t = \left[(1 - T_t) \cdot INT_t \right] - \left[\frac{WPI_t - WPI_{t-1}}{WPI_t} \right] \tag{6}$$

where T_t = taxation rate of lowest bracket of corporate taxation;

INT_t = prime interest rate; and

WPI_t = wholesale price index.

With the annual net borrowing cost as the discount rate, annuities

---

[32]The degree of availability of subsidized Federal Crop Insurance Corporation (FCIC) insurance in county i during the time t-1 to t, $FCIC_{it}$, was considered as a weighted average of the number of years which FCIC insurance was available during given quinquennia for the four major crops -- soybeans, cotton, rice, and corn. Preliminary analysis indicated that FCIC insurance did not play a discernable role in landowner conversion and abandonment decisions.

were calculated as indicated in the various equations of Chapter II.[33]
The planning horizon utilized for these calculations was of twenty-year
duration, selected to reflect the findings of empirical research on
farmer' implicit planning horizons for various investment decisions
(Nelson, Lee, and Murray 1973; Seitz and Swanson 1980).[34]

Urbanization Measures

The analytical model developed in Chapter II focuses on landowners'
decisions regarding the alternative use of their property as forested
wetland or agricultural cropland. The relevance of this model is
supported by previous empirical research on the subject, as described in
Chapter I and Appendix 5. Despite the fact that urbanization pressure
has apparently played an insignificant role in the depletion of forested
wetlands in the Lower Mississippi Alluvial Plain during the period of
interest, alternative measures of such pressure were considered. None
of these measures, however, were found to be significant in the land
conversion/abandonment decision.[35]

---

[33]Summary data of the prime interest rate, the wholesale price index,
and the annual net borrowing cost, r_t, are presented in Stavins 1986.

[34]Some would argue that the proper planning horizon in a model based
upon the notion of rational landowner decision making is an infinite
one. Note that the results of the econometric analysis are not
materially affected by using an infinite planning horizon for the
calculations of the respective annuities.

[35]The primary measures considered were: population change (U.S.
Department of Commerce, Bureau of the Census, 1924-1984); share of the
population living in urban areas (U.S. Department of Commerce, Bureau of
the Census, 1924-1984); and per capita personal income. Despite the
lack of evidence of urbanization playing a significant role in wetland
conversion, to prevent the possibility of omitted variable bias in the
econometric estimation process, the one county which experienced a
substantial degree of urban growth during the period, Orleans Parish in
Louisiana, was eliminated from the sample.

APPENDIX 7: SIZE DISTRIBUTION OF FARMS
LOWER MISSISSIPPI ALLUVIAL PLAIN, 1935 and 1982

Size Class	ARKANSAS		LOUISIANA		MISSISSIPPI		TOTAL AREA	
(acres)	1935	1982	1935	1982	1935	1982	1935	1982
				(percent)				
≤49	58.7	25.2	74.3	37.5	70.0	24.3	67.1	28.1
50-99	21.0	19.3	13.9	16.7	14.3	20.9	16.5	19.2
100-179	13.6	16.2	6.9	13.6	9.3	20.0	10.2	16.9
180-259	3.5	10.4	2.0	7.5	2.9	9.4	2.9	9.3
260-499	2.3	13.4	1.7	10.3	2.3	11.9	2.2	12.1
500-999	0.6	9.2	0.7	8.3	0.8	7.3	0.7	8.3
1000-4999	0.2	6.0	0.5	5.8	0.3	5.9	0.3	5.9
≥5000	0.0	0.2	0.0	0.3	0.0	0.3	0.0	0.3
TOTAL[a]	100.0	100.0	100.0	100.0	100.0	100.0	100.0	100.0

[a]Columns may not add to 100 due to rounding error.

SOURCE: 1935 - Census of Agriculture 1935, Vol. 2, State Table 3.
1982 - Census of Agriculture 1982, Vol. 1, Table 4.

163

APPENDIX 8: LAND VALUES AND THE ANTICIPATION OF FUTURE CAPITAL GAINS

With no loss of generality, explicit consideration of the possibility of selling a land parcel may be excluded from the analysis. Following a line of argument due to Randall and Castle (1985), assume, first, that land is used for producing a vector, z, of goods and services, given a transformation function, $T(z,x,h,b)$, where x is a vector of inputs other than land and labor, h is the quantity of land, and b is the quantity of labor. The momentary rent accruing to a unit of land, p_h, may be defined as

$$p_h = (p_z \cdot z - p_x \cdot x - w \cdot b)/h \qquad (1)$$

where p_z is a vector of product prices, p_x is a vector of input prices, and w is the wage rate.

The present value of a stream of rents beginning at time $t = 0$, is:

$$V_0 = \int_0^\infty \left[p_h(t) \cdot e^{-rt} \right] dt \qquad (2)$$

where V_0 = the present value of an infinitely long stream of rents beginning at time $t=0$;

$p_h(t)$ = unit land rent at time t; and

r = real interest rate.

If the land parcel were sold at time $t = 0$, and $p_h(t)$ represented the anticipated stream of future rents, the land's real market value as a productive asset would be V_0.

164

If the land were owned by a producer who planned to sell it at a future time, T, then the present value of the land to its owner would be:

$$V_0' = \int_0^T \left[p_h(t) \cdot e^{-rt} \right] dt + P_h^T \cdot e^{-rT} \tag{3}$$

where P_h^T = the real market price of land at time T. If markets are efficient, then P_h^T will be equal to the present value (at time T) of the anticipated (future) stream of rents:

$$P_h^T = \int_T^\infty \left[p_h(t) \cdot e^{-r(t - T)} \right] dt \tag{4}$$

Substituting equation 4 into equation 3, and comparing the result with equation 2, it is clear that $V_0 = V_0'$. If expectations are unchanging, the land price at each point in time reflects the discounted value of future production.

Thus, under these conditions, there is no fundamental economic difference between, on the one hand, utilizing land for forest (agricultural) production in the anticipation of future capital gains from the sale of the land, and, on the other hand, utilizing the land for forest (agricultural) production in the anticipation of continuing such productive activities indefinitely. With no loss of generality, the possibility of land sales may be excluded from (kept implicit within) the relevant optimization problem.

165

In the static model, it is possible to divide the landowner's decision into two distinct optimization problems, only one of which is relevant at any time, depending upon the current condition of the land. A parcel of land, j (in county i), is conceived of as being sufficiently small such that it must be either entirely forested or entirely in an agricultural state. Therefore, at each time t, for each parcel, j, the landowner faces one of two decisions: if the parcel of land is currently forested, the landowner must decide whether and at what time, T, to convert that parcel to agricultural use; and if the parcel of land is currently in agricultural use, he must decide whether and at what time, τ, to abandon agricultural production and allow the parcel to revert gradually to a forested state.

Beginning with the decision of whether and when to convert a forested parcel to agricultural use, and following the overall model developed in the main text, a risk-neutral landowner may be expected to seek to maximize the present discounted value of the stream of expected future returns to his land:

$$\max_{\{T\}} L(T) = \int_0^T f_{it} e^{-rt} dt + \int_T^\infty \left[a_{it} q_{ijt} - ac_{it} \right] e^{-rt} dt + \left[W_{iT} - C_{iT} \right] e^{-rT} \quad (1)$$

$$\text{subject to } T \geq 0 \quad (2)$$

where T is the time of conversion, and all variables are defined as in the main text (and, again, lower-case letters refer to current, annual values of respective variables, and upper-case letters indicate one-time, present values).

A first-order, necessary condition for maximizing L(T) is:

$$\left[\frac{\partial L(T)}{\partial T}\right] \cdot T = 0 \tag{3}$$

Combining equations 2 and 3,

$$\frac{\partial L(T)}{\partial T} \leq 0 \tag{4}$$

Evaluation of this partial derivative yields:

$$\left[f_{iT} - a_{iT}q_{ijT} + ac_{iT} - r \cdot W_{iT} + \frac{\partial W_{iT}}{\partial T} + r \cdot C_{iT} - \frac{\partial C_{iT}}{\partial T}\right] \cdot e^{-rT} \leq 0 \tag{5}$$

Dividing by e^{-rT}, multiplying by -1, and rearranging terms, conversion will occur at time T such that:

$$a_{iT}q_{ijT} - ac_{iT} - f_{iT} + r \cdot W_{iT} - r \cdot C_{iT} > \frac{\partial W_{iT}}{\partial T} - \frac{\partial C_{iT}}{\partial T} \tag{6}$$

Dividing by r, the relationship is re-expressed in terms of present values:

$$A_{1T}q_{1jT} - AC_{1T} - FN_{1T} - C_{1T} > \frac{1}{r}\left[\frac{\partial W_{1T}}{\partial T} - \frac{\partial C_{1T}}{\partial T}\right] \tag{7}$$

If it is assumed, as in the text, that prices are exogenous, and the target, steady-state condition is of interest, then the necessary condition which emerges is:

$$\text{Conversion occurs if } \{A_{1t}q_{1jt} - AC_{1t} - FN_{1t} - C_{1t}\} > 0 \tag{8}$$

which is the same necessary condition expressed in the main text in equation 24. Note that the left-hand side of the above inequality is equal to the quantity defined in the text as X_{1jt}.

Next, the decision of whether and when to abandon a parcel of cropland is examined. Again, it is assumed that a private landowner will seek to maximize the present discounted value of the stream of expected future returns to his land:

$$\max_{\{\tau\}} A(\tau) = \int_{0}^{\tau}\left[a_{1t}q_{1jt} - ac_{1t}\right]e^{-rt}dt + \int_{\tau}^{\infty}f_{1t}e^{-rt}dt - \int_{\tau}^{R}f_{1t}e^{-rt}dt \tag{9}$$

$$\text{subject to:} \quad \tau \geq 0 \tag{10}$$

where τ is the time of abandonment, R is rotation length, and all other variables are as defined in the main text. Note that the third and last term in the maximand above is the loss of forest revenue due to gradual regrowth of the forest subsequent to abandonment, $D_{j\tau}$.

A first-order necessary condition for maximizing $A(\tau)$ is:

$$\left[\frac{\partial A(\tau)}{\partial \tau}\right] \cdot \tau = 0 \qquad (11)$$

Combining equations 10 and 11,

$$\frac{\partial A(\tau)}{\partial \tau} \leq 0 \qquad (12)$$

Evaluation of this partial derivative yields:

$$\left[a_{i\tau} q_{ij\tau} - ac_{i\tau} - f_{i\tau} + r \cdot D_{i\tau} - \frac{\partial D_{i\tau}}{\partial \tau}\right] \cdot e^{-r\tau} \leq 0 \qquad (13)$$

Dividing by $e^{-r\tau}$, multiplying by -1, and rearranging terms, abandonment will occur at time τ such that:

$$f_{i\tau} - a_{i\tau} q_{ij\tau} + ac_{i\tau} - r \cdot D_{i\tau} > -\left[\frac{\partial D_{i\tau}}{\partial \tau}\right] \qquad (14)$$

Dividing by r, the relationship is re-expressed in terms of present values:

$$F_{i\tau} - A_{i\tau} q_{ij\tau} + AC_{i\tau} - D_{i\tau} = -\frac{1}{r} \cdot \left[\frac{\partial D_{i\tau}}{\partial \tau}\right] \qquad (15)$$

169

Recalling from the text that $\tilde{F}_{it} = F_{it} \quad D_{it}$, and again assuming that prices are exogenous and the steady-state condition is of interest, the necessary condition which emerges is:

$$\text{Abandonment occurs if } \{\tilde{F}_{it} - A_{it} \cdot q_{ijt}\} > 0 \qquad (16)$$

which is the same necessary condition expressed in the main text in equation 25, and where the left-hand side of the above inequality is equal to the quantity defined in the text as Y_{ijt}.

170

APPENDIX 10: MUTUAL EXCLUSIVITY
OF FARMLAND ABANDONMENT AND FOREST CONVERSION

It is not possible for X_{ijt} and Y_{ijt} to be positive simultaneously. In order for X and Y to be greater than zero, it is necessary that:

$$X > 0 \rightarrow (Aq - AC - C - FN) > 0 \rightarrow \{Aq > AC + C + FN\} \quad (1)$$

$$Y > 0 \rightarrow (\tilde{F} - Aq + AC) > 0 \rightarrow \{Aq < \tilde{F} + AC\} \quad (2)$$

These two conditions can hold simultaneously only if

$$\{\tilde{F} > C + FN\} \rightarrow \tilde{F} > (C + (F - W)) \rightarrow (F - D) > (C + F - W) \quad (3)$$

$$- D + W > C \rightarrow \{W - D > C\} \quad (4)$$

But, $W = \int_{0}^{R} f \cdot e^{-rt} dt$ (where R is the rotation length), and D is equal to this same integral. Thus, $W = D$. This implies that $C < 0$, i.e. that conversion costs must be negative, which is, of course, impossible. This confirms one's intuition that as long as conversion costs are non-negative, it would not make sense to abandon farmland on one parcel while tearing down forest to make way for cropland on another parcel.

171

$$\text{FORCH}_{it} = \text{FORCH}_{it}^c \cdot D_{it}^c + \text{FORCH}_{it}^a \cdot D_{it}^a + \lambda_i + \phi_{it}$$

$$\text{FORCH}_{it}^c \cdot (-1) = \gamma_c \left[d_{it} \cdot \left[1 - \mathbf{F}\left[\left[q_{it}^x - \mu(1 + \beta_2 \text{PROJ}_{it}) \right] \right/ \sigma_i (1 + \beta_3 \text{PROJ}_{it}) \right] \right] + \left[\frac{S}{T} \right]_{i,t-1} - 1 \right]$$

$$\text{FORCH}_{it}^a = \gamma_a \left[d_{it} \cdot \left[\mathbf{F}\left[\left[q_{it}^y - \mu(1 + \beta_2 \text{PROJ}_{it}) \right] \right/ \sigma_i (1 + \beta_3 \text{PROJ}_{it}) \right] \right] + \left[1 - d_{it} \right] - \left[\frac{S}{T} \right]_{i,t-1} \right]$$

$$d_{it} = \left[\frac{1}{1 + \left[\dfrac{1}{e^{\pi(z)}} \right]} \right] \qquad \text{where } \pi(z) = \text{DRY}_i + \beta_1 \text{PROJ}_{it}$$

$$q_{it}^x = \left[\frac{\text{FN}_{it} + \text{AC}_{it}}{A_{it} - \alpha_1 C_{it} \cdot \exp\{\alpha_2 \text{PHDI}_{it}\}} \right] \qquad q_{it}^y = \left[\frac{\tilde{F}_{it} + \text{AC}_{it}}{A_{it}} \right]$$

APPENDIX 12: ECONOMETRIC MODEL OF FORESTED WETLAND CONVERSION AND AGRICULTURAL CROPLAND ABANDONMENT UNIFORM DISTRIBUTION OF HETEROGENEITY

$$FORCH_{it} = FORCH_{it}^{c} \cdot D_{it}^{c} + FORCH_{it}^{a} \cdot D_{it}^{a} + \lambda_i + \phi_{it}$$

$$FORCH_{it}^{c} \cdot (-1) = \gamma_c \left[d_{it} \left[\left[\omega(1 + \beta_2 PROJ_{it}) - q_{it}^{x} \right] \right. \right.$$

$$\left. \left. / \theta_1 (1 + \beta_3 PROJ_{it}) \right] + \left[\frac{S}{T} \right]_{i,t-1} - 1 \right]$$

$$FORCH_{it}^{a} = \gamma_a \left[d_{it} \cdot \left[\left[q_{it}^{y} - \omega(1 + \beta_2 PROJ_{it}) \right] \right. \right.$$

$$\left. \left. / \theta_1 (1 + \beta_3 PROJ_{it}) \right] - \left[\frac{S}{T} \right]_{i,t-1} + 1 \right]$$

$$d_{it} = \left[\frac{1}{1 + \left[\frac{1}{e^{\pi(z)}} \right]} \right] \qquad \text{where } \pi(z) = DRY_i + \beta_1 PROJ_{it}$$

$$q_{it}^{x} = \left[\frac{FN_{it} + AC_{it}}{A_{it} - \alpha_1 C_{it} \cdot \exp\{\alpha_2 PHDI_{it}\}} \right] \qquad q_{it}^{y} = \left[\frac{\tilde{F}_{it} + AC_{it}}{A_{it}} \right]$$

where ω = upper limit of uniform distribution; and

θ_1 = range of uniform distribution.

173

ARKANSAS	LOUISIANA	MISSISSIPPI
(1) Chicot	(14) Concordia	(27) Bolivar
(2) Clay	(15) East Carroll	(28) Coahoma
(3) Craighead	(16) Franklin	(29) Humphreys
(4) Crittenden	(17) Iberville	(30) Issaquena
(5) Cross	(18) Madison	(31) Leflore
(6) Desha	(19) Pointe Coupee	(32) Quitman
(7) Greene	(20) Richland	(33) Sharkey
(8) Lee	(21) St. Charles	(34) Sunflower
(9) Mississippi	(22) St. James	(35) Tunica
(10) Phillips	(23) St. John/Bapt.	(36) Washington
(11) Poinsett	(24) Tensas	
(12) St. Francis	(25) West Baton Rouge	
(13) Woodruff	(26) West Carroll	

**APPENDIX 14: FOREST AND AGRICULTURAL ACREAGE
THIRTY-SIX INTERIOR COUNTIES
LOWER MISSISSIPPI ALLUVIAL PLAIN, 1934 - 1984**

Year	Forest Acreage	Acreage of Four[a] Major Crops
	(thousands of acres)	
1934	6,274	3,661
1939	5,970	3,648
1944	5,730	3,688
1949	5,341	3,934
1954	5,201	4,156
1959	4,826	4,329
1964	4,170	4,894
1969	3,506	5,758
1974	3,063	6,311
1979	2,927	7,015
1984	2,638	6,808

[a]Soybeans, cotton, rice, and corn.

Parameter	County	Parameter Estimate	Standard Error Estimate
λ_1	Chicot, AR	.01877	.01545
λ_2	Clay, AR	.00347	.01425
λ_3	Craighead, AR	.00110	.00513
λ_4	Crittenden, AR	- .00218	.00678
λ_5	Cross, AR	.01170	.01012
λ_6	Desha, AR	.00297	.01450
λ_7	Greene, AR	.00665	.01035
λ_8	Lee, AR	- .00552	.00887
λ_9	Mississippi, AR	.00985	.00906
λ_{10}	Phillips, AR	.00790	.00887
λ_{11}	Poinsett, AR	- .00263	.00752
λ_{12}	St. Francis, AR	.01278	.00813
λ_{13}	Woodruff, AR	.02003*	.01205
λ_{14}	Concordia, LA	.00994	.01289
λ_{15}	East Carroll, LA	.00505	.01141
λ_{16}	Franklin, LA	.01409	.01247
λ_{17}	Iberville, LA	.02306***	.00711
λ_{18}	Madison, LA	.01870	.01324
λ_{19}	Pointe Coupee, LA	.01994**	.01014
λ_{20}	Richland, LA	.01728	.01158
λ_{21}	St. Charles, LA	- .00012	.01142
λ_{22}	St. James, LA	.02855***	.00840
λ_{23}	St. John Baptist, LA	.05170***	.00951
λ_{24}	Tensas, LA	.01864*	.01036
λ_{25}	West Baton Rouge, LA	.02735***	.00791
λ_{26}	West Carroll, LA	- .00412	.01160
λ_{27}	Bolivar, MS	.01804**	.00808
λ_{28}	Coahoma, MS	.01208**	.00556
λ_{29}	Humphreys, MS	.00653	.00825
λ_{30}	Issaquena, MS	.01280**	.00589
λ_{31}	Leflore, MS	.02317***	.00778
λ_{32}	Quitman, MS	.01024	.00688
λ_{33}	Sharkey, MS	.00492	.00869
λ_{34}	Sunflower, MS	.02311***	.00849
λ_{35}	Tunica, MS	.01986***	.00699
λ_{36}	Washington, MS	.01880***	.00673

***Significant at the 1% level, 2-tailed test.
**Significant at the 5% level, 2-tailed test.
*Significant at the 10% level, 2-tailed test.

APPENDIX 16: ECONOMETRIC ESTIMATION RESULTS
SPECIFICATIONS U1 THROUGH U3
UNIFORM DISTRIBUTION OF HETEROGENEITY

Parameter	Interpretation	Alternative Specifications[a]		
		U1	U2	U3
γ_a	Abandonment Partial Adjustment	0.22153 (0.052)[b]	0.13246 (0.079)	0.18288 (0.075)
γ_c	Conversion Partial Adjustment	0.54997 (0.092)	0.56427 (0.097)	0.29872 (0.114)
ω	Upper Limit of Heterogeneity	4.14360 (1.313)	5.93140 (2.210)	4.64267 (2.173)
θ	Range of of Heterogeneity	1.68770 (0.664)	1.76840 (0.703)	1.34980 (0.855)
β_1	Project Impact on Agric. Feasibility	9.15760 (3.452)	8.42410 (2.600)	8.94940 (3.705)
α_1	Relative Conversion- Cost Impact	1.51200 (1.360)	2.03140 (1.551)	-
α_2	Weather Impact on Conversion Cost	-	-	1.58600 (0.302)
δ	Intercept	-	0.03365 (0.014)	-
logL	Log Likelihood Value	758.716	763.505	787.892
df	Degrees of Freedom	354	353	318

[a]The specifications are described in the text:

U1 -- uniform distribution of heterogeneity
U2 -- intercept term; uniform distribution of heterogeneity
U3 -- fixed effects; uniform distribution of heterogeneity

[b]Robust standard error estimates appear below coefficients.

Parameter	Interpretation	Alternative Specifications[a]			
		L4	L5	L6	L7
γ_a	Abandonment Partial Adjustment	0.36987 (0.193)[b]	0.38328 (0.192)	0.38010 (0.192)	0.36883 (0.192)
γ_c	Conversion Partial Adjustment	0.42384 (0.146)	0.41445 (0.140)	0.40686 (0.139)	0.43903 (0.144)
μ	Mean of Heterogeneity	1.10830 (0.403)	0.80798 (0.349)	0.87093 (0.319)	0.76765 (0.368)
σ	Standard Deviation of Heterogeneity	0.36753 (0.088)	0.37112 (0.090)	0.36648 (0.089)	0.37750 (0.089)
β_1	Project Impact on Agric. Feasibility	8.01280 (2.657)	8.84720 (3.149)	8.56730 (3.011)	-
β_4	COE Project Impact on Ag Feasibility	-	-	-	10.3690 (3.961)
β_5	SCS Project Impact on Ag Feasibility	-	-	-	2.68320 (5.521)
α_1	Relative Conversion-Cost Impact	-	1.19390 (0.279)	-	1.57910 (0.939)
α_2	Weather Impact on Conversion Cost	1.63970 (0.261)	-	1.13670 (0.092)	-
logL	Log Likelihood	787.840	786.523	786.894	786.180
df	Degrees of Freedom	318	318	318	317

[a]The specifications are described in the text:

L4 -- fixed effects; lognormal distribution of heterogeneity
L5 -- heterogeneity on feasibility and conversion cost; fixed effects; lognormal distribution of heterogeneity
L6 -- heterogeneity on feasibility and conversion cost; fixed effects; lognormal distribution of heterogeneity
L7 -- separate parameters for Corps and SCS; fixed effects; lognormal distribution of heterogeneity

[b]Robust standard error estimates appear below coefficients.

Parameter	Interpretation	Alternative Specifications[a]			
		N1	N2	N3	N4
γ_a	Abandonment Partial Adjustment	0.47605 (0.196)[b]	0.42903 (0.195)	0.48283 (0.198)	0.41883 (0.190)
γ_c	Conversion Partial Adjustment	0.49512 (0.150)	0.41753 (0.139)	0.46799 (0.153)	0.62814 (0.150)
μ	Mean of Heterogeneity	1.43370 (0.391)	1.88280 (0.384)	1.39370 (0.360)	2.26650 (0.419)
σ	Standard Deviation of Heterogeneity	0.41512 (0.089)	0.36998 (0.086)	0.41151 (0.093)	0.43538 (0.067)
β_1	Project Impact on Agric. Feasibility	10.2810 (4.017)	8.78760 (3.094)	10.5050 (4.224)	8.69140 (2.394)
β_2	Project Impact on Heterogeneity Mean	-	-	-	0.24691 (0.317)
β_3	Project Impact on Heterogeneity S.D.	-	-	-	0.39361 (0.176)
α_1	Relative Conversion Cost Impact	1.02400 (0.546)	-	0.81565 (0.238)	-
α_2	Weather Impact on Conversion Cost	-	1.36090 (0.166)	-	1.41720 (0.193)
logL	Log Likelihood	786.972	787.919	786.967	791.565
df	Degrees of Freedom	318	318	318	316

[a]The specifications are described in the text:

N1 -- fixed effects; normal distribution of heterogeneity
N2 -- fixed effects; normal distribution of heterogeneity
N3 -- heterogeneity on feasibility and conversion cost; fixed effects; normal distribution of heterogeneity
N4 -- projects affect heterogeneity; fixed effects; normal distribution of heterogeneity

[b]Robust standard error estimates appear below coefficients.

APPENDIX 19: SIMULATED CHANGES IN AREA OF FORESTED WETLANDS
IN THIRTY-SIX COUNTIES OF THE LOWER MISSISSIPPI ALLUVIAL PLAIN,
1935-1984
USING ALTERNATIVE ECONOMETRIC SPECIFICATIONS

Five-Yr Period	Actual Change	Simulated Changes using Alternative Specifications[a]					
		L1	L2	L3	L4	L5	L6
		(1,000 acres)					
1935-39	-304	-243	-254	-287	-274	-246	-251
1940-44	-240	-334	-351	-348	-329	-329	-328
1945-49	-390	-371	-394	-377	-356	-368	-365
1950-54	-140	-273	-269	-263	-261	-269	-267
1955-59	-375	-422	-416	-412	-417	-424	-423
1960-64	-656	-554	-528	-524	-539	-545	-542
1965-69	-664	-554	-537	-570	-585	-554	-560
1970-74	-443	-341	-344	-326	-338	-344	-342
1975-79	-136	-291	-289	-267	-273	-297	-293
1980-84	-290	-316	-303	-303	-326	-325	-330
Total Change	-3,637	-3,698	-3,684	-3,677	-3,697	-3,701	-3,701

[a]Alternative specifications are described in the text.

180

Year	Actual Forested Area	Simulations using Alternative Specifications[a]					
		L1	L2	L3	L4	L5	L6
				(1,000 acres)			
1935	6,275	6,275	6,275	6,275	6,275	6,275	6,275
1939	5,970	6,033	6,022	5,989	6,003	6,031	6,025
1944	5,730	5,702	5,674	5,644	5,677	5,705	5,700
1949	5,341	5,337	5,285	5,272	5,326	5,342	5,340
1954	5,201	5,069	5,021	5,014	5,070	5,078	5,079
1959	4,826	4,652	4,610	4,607	4,658	4,659	4,660
1964	4,170	4,106	4,091	4,093	4,128	4,122	4,127
1969	3,506	3,563	3,565	3,534	3,555	3,579	3,578
1974	3,063	3,229	3,228	3,213	3,223	3,241	3,242
1979	2,927	2,947	2,948	2,954	2,959	2,953	2,958
1984	2,638	2,642	2,655	2,662	2,644	2,639	2,639
Total Change	-3,637	-3,698	-3,684	-3,677	-3,697	-3,701	-3,701
Error		1.7%	1.3%	1.1%	1.6%	1.8%	1.8%

[a]Alternative specifications are described in the text.

Five-Yr Period	Actual Change	Factual Simula-tion	Counterfactually Simulated Changes[b]				
			$PROJ_{it}$	DRY_{it}	$PHDI_{it}$	C_{it}	FN_{it}
			(1,000 acres)				
1935-39	-304	-287	-283	-151	-183	-386	-388
1940-44	-240	-348	-335	-206	-249	-445	-445
1945-49	-390	-377	-365	-238	-288	-464	-474
1950-54	-140	-263	-250	-149	-186	-338	-337
1955-59	-375	-412	-313	-296	-345	-476	-488
1960-64	-656	-524	-379	-412	-447	-595	-599
1965-69	-664	-570	-303	-523	-535	-592	-602
1970-74	-443	-326	-101	-303	-383	-389	-343
1975-79	-136	-267	-29	-259	-333	-337	-270
1980-84	-290	-303	-169	-294	-325	-331	-313
50-Year Change	-3,637	-3,677	-2,527	-2,831	-3,273	-4,354	-4,259
1985-89	-	-106	-59	-103	-114	-117	-109
1990-94	-	-37	-21	-36	-40	-41	-38
1995-99	-	-13	-5	-13	-14	-14	-13
65-Year Change	-	-3,834	-2,612	-2,984	-3,442	-4,526	-4,419
Long Term Change	-	-3,841	-2,614	-2,990	-3,449	-4,534	-4,427

[a]The final model, specification L3, is utilized throughout.

[b]Counterfactually simulated changes refer to simulated changes with respective variables held at zero for all counties for all years.

APPENDIX 22: SENSITIVITY ANALYSIS
SIMULATED AREA OF FORESTED WETLANDS
UNDER VARIOUS SCENARIOS
LOWER MISSISSIPPI ALLUVIAL PLAIN, 1935-1999[a]

Year	Actual Forested Area	Factual Simula- tion	Counterfactual Simulations[b]				
			$PROJ_{it}$	DRY_{it}	$PHDI_{it}$	C_{it}	FN_{it}
			(1,000 acres)				
1939	5,970	5,989	5,994	6,125	6,094	5,889	5,887
1944	5,730	5,644	5,661	5,921	5,847	5,444	5,442
1949	5,341	5,272	5,302	5,688	5,563	4,980	4,968
1954	5,201	5,014	5,056	5,543	5,382	4,642	4,631
1959	4,826	4,607	4,746	5,251	5,042	4,166	4,143
1964	4,170	4,093	4,375	4,847	4,603	3,571	3,544
1969	3,506	3,534	4,079	4,334	4,078	2,979	2,942
1974	3,063	3,213	3,979	4,037	3,703	2,590	2,599
1979	2,927	2,954	3,953	3,785	3,379	2,253	2,329
1984	2,638	2,662	3,789	3,500	3,063	1,922	2,016
1989	-	2,556	3,731	3,399	2,952	1,805	1,907
1994	-	2,520	3,711	3,364	2,913	1,764	1,869
1999	-	2,507	3,706	3,351	2,899	1,750	1,856
Steady State	-	2,500	3,704	3,345	2,892	1,742	1,848

[a]The final model, specification L3, is utilized throughout.

[b]The counterfactual simulations refer to simulations with the respective variables held at a zero level for all counties for all years.

APPENDIX 23: QUINQUENNIAL IMPACTS OF FEDERAL FLOOD-CONTROL PROJECTS
ON FORESTED WETLAND DEPLETION IN THIRTY-SIX COUNTIES
OF THE LOWER MISSISSIPPI ALLUVIAL PLAIN, 1935-1999[a]

| Five-Year Period | Forested Wetland Depletion Due to Federal Projects | | | | | |
| | Impact on Agric. Feasibility | | Impact on Heterogeneity | | Total Project Impacts | |
	Level	Share[b]	Level	Share	Level	Share
	(1,000 acres)					
1935-1939	-5	1.7%	0	0.0%	-5	1.7%
1940-1944	-14	4.0%	+1	0.3%	-13	3.7%
1945-1949	-13	3.4%	+1	0.3%	-12	3.2%
1950-1954	-13	4.9%	0	0.0%	-13	4.9%
1955-1959	-120	29.1%	+20	4.9%	-100	24.3%
1960-1964	-187	35.7%	+42	8.0%	-145	27.7%
1965-1969	-318	55.8%	+51	8.9%	-267	46.8%
1970-1974	-247	75.8%	+22	6.7%	-225	69.0%
1975-1979	-250	93.6%	+12	4.5%	-238	89.1%
1980-1984	-153	50.7%	+19	6.4%	-134	44.3%
50-Year Impact	-1,319	35.9%	+168	4.6%	-1,150	31.3%
1985-1989	-54	50.7%	+7	6.4%	-47	44.3%
1990-1994	-19	50.7%	+2	6.4%	-17	44.3%
1995-1999	-12	67.8%	+1	3.5%	-8	64.4%
65-Year Impact	-1,401	36.5%	+178	4.6%	-1,223	31.9%

[a]The final model, specification L3, is utilized throughout.

[b]Percentage of simulated change in forested acreage due to projects.

APPENDIX 24: TAXONOMY OF MAJOR WETLAND VALUES

FISH AND WILDLIFE VALUES

  o Fish and Shellfish Habitat
  o Waterfowl and Other Bird Habitat
  o Furbearer and Other Wildlife Habitat

ENVIRONMENTAL QUALITY VALUES

  o Water Quality Maintenance
  o Pollution Filter
  o Sediment Removal
  o Oxygen Production
  o Nutrient Recycling
  o Chemical and Nutrient Absorption
  o Aquatic Productivity
  o Microclimate Regulator
  o World Climate (Ozone layer)

SOCIO-ECONOMIC VALUES

  o Flood Control
  o Wave Damage Protection
  o Erosion Control
  o Groundwater Recharge and Water Supply
  o Timber and Other Natural Products
  o Energy Source (Peat)
  o Livestock Grazing
  o Fishing and Shellfishing
  o Hunting and Trapping
  o Recreation
  o Aesthetics
  o Education and Scientific Research

SOURCE: Tiner, Ralph W., Jr. _Wetlands of the United States: Current Status and Recent Trends_. Washington, D.C.: U.S. Department of the Interior, Fish and Wildlife Service, March 1984.

APPENDIX 25: SIMULATED SOCIALLY OPTIMAL CHANGES IN FORESTED WETLANDS
VALUE OF ENVIRONMENTAL BENEFITS = $50 AND $200 PER ACRE
1935-1984[a]

| 5-Year Period | Actual Change | Simulated Socially Optimal Changes | | | |
| | | Externality = $50/Acre | | Externality = $200/Acre | |
		With Federal Projects[b]	No Federal Projects[c]	With Federal Projects	No Federal Projects
		(1,000 acres)			
1935-39	-304	+14	+17	+657	+657
1940-44	-240	-74	-60	+328	+364
1945-49	-390	-263	-249	+61	+70
1950-54	-140	-16	+1	+301	+346
1955-59	-375	-260	-162	+55	+155
1960-64	-656	-578	-429	-310	-171
1965-69	-664	-538	-275	-204	+77
1970-74	-443	-341	-62	-127	+145
1975-79	-136	-55	+252	+150	+470
1980-84	-290	-201	+127	+25	+37
TOTAL CHANGE	-3,637	-2,313	-839	+938	+2,491

[a]The final model, specification L3, is utilized throughout.

[b]Simulated socially optimal changes in forested wetland acreage, given the existence of Federal flood-control and drainage projects.

[c]Simulated socially optimal changes in forested wetland acreage in the absence of any Federal flood-control and drainage projects.

APPENDIX 26: ESTIMATED FUTURE SOCIALLY OPTIMAL QUINQUENNIAL CHANGES
IN FORESTED WETLANDS FOR ALTERNATIVE ANNUAL VALUES
OF ENVIRONMENTAL BENEFITS,
THIRTY-SIX COUNTIES, LOWER MISSISSIPPI ALLUVIAL PLAIN, 1985-1999[a]

Annual Value of Environmental Benefits Per Acre	Simulated Socially Optimal Changes in Forested Wetlands Given the Existence of Federal Projects			
	1985-1989	1990-1994	1995-1999	Total
(dollars)	(1,000 acres)			
0	- 106	- 37	- 13	- 156[b]
50	- 71	- 25	- 9	- 105
100	- 39	- 14	- 5	- 58
150	- 12	- 4	- 2	- 18
200	+ 16	+ 10	+ 6	+ 32
250	+ 51	+ 32	+ 21	+ 104
500	+ 168	+ 106	+ 67	+ 341
750	+ 222	+ 141	+ 89	+ 452
1,000	+ 269	+ 170	+ 108	+ 547

[a]The final model, specification L3, is utilized.

[b]Totals may not add due to rounding error.

APPENDIX 27: SIMULATED FUTURE CHANGES IN FORESTED WETLANDS
FOR ALTERNATIVE LEVELS OF FUTURE AGRICULTURAL PRICES,
THIRTY-SIX COUNTIES, LOWER MISSISSIPPI ALLUVIAL PLAIN[a]

Relative Level of Real Agricultural Prices[b]	Simulated Long-Term Change in Forested Wetland Acreage (from 1989 until steady state)
	(1,000 acres)
1.0	- 58
1.1	- 98
1.2	- 120
1.3	- 134
1.4	- 143
1.5	- 148
1.6	- 152
1.7	- 155
1.8	- 157
1.9	- 159
2.0	- 160

[a]The final model, specification L3, is utilized.

[b]Real agricultural prices subsequent to 1989, relative to real 1984 prices.

APPENDIX 28: DISTRIBUTION OF SOYBEAN PRODUCTION

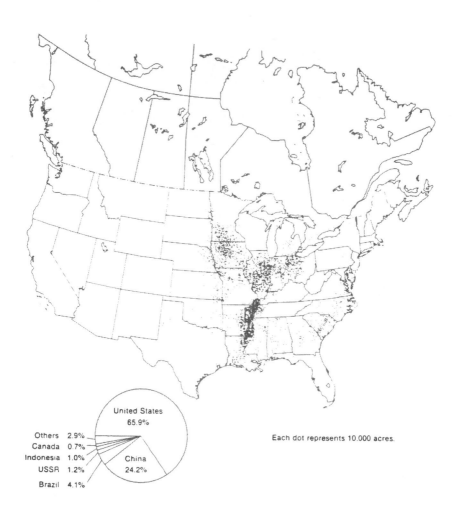

Each dot represents 10.000 acres.

United States
65.9%

Others 2.9%
Canada 0.7%
Indonesia 1.0%
USSR 1.2%
Brazil 4.1%

China
24.2%

<u>SOURCE</u>: Chapman and Carter 1976, p. 344.

189

APPENDIX 29:   DISTRIBUTION OF COTTON PRODUCTION

China 12.6%

India 10.1%

United
States
19.0%

Pakistan 6.0%

Turkey 4.3%

Others
48.0%

Each dot represents 5,000 acres.

SOURCE: Chapman and Carter 1976, p. 382.

APPENDIX 30: DISTRIBUTION OF RICE PRODUCTION

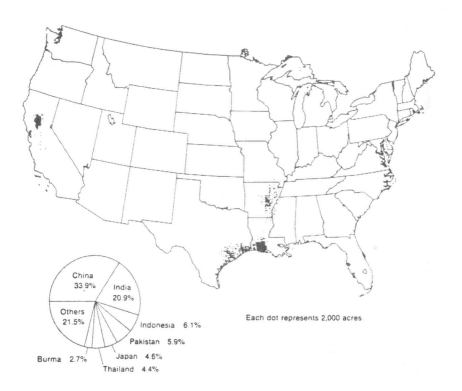

China 33.9%

India 20.9%

Others 21.5%

Indonesia 6.1%

Pakistan 5.9%

Burma 2.7%

Japan 4.6%

Thailand 4.4%

Each dot represents 2,000 acres

SOURCE: Chapman and Carter 1976, p. 280.

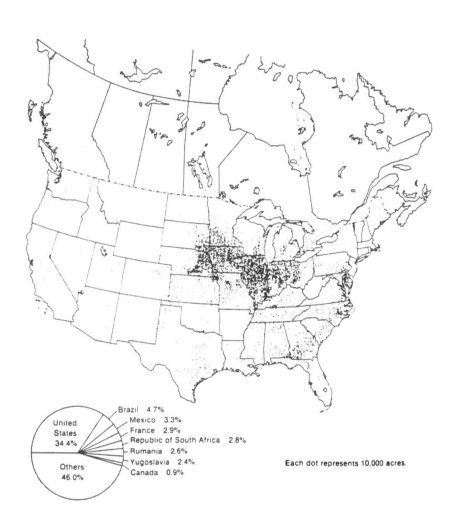

SOURCE: Chapman and Carter 1976, p. 258.

APPENDIX 32:

MAJOR AGRICULTURAL CROP ACREAGES
INTERIOR COUNTIES, 1929 – 1984

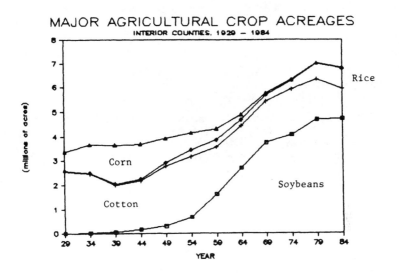

AGRICULTURAL REVENUE PER ACRE
INTERIOR COUNTIES, 1934 – 1984

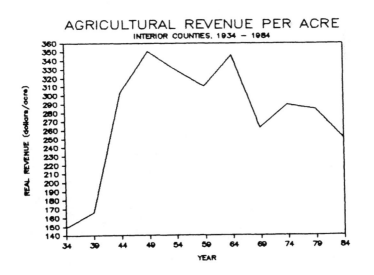

193

APPENDIX 33: AVERAGE ANNUAL YIELD OF MAJOR AGRICULTURAL CROPS
LOWER MISSISSIPPI ALLUVIAL PLAIN, 1929-1984

Year	Soybeans (bushels/acre)	Cotton (lbs/acre)	Rice (bushels/acre)	Corn (bushels/acre)
1929	-	238.6	45.0	17.0
1934	-	259.1	50.7	15.7
1939	-	338.3	55.0	15.9
1944	10.0	428.2	54.5	17.7
1949	15.5	379.2	51.4	17.9
1954	13.3	366.4	56.6	17.1
1959	19.8	481.0	64.0	19.7
1964	21.0	630.9	82.8	31.2
1969	19.8	614.4	100.0	35.2
1974	20.4	457.4	102.3	40.1
1979	22.9	459.2	97.7	45.7
1984	25.1	688.7	98.1	96.1

APPENDIX 34: AVERAGE NOMINAL PRICES OF MAJOR CROPS
LOWER MISSISSIPPI ALLUVIAL PLAIN, 1929-1984

Year	Soybeans ($/bushel)	Cotton ($/pound)	Rice ($/CWT)	Corn ($/bushel)
1929	2.96	0.17	1.05	0.98
1934	1.87	0.09	0.66	0.66
1939	1.61	0.10	0.73	0.71
1944	1.96	0.17	1.45	1.04
1949	2.58	0.30	2.13	1.64
1954	2.53	0.36	2.24	1.59
1959	2.04	0.32	2.22	1.17
1964	2.35	0.32	2.27	1.21
1969	2.56	0.26	2.26	1.30
1974	4.52	0.32	3.84	2.01
1979	6.08	0.58	3.90	2.56
1984	6.86	0.62	4.28	3.15

APPENDIX 35:   AVERAGE NOMINAL PRODUCTION COSTS OF MAJOR CROPS
AND AVERAGE NOMINAL CONVERSION COST
LOWER MISSISSIPPI ALLUVIAL PLAIN, 1929-1984

Year	Soybeans	Cotton	Rice	Corn	Conversion Cost
			(dollars/acre)		
1929	8.53	40.14	27.07	6.99	-
1934	6.37	30.10	20.25	5.10	-
1939	8.05	38.34	26.43	7.88	2.06
1944	10.70	49.96	34.95	12.09	21.01
1949	13.22	65.17	43.37	16.64	33.42
1954	15.62	82.39	52.11	21.08	39.80
1959	18.27	95.27	62.12	26.41	48.60
1964	24.76	96.75	85.46	41.06	63.77
1969	39.42	126.11	140.87	69.68	93.28
1974	59.97	166.36	206.72	102.53	159.37
1979	83.52	267.44	245.18	126.39	210.53
1984	118.13	372.43	322.33	200.73	250.77

APPENDIX 36: AVERAGE NOMINAL FORESTRY PRICES, VOLUMES, AND YIELDS LOWER MISSISSIPPI ALLUVIAL PLAIN, 1939-1984

Year	Sawlogs			Pulpwood		
	Price ($/MBF)	Volume (1000MBF)	Yield (boardfeet/ acre/yr)	Price ($/cord)	Volume (K cords)	Yield (cords/ acre/yr)
1939	5.19	18,529	158	0.51	44,645	0.37
1944	6.29	17,217	155	0.59	39,973	0.35
1949	8.79	15,898	151	0.94	35,336	0.33
1954	15.92	14,329	144	1.20	31,370	0.30
1959	16.25	12,286	129	1.86	27,774	0.29
1964	18.14	10,786	126	2.53	24,056	0.28
1969	23.75	9,569	131	3.05	20,121	0.27
1974	38.27	8,929	135	3.23	17,241	0.25
1979	65.61	8,908	148	4.24	15,821	0.23
1984	81.08	9,212	166	5.87	14,987	0.23

PERSONAL COMMUNICATIONS

Ahlrich, V.C. U.S. Army Corps of Engineers, Vicksburg District. Vicksburg, Mississippi.

Altman, James. American Pulpwood Association. Jackson, Mississippi.

Anderson, David. U.S. Soil Conservation Service. Jackson, Mississippi.

John L. Arendale. Data Automation Division, Federal Crop Insurance Corporation. Kansas City, Missouri.

Ashley, Roy C. Division of Forestry, Tennessee Department of Conservation. Nashville, Tennessee.

Baxter, Charles. Division of Ecological Services, Fish and Wildlife Service, U.S. Department of the Interior. Vicksburg, Mississippi.

Beltz, Roy. Southern Forest Experiment Station, Forest Service, U.S. Department of Agriculture. Starkville, Mississippi.

Benney, James. Arkansas State Forestry Commission. Little Rock, Arkansas.

Birdsey, Richard. Southern Forest Experiment Station, Forest Service, U.S. Department of Agriculture. Starkville, Mississippi.

Birdwell, Robert. Natural Resource Assessments, Soil Conservation Service, U.S. Department of Agriculture. Washington, D.C.

Blackmun, Robert. University of Arkansas. Monticello, Arkansas.

Bloom, David. Department of Economics, Harvard University. Cambridge, Massachusetts.

Branard, Joseph. Northeastern Forest Experiment Station, Forest Service, U.S. Department of Agriculture. Bromall, Pennsylvania.

Broadnax, Angel. Regional Office, Bureau of the Census, U.S. Department of Commerce. Boston, Massachusetts.

Brown, John P. Chase, Brown, and Blaxall, Inc. Washington, D.C.

Burkhardt, E.C. Forestry Consultant, Vicksburg, Mississippi.

Burt, Oscar. Department of Agricultural Economics and Economics, Montana State University. Bozeman, Montana.

Caldwell, Noel D. U.S. Army Corps of Engineers, Lower Mississippi Valley Division. Vicksburg, Mississippi.

Cantrell, Charles. Data Automation Division, Federal Crop Insurance Corporation. Kansas City, Missouri.

Cavanagh, Christopher. Department of Economics, Harvard University. Cambridge, Massachusetts.

Carlton, Charles. International Paper Company. Vicksburg, Mississippi.

Ceraso, Jane. Environmental Defense Fund. New York, New York.

Chuang, John. Environmental Defense Fund. New York, New York.

Collins, Susan M. Department of Economics, Harvard University. Cambridge, Massachusetts.

Cooke, Fred. Delta Branch Experiment Station, U.S. Department of Agriculture. Stoneville, Mississippi.

Corbett, Stephen. Southern Forest Products Association. Kenner, Louisiana.

Corty, Floyd. Louisiana State University. Baton Rouge, Louisiana.

Dasgupta, Partha. London School of Economics. London, England.

Davis, Charles. Fish and Wildlife Service, U.S. Department of the Interior. Washington, D.C.

Davis, Jack C. U.S. Soil Conservation Service. Little Rock, Arkansas.

Dennis, Tom. U.S. Soil Conservation Service. Little Rock, Arkansas.

DeSeve, Richard. Office of Congressional and Public Affairs, Federal Crop Insurance Corporation. Washington, D.C.

Dodson, Gene A. Engineering Division, Hydraulics Branch, Memphis District, U.S. Army Corps of Engineers. Memphis, Tennessee.

Dudek, Daniel. Environmental Defense Fund. New York, New York.

Dykes, J.L. U.S. Army Corps of Engineers, New Orleans District. New Orleans, Louisiana.

Easterling, Jeffrey. Arkansas State Forestry Commission. Little Rock, Arkansas.

Ellis, Wayne. Soil Conservation Service, U.S. Department of Agriculture. Jackson, Mississippi.

Essex, Bert. North Central Forest Experiment Station, Forest Service, U.S. Department of Agriculture. St. Paul, Minnesota.

Estes, Leon. Mississippi State Forestry Commission. Jackson, Mississippi.

Fergurson, David. Arkansas Soil and Water Conservation Commission. Little Rock, Arkansas.

Fields, Gordon. Asby Veneer Company. Jackson, Tennessee.

Fielder, Lonnie. Louisiana State University. Baton Rouge, Louisiana.

Forgash, Michael A. Congressional and Public Affairs, Federal Crop Insurance Corporation. Washington, D.C.

Forsythe, Stephen W. Division of Ecological Services, Fish and Wildlife Service, U.S. Department of the Interior. Vicksburg, Mississippi.

Foster, David. Louisiana Department of Agriculture. Baton Rouge, Louisiana.

Frayer, Warren E. School of Forestry and Wood Products, Michigan Technological University. Houghton, Michigan.

Frey, Paul D. Office of Forestry, Louisiana Department of Natural Resources. Baton Rouge, Louisiana.

Furnival, George. School of Forestry, Yale University. New Haven, Connecticut.

Gallogly, James P. Data Automation Division, Federal Crop Insurance Corporation. Kansas City, Missouri.

Geisler, James. Arkansas Cooperative Extension Service. Little Rock, Arkansas.

Goebel, J. Jeffery. Resources Inventory Division, Soil Conservation Service, U.S. Department of Agriculture. Washington, D.C.

Goldstein, Jon H. Office of Policy Analysis, U.S. Department of the Interior. Washington, D.C.

Gosselink, James G. Center for Wetland Resources, Louisiana State University. Baton Rouge, Louisiana.

Goulder, Lawrence. Department of Economics, Harvard University. Cambridge, Massachusetts.

Griliches, Zvi. Department of Economics, Harvard University. Cambridge, Massachusetts.

Gudmund, Max. Soil Conservation Service, U.S. Department of Agriculture. Jackson, Mississippi.

Guedry, Leo J. Louisiana State University. Baton Rouge, Louisiana.

Hackbart, Dennis. Soil Conservation Service, U.S. Department of Agriculture. Little Rock, Arkansas.

Hardy, Philip. Mississippi Crop and Livestock Reporting Service. Jackson, Mississippi.

Hawkins, Douglas. Soil Conservation Service, U.S. Department of Agriculture. Washington, D.C.

Hoskins, David W. Appalachian Mountain Club. Boston, Massachusetts

Houck, Oliver. Tulane Law School, Tulane University. New Orleans, Louisiana.

Houthakker, Hendrik S. Department of Economics, Harvard University. Cambridge, Massachusetts.

Jaffe, Adam. Department of Economics, Harvard University. Cambridge, Massachusetts.

Johnson, Robert. Forest Service, U.S. Department of Agriculture. Starkville, Mississippi.

Jones, Donald. Economics Division, Soil Conservation Service, U.S. Department of Agriculture. Washington, D.C.

Kalt, Joseph P. John F. Kennedy School of Government, Harvard University. Cambridge, Massachusetts.

Karl, Thomas R. National Climatic Data Center. Asheville, North Carolina.

Knight, George. Mississippi Crop and Livestock Reporting Service. Jackson, Mississippi.

Kramer, Randall A. Department of Agricultural Economics, Virginia Polytechnic Institute and State University. Blacksburg, Virginia.

Krenz, Ronald D. Department of Agricultural Economics, Oklahoma State University. Stillwater, Oklahoma.

Krouse, Michael R. Research Division, Institute for Water Resources, U.S. Army Corps of Engineers. Fort Belvoir, Virginia.

Krueger, Alan. Department of Economics, Princeton University. Princeton, New Jersey.

Kuttner, Kenneth. Department of Economics, Harvard University. Cambridge, Massachusetts.

Lehr, Samual. Hydraulics Branch, Engineering Division, U.S. Army Corps of Engineers. Memphis, Tennessee.

Lipinski, Mary. U.S. Department of Commerce. Boston, Massachusetts.

Luciano, Anthony. Division of Forestry, Kentucky Department of Natural Resources. Frankfurt, Kentucky.

Martin, Gale. Mississippi Soil and Water Conservation Commission. Jackson, Mississippi.

Marx, Robert W. Geography Division, Bureau of the Census, U.S. Department of Commerce. Washington, D.C.

Massengale, Robert. Forestry Division, Missouri Department of Conservation. Jefferson City, Missouri.

Mathis, William. U.S. Army Corps of Engineers, Little Rock District. Little Rock, Arkansas.

McCracken, Ralph J. Soil Conservation Service, U.S. Department of Agriculture. Washington, D.C.

Miranda, Marie Lynn. Department of Economics, Harvard University. Cambridge, Massachusetts.

Miranowski, John A. Natural Resource Economics Division, Economic Research Service, U.S. Department of Agriculture. Washington, D.C.

Moser, David. Institute for Water Resources, U.S. Army Corps of Engineers. Fort Belvoir, Virginia.

Nelson, Bergen. Louisiana Crop and Livestock Reporting Service. Alexandria, Louisiana.

Nelson, Richard. Fish and Wildlife Service, U.S. Department of the Interior. Washington, D.C.

Nordstrom, Gary R. Resources Inventory Division, Soil Conservation Service, U.S. Department of Agriculture. Washington, D.C.

Paris, Michael. Regional Economic Measurement Division, Bureau of Economic Analysis, U.S. Department of Commerce. Washington, D.C.

Parvin, D. W. Agricultural Economics Department, Mississippi State University. Mississippi State, Mississippi.

Patterson, Curtis. Louisiana Department of Transportation and Development. Baton Rouge, Louisiana.

Paulus, E. F. Potlach Lumber Company. Warren, Arkansas.

Peterson, John W. Project Development and Maintenance Division, Soil Conservation Service, U.S. Department of Agriculture. Washington, D.C.

Pierce, Richard S. Center For Wetland Resources, Louisiana State University. Baton Rouge, Louisiana.

Pindyck, Robert. Sloan School, Massachusetts Institute of Technology, Cambridge, Massachusetts.

Reno, W. M. Caterpillar Tractor Company. Dallas, Texas.

Riekert, Edward. Basin and Area Planning Division, Soil Conservation Service, U.S. Department of Agriculture. Washington, D.C.

Rogers, Peter. Division of Engineering and Applied Physics, Harvard University. Cambridge, Massachusetts.

Ross, John. Arkansas Forestry Commission, Forest City, Arkansas.

Rosson, James. Forest Service, U.S. Department of Agriculture. Starkville, Mississippi.

Rowe, Oscar. U.S. Army Corps of Engineers, New Orleans District. New Orleans, Louisiana.

Rucker, Harry S. U.S. Soil Conservation Service. Alexandria, Louisiana.

Samuels, Deanne. Department of Economics, Harvard University. Cambridge, Massachusetts.

Sands, General Thomas A. U.S. Army Corps of Engineers. Vicksburg, Mississippi.

Schmude, Keith. Resources Inventory Division, Soil Conservation Service, U.S. Department of Agriculture. Washington, D.C.

Schwartz, Gary M. Data Automation Division, Federal Crop Insurance Corporation. Kansas City, Missouri.

Shropshire, Frank. U.S. Forest Service, Jackson, Mississippi.

Shulstad, Robert. Department of Agricultural Economics. University of Arkansas. Fayetteville, Arkansas.

Shumway, C. Richard. Department of Agricultural Economics, Texas A & M University. College Station, Texas.

Simmons, Gene. Soil Conservation Service, U.S. Department of Agriculture. Alexandria, Louisiana.

Slater, Wayne R. Center For Wetland Resources, Louisiana State University. Baton Rouge, Louisiana.

Solomon, Mark. U.S. Army Corps of Engineers, New Orleans District. New Orleans, Louisiana.

Sorenson, David. Division of Forestry, Kentucky Department of Natural Resources. Frankfurt, Kentucky.

Spann, Quinn. U.S. Army Corps of Engineers, Little Rock District. Little Rock, Arkansas.

Strohn, Bert. U.S. Army Corps of Engineers, Memphis District. Memphis, Tennessee.

Stuart, Richard. Lower Mississippi Valley Division, U.S. Army Corps of Engineers. Vicksburg, Mississippi.

Sullivan, Albert E. Soil Conservation Service, U.S. Department of Agriculture. Jackson, Mississippi.

Taylor, Hattie. U.S. Army Corps of Engineers, Vicksburg District. Vicksburg, Mississippi.

Thomas, Carl. Ecological Sciences Division, Soil Conservation Service, U.S. Department of Agriculture. Washington, D.C.

Timmer, Peter. Department of Economics, Harvard University. Cambridge, Massachusetts.

Tiner, James. Arkansas State Forestry Commission. Little Rock, Arkansas.

Tribble, Ray. Office of the County Supervisor, LeFlore County. Greenwood, Mississippi.

Tripp, James T. B. Environmental Defense Fund. New York, New York.

Turner, R. E. Center for Wetland Resources, Coastal Ecology Institute, Louisiana State University.

Van Beek, Johannes L. Coastal Environments, Inc. Baton Rouge, Louisiana.

Von Steen, Donald H. Arkansas Crop and Livestock Reporting Service. Little Rock, Arkansas.

Wallis, Alan. National Climatic Data Center. Asheville, North Carolina.

Watson, Mark. Department of Economics, Northwestern University. Evanston, Illinois.

Willey, W. R. Z. Environmental Defense Fund. Berkeley, California.

Williams, Robert. Department of Agricultural Economics, Mississippi State University. Mississippi State, Mississippi.

Williamson, Jeffrey G. Department of Economics, Harvard University. Cambridge, Massachusetts.

Young, Keith. Soils Technology Branch, Soil Conservation Service, U.S. Department of Agriculture. Washington, D.C.

REFERENCES

Allen, H. H. "Role of Wetland Plants in Erosion Control of Riparian
    Shorelines." Wetland Functions and Values: The State of our
    Understanding, ed. P. E. Greeson, J. R. Clark, and J. E. Clark, pp.
    403-414. Minneapolis: American Water Resources Association, 1979.

Amemiya, Takeshi. Advanced Econometrics. Cambridge, Massachusetts:
    Harvard University Press, 1985.

_____. "The Maximum Likelihood Estimator and the Nonlinear Three-
    Stage Least Squares Estimator in the General Nonlinear Simultaneous
    Equation Model." Econometrica 45(1977):955-968.

_____. "Non-Linear Regression Models." Handbook of Econometrics,
    Volume I, ed. Zvi Griliches and Michael D. Intrilligator,
    pp.333-389. Amsterdam: North-Holland Publishing Company, 1983.

American Society of Agricultural Engineers. Problems and Needs in
    Agricultural Drainage. St. Joseph, Mississippi, 1946.

Arkansas Agriculture Experiment Station. Crop Enterprises on Cotton
    Farms in Northeast Arkansas: Production Requirements, Estimated
    Costs, and Returns. Report Series 131, University of Arkansas,
    Fayetteville, December 1964.

Arkansas Crop and Livestock Reporting Service. Arkansas County
    Estimates. Division of Agriculture, University of Arkansas, years
    1947 -1984 inclusive.

_____. 1982 Agricultural Statistics for Arkansas. Little Rock,
    Arkansas: Statistical Reporting Service, U.S. Department of
    Agriculture, Report Series 280, August 1983.

Arkansas Forestry Commission. "Forest Price Statistics", Little Rock
    Arkansas, unpublished.

Arnott, R. J. and F. D. Lewis. "The Transition of Land to Urban Use."
    Journal of Political Economy 87(1979):161-170.

Arrow, Kenneth J. and Anthony C. Fisher. "Environmental Preservation,
    Uncertainty, and Irreversibility." American Economic Review
    60(1970): 364-378.

Bardecki, Michael J. "What Value Wetlands?" Journal of Soil and Water
    Conservation, May-June 1984, pp. 166-169.

Barlow, Frank D. The Cost of Producing Cotton in Louisiana.
    Agricultural Experiment Station Mimeograph Circular No. 84,
    Louisiana State University and Agricultural and Mechanical College,
    July 1948.

Barton, Katherine. "Wetlands Preservation." Audubon Wildlife Report 1985, ed. Roger L. Di Silvestro, pp. 213-264. New York: The National Audubon Society, 1985.

Baumol, William J. and Wallace E. Oates. The Theory of Environmental Policy. Englewood Cliffs, New Jersey: Prentice Hall, 1975.

Beasley, Lynn W., and Williard F. Woolf. The Effects of Production Practice on Soybean Yields, Costs and Returns in the Mississippi River Delta of Louisiana. Department of Agricultural Economics and Agribusiness Research Report No. 435, Louisiana State University and Agricultural and Mechanical College, February 1972.

Berndt, E. R., B. H. Hall, and R. E. Hall, and J. A. Hausman. "Estimation and Inference in Nonlinear Structural Models." Annals of Economic and Social Measurement 3(1975):653-665.

Berndt, E. R., and N. E. Savin. "Conflict among Criteria for Testing Hypotheses in the Multivariate Linear Regression Model." Econometrica 45(1977):1263-1275.

Bohi, Douglas R. and Michael A. Toman. Analyzing Nonrenewable Resource Supply. Washington, D.C.: Resources for the Future, 1984.

Boto, K. G. and W. H. Patrick, Jr. "Role of Wetlands in the Removal of Suspended Sediments." Wetland Functions and Values: The State of our Understanding, ed. P. E. Greeson, J. R. Clark, and J. E. Clark, pp. 479-489. Minneapolis: American Water Resources Association, 1979.

Boyt, F. L., S. E. Bayley, and J. Zoltek. "Removal of Nutrients from Treated Municipal Wastewater by Wetland Vegetation." Journal of the Water Pollution Control Federation 49(1977):789-799.

Brehm, C.T. and T.R. Saving. "The Demand for General Assistance Payments." American Economic Review 59(1964):1002-1018.

Breusch, T. S. "Testing for Autocorrelation in Dynamic Linear Models." Australian Economic Papers 17(1978):334-355.

Brown, John P. The Economic Effects of Floods: Investigations of a Stochastic Model of Rational Investment Behavior in the Face of Floods. New York: Springer-Verlag, 1972.

_____. "Stream Channelization: The Economics of the Controversy." Natural Resources Journal 14 (1974):557-576.

Brown, John P., Bruno Contini, and C. B. McGuire. "An Economic Model of Floodplain Land Use and Land Use Policy." Water Resources Research 8(1972):18-32.

Buse, A. "The Likelihood Ratio, Wald, and Lagrange Multiplier Tests: An Expository Note." The American Statistician 36(1982):153-157.

Chamberlain, Gary. "Multivariate Regression Models for Panel Data." Journal of Econometrics 18(1982):5-46.

_____. "Panel Data." Handbook of Econometrics, Volume II, ed. Zvi Griliches and Michael D. Intrilligator, pp.1247-1318. Amsterdam: North- Holland, 1984.

Chapman, Stephen R. and Lark P. Carter. Crop Production: Principles and Practices. San Francisco: W. H. Freeman and Company, 1976.

Chicoine, D. L. "Farmland Values at the Urban Fringe: An Analysis of Sales Prices." Land Economics 57(1981):353-362.

Cicchetti, Charles J. and A. Myrick Freeman III. "Option Demand and Consumer Surplus: Further Comment." Quarterly Journal of Economics 85(1971): 528-539.

Clark, Colin W. Mathematical Bioeconomics: The Optimal Management of Renewable Resources. New York: John Wiley, 1976.

Conrad, Jon M. "Quasi-Option Value and the Expected Value of Information." Quarterly Journal of Economics 94(1980):813-820.

Cooke, Fred T., J.M. Anderson, and Arthur M. Heagler. Crop Budgets and Planning Data for Major Farm Enterprises in the Yazoo-Mississippi Delta. Mississippi Agricultural and Forest Experiment Station Bulletin 794, July 1972.

Cory, Dennis C. and Bonnie Colby Saliba. "Requiem for Option Value." Land Economics 63(1987):1-10.

Cowardin, L. M., V. Carter, F. C. Golet, and E. T. LaRoe. Classification of Wetlands and Deepwater Habitats of the United States. Washington, D.C.: U.S. Fish and Wildlife Service, FWS/OBS-79/31, 1979.

Cox, J. C. and A. W. Wright. "The Determinants of Investment in Petroleum Reserves and Their Implication s for Public Policy." American Economic Review 66(1976):153-167.

Crocker, Thomas D. "On the Value of the Condition of a Forest Stock." Land Economics 61(1985):244-254.

Cropper, Maureen L. "Regulating Activities with Catastrophic Environmental Effects." Journal of Environmental Economics and Management 3(1976):1-15.

Crowe, Grady B. Specified Production Costs for Cotton and Alternative Crops, Yazoo-Mississippi Delta. Mississippi Agricultural Experiment Station, March 1956.

Cummings, Ronald G. "Some Extensions of the Economic Theory of Natural Resources." Western Economic Journal 7(1969):201-210.

Dasgupta, Partha S. and Geoffrey M. Heal. Economic Theory and Exhaustible Resources. Cambridge, England: Cambridge University Press, 1979.

David, Paul. "The Mechanization of Reaping in the Ante-Bellum Midwest." Industrialization in Two Systems, ed. Henry Rosovsky, pp. 3-39. Cambridge: Harvard University Press, 1966.

_____. "A Contribution of the Theory of Diffusion." Stanford University CREG Memorandum #71, June 1969.

Davies, Stephen. The Diffusion of Process Innovations. Cambridge, England: Cambridge University Press, 1979.

Davis, Robert. Economic Potential for Converting Woodland and Pasture to Cropland: Lower Mississippi Valley and Southeast. Economic Research Service Bulletin 495. Washington, D.C.: U.S. Department of Agriculture, 1972.

Department of Agricultural Economics. Budgets for Major Farm Enterprises in the Mississippi River Delta of Arkansas, Louisiana, and Mississippi. Circular 281, Louisiana State University and Agricultural and Mechanical College, June 1961.

Dideriksen, R. I., A. R. Hidlebaugh, and K. O. Schmude. Potential Cropland Study. SB-578. Washington, D.C.: U.S. Department of Agriculture, Soil Conservation Service, October 1977.

Dorland, Douglas, Carl Farler, Carrol R. Garner, Don Smith, Robert W. hale, and Clyde A. Stuart, Jr. Arkansas Cotton Budgets, 1982 Production Cost Estimates. Agricultural Experiment Station Special Report No. 102, University of Arkansas, February 1982a.

_____. Arkansas Feed Grain Budgets, 1982 Production Cost Estimates. Agricultural Experiment Station Special Report No. 103, University of Arkansas, February 1982b.

_____. Arkansas Soybean Budgets, 1982 Production Cost Estimates. Agricultural Experiment Station Special Report No. 104, University of Arkansas, March 1982c.

Duerr, William A. Basic Data on Forest Area and Timber Volumes from the Southern Forest Survey, 1932-36. U.S. Department of Agriculture Forest Survey Release No. 54, February 1946.

Dunnuck, Gene, Miles McPeek, and Hillard Jackson. Prices and Price Indexes for Arkansas Farm Products, 1910-1959. Agriculture Experiment Station Bulletin No. 627, University of Arkansas, June 1960.

Durbin, J. "Testing for Serial Correlation in Least Squares Regression when Some of the Regressors are Lagged Dependent Variables." Econometrica 38(1970):410-421.

Earles, J.M. Forest Area Statistics for Midsouth Counties. U.S. Department of Agriculture Forest Service Resource Bulletin SO-40, 1973.

_____. Forest Statistics for Louisiana Parishes. U.S. Department of Agriculture Forest Service Resource Bulletin SO-52, 1975.

Ehui, Simeon K., Thomas W. Hertel, and Paul V. Preckel. Forest Resource Depletion, Soil Dynamics and Agricultural Productivity in the Tropics. Department of Agricultural Economics, Purdue University, Staff Paper #87-22, West Lafayette, Indiana, July 1987.

Engle, Robert F. "Wald, Likelihood Ratio, and Lagrange Multiplier Tests in Econometrics." Handbook of Econometrics, Volume II, ed. Zvi Griliches and Michael D. Intrilligator, pp.775-826. Amsterdam: North-Holland, 1984.

Farber, Stephen. "The Value of Coastal Wetlands for Protection of Property against Hurricane Wind Damage." Journal of Environmental Economics and Management 14(1987):143-151.

Fielder, Lonnie. Agricultural Statistics and Prices for Louisiana, 1924-1981. Louisiana State University, Department of Agricultural Economics and Agribusiness, D.A.E. Research Report No. 583, August 1981.

Fielder, Lonnie and Bergen Nelson. Agricultural Statistics and Prices for Louisiana, 1924-1981.. Louisiana State University, Department of Agricultural Economics and Agribusiness, D.A.E. Research Report No. 600, August 1982.

_____. Agricultural Statistics and Prices for Louisiana, 1975-1978. Louisiana State University, Department of Agricultural Economics and Agribusiness, D.A.E. Research Report No. 554, July 1979.

_____. Agricultural Statistics and Prices for Louisiana, 1978 - 1983. Louisiana Agricultural Experiment Station, Department of Agricultural Economics and Agribusiness Research Report No. 631, Louisiana State University, August 1984.

Fielder, Lonnie and Clarence O. Parker. Louisiana Crop Statistics, by Parishes, Through 1970. Louisiana State University, Department of Agricultural Economics and Agribusiness, D.A.E. Research Report No. 436,   April 1972.

Fisher, Anthony C. and W. Michael Hanemann. Option Value and the Extinction of Species. Giannini Foundation of Agricultural Economics, Working Paper No. 269, University of California, Berkeley, October 1984.

Fisher, Anthony C. and John V. Krutilla. "Economics of Nature Preservation." Handbook of Natural Resource and Energy Economics, Volume I, eds. Allen V. Kneese and James L. Sweeney, pp. 165-189. Amsterdam: North Holland, 1985.

Fisher, Anthony C. and Frederick M. Peterson. "The Environment in Economics: A Survey." The Journal of Economic Literature 14(1976):1-33.

Forster, B. A. "Optimal Consumption Planning in a Polluted Environment." Economic Record 49(1973):534-545.

Frayer, Warren E. Land Use Trends in the Lower Mississippi Alluvial Plain, 1937-1974. Unpublished report submitted to HRB Singer, Inc., February, 1979.

_____. Status and Trends of Wetlands and Deepwater Habitats in the Coterminous United States, 1950's to 1970's. Ft. Collins: Colorado State University, Department of Forest and Wood Sciences, April 1983.

Freeman, A. Myrick III. The Benefits of Environmental Improvement: Theory and Practice. Baltimore: Johns Hopkins University Press, 1979.

_____. "Methods for Assessing the Benefits of Environmental Programs." Handbook of Natural Resource and Energy Economics, Volume I, eds. Allen V. Kneese and James L. Sweeney, pp. 223-270. Amsterdam: North Holland, 1985.

Frey, H. Thomas, and Henry W. Dill. Land Use Change in the Southern Mississippi Alluvial Valley: 1950-1969. Washington, D.C.: U.S. Department of Agriculture, Economic Research Service, Agriculture Economic Report 215, October 1971.

Frey, H. Thomas, and Roger W. Hexem. Major Uses of Land in the United States: 1982. Washington, D.C.: U.S. Department of Agriculture, Natural Resource Economics Division, Economic Research Service, Agricultural Economic Report No. 535, June 1985.

Gallagher, Paul. "The Effectiveness of Price Support Policy -- Some Evidence for U.S. Corn Acreage Response." Agricultural Economics Research 30(1978):8-14.

Gallagher, Paul and Robert C. Green. A Cropland Use Model: Theory and Suggestions for Estimating Planted Acreage Response. National Economics Division, Economic Research Service, U.S. Department of Agriculture, ERS Report No. AGES840410, November 1984.

Galloway, Gerald E. Ex Post Evaluation of Regional Water Resources Development: The Case of the Yazoo-Mississippi Delta. Ft. Belvoir, Virginia: Institute for Water Resources, U.S. Army Corps of Engineers, October 1980.

Gardner, Bruce L. "Futures Prices in Supply Analysis." _American Journal of Agricultural Economics_ 58(1976):81-84.

Gardner, Bruce L. and J. P. Chavas. "Market Equilibrium with Random Production." Paper presented at AAEA Annual Meeting, Pullman, Washington, August 1979.

Gardner, Bruce L. and Randall A. Kramer. "Experience with Crop Insurance Programs in the United States." _Agricultural Risks and Insurance: Issues and Policies_, ed. P. Hazell, C. Pomareda and A. Valdes. Baltimore: Johns Hopkins University Press, forthcoming.

Gibbons, Diana C. _The Economic Value of Water_. Washington, D.C.: Resources for the Future, Inc., 1986.

Godfrey, L. G. "Testing Against General Autoregressive and Moving Average Error Models When the Regressors Include Lagged Dependent Variables." _Econometrica_ 46(1978):1293-1302.

Goldstein, Jon H. _Competition for Wetlands in the Midwest: An Economic Analysis_. Washington, D.C.: Resources for the Future, Inc., 1971.

_____. "The Impact of Federal Programs and Subsidies on Wetlands." Paper presented at National Wetlands Inventory Conference, Denver, Colorado, March 1988.

Gordon, Richard L. "A Reinterpretation of the Pure Theory of Exhaustion." _Journal of Political Economy_ 75(1967):274-286.

Gosselink, James G., E. P. Odum, and R. M. Pope. _The Value of a Tidal Marsh_. LSU-56-74-03. Baton Rouge: Center for Wetland Resources, Louisiana State University, 1973.

Gotz, Glenn A. and John J. McCall. _A Dynamic Retention Model for Air Force Officers_. Rand Report R-3028-AF, Santa Monica, California, December 1984.

_____. "Estimation in Sequential Decisionmaking Models." _Economic Letters_ 6(1980):131-136.

Graham, Daniel A. "Cost-Benefit Analysis under Uncertainty." _American Economic Review_ 71(1981):715-725.

Gray, L. C. "Utilization of Our Lands for Crops, Pasture, and Forests." _Agriculture Yearbook 1923_, pp. 415-506. Washington, D.C.: U.S. Department of Agriculture, 1924.

Greeson, P. E., J. R. Clark, and J. E. Clark. _Wetland Functions and Values: The State of our Understanding_, Proceedings of the National Symposium on Wetlands, November 7-10, 1978. Minneapolis: American Water Resources Association, 1979.

Griliches, Zvi. "Hybrid Corn: An Exploration in the Economics of Technological Change." Econometrica 25(1957):501-522.

Griliches, Zvi, and Michael D. Intrilligator. Handbook of Econometrics, Volume I. Amsterdam: North-Holland Publishing Company, 1983.

_____. Handbook of Econometrics, Volume II. Amsterdam: North-Holland, 1984.

Hall, Peter, ed. Von Thunen's Isolated State. London: Pergamon Press, 1966.

Hammack, Judd, and Gardner Mallard Brown, Jr. Waterfowl and Wetlands: Toward Bioeconomic Analysis. Baltimore: Resources for the Future, 1974.

Hanemann, W. Michael. Information and the Concept of Option Value. Giannini Foundation of Agricultural Economics, Working Paper No 228, University of California, Berkeley, November 1983.

Harrison, Robert W. Alluvial Empire: A Study of State and Local Efforts Toward Land Development in the Alluvial Valley of the Lower Mississippi River, Volume I. Little Rock, Arkansas: U.S. Department of Agriculture, Economic Research Service, 1961.

Harsch, Jeanne H., Mississippi Agricultural Statistics, 1974-1980. Jackson: Mississippi: Mississippi Crop and Livestock Reporting Service Supplement Number 15, 1981.

_____. Mississippi Agricultural Statistics 1969 - 1977. Jackson: Mississippi Crop and Livestock Reporting Service Supplement Number 12, 1978.

_____. Mississippi Agricultural Statistics 1982 - 1983. Jackson: Mississippi Crop and Livestock Reporting Service Supplement Number 18, December 1984.

Hedlund, Arnold, and J.M. Earles. Forest Statistics for Arkansas Counties. U.S. Department of Agriculture Forest Service Resource Bulletin SO-22, 1970.

_____. Forest Statistics for Mississippi Counties. U.S. Department of Agriculture Forest Resource Bulletin SO-15, 1969.

Heimlich, Ralph E., and Linda L. Langner. Swampbusting: Wetland Conversion and Farm Programs. Agricultural Economic Report Number 551. Washington, D.C.: U.S. Department of Agriculture, Economic Research Service, Natural Resource Economics Division, August 1986.

Herrington, Billy E., Jr. "The Economic Feasibility of Increasing Crop Production in the Mississippi Delta Region through the Conversion of Non- Cropland to Cropland, and the Upgrading of Existing Cropland." M.S. thesis, University of Arkansas, 1979.

Herrington, Billy E. and Robert N. Shulstad. Conversion of Delta Woodland and Pasture to Cropland: Economic Feasibility and Implications. Agricultural Experiment Station, University of Arkansas, Fayetteville, March 1982.

Holmes, B. H. A History of Federal Water Resources Programs, 1800-1959. Miscellaneous Publication 1233. Washington, D.C.: U.S. Department of Agriculture, 1972.

_____. History of Federal Water Resources Programs and Policies, 1961- 1970. Miscellaneous Publication 1379. Washington, D.C.: U.S. Department of Agriculture, 1979.

Hotelling, Harold. "The Economics of Exhaustible Resources." Journal of Political Economy 39(1931):137-175.

Houck, James P., Martin E. Abel, Mary E. Ryan, Paul W. Gallagher, Robert G. Hoffmann and J. B. Penn. Analyzing the Impact of Government Programs on Crop Acreage. Technical Bulletin No. 1548, Economic Research Service, U.S. Department of Agriculture, August 1976.

Houck, James P. and Abraham Subotnik. "The U.S. Supply of Soybeans: Regional Acreage Functions." Agricultural Economics Research 21(1969):99-108.

Jackson, Hillard, and Donald Van Steen. Prices and Price Indexes for Arkansas Farm Products, 1960-1977. Agriculture Experiment Station Bulletin No. 830, University of Arkansas, September 1978.

Jaworski, E. and C. N. Raphael. Fish, Wildlife and Recreational Values of Michigan's Coastal Wetlands. East Lansing: Michigan Department of Natural Resources, 1978.

Jones, L. R. "The Mechanization of Reaping and Mowing in American Agriculture, 1833-1870: Comment." Journal of Economic History 37(1977):451-455.

Jorgenson, Dale W. and Jean-Jacques Laffont. "Efficient Estimation of Nonlinear Simultaneous Equations with Additive Disturbances." Annals of Economic and Social Measurement 3(1975):615-640.

Judge, George G., W. E. Griffiths, R. Carter Hill, Helmut Lutkepohl, and Tsoung-Chao Lee. The Theory and Practice of Econometrics. New York: John Wiley and Sons, 1985.

Kamien, Morton I. and Nancy L. Schwartz. "Disaggregated Intertemporal Models with an Exhaustible Resource and Technical Advance." Journal of Environmental Economics and Management 4(1977):271-288.

_____. "The Role of Common Property Resources in Optimal Planning Models with Exhaustible Resources." Explorations in Natural Resource Economics, ed., V. Kerry Smith and John V. Krutilla, pp. 45-71. Baltimore: The Johns Hopkins University Press, 1982.

Karl, Thomas R. "Some Spatial Characteristics of Drought Duration in the United States." <u>Journal of Climate and Applied Meteorology</u> 22(1983): 1356-1366.

_____. "The Sensitivity of the Palmer Drought Severity Index and Palmer's Z-Index to Their Calibration Coefficients Including Potential Evapotransporation." Paper presented at the Eighth National Conference on Fire and Forest Meteorology, Detroit, Michigan, April 29 - May 3, 1985.

Karl, Thomas R., Laura K. Metcalf, M. Lawrence Nicodemus, and Robert G. Quayle. <u>Statewide Average Climatic History: Arkansas 1891 - 1982</u>. Asheville, North Carolina: National Climatic Data Center, Historical Climatology Series 6-1, September 1983a.

_____. <u>Statewide Average Climatic History: Louisiana 1891 - 1982</u>. Asheville, North Carolina: National Climatic Data Center, Historical Climatology Series 6-1, September 1983b.

_____. <u>Statewide Average Climatic History: Mississippi 1891 - 1982</u>. Asheville, North Carolina: National Climatic Data Center, Historical Climatology Series 6-1, September 1983c.

Keeler, Emmett, Michael Spence, and Richard Zeckhauser. "The Optimal Control of Pollution." <u>Journal of Economic Theory</u> 4(1972):19-34.

Kneese, Allen V., and James L. Sweeney, ed. <u>Handbook of Natural Resource and Energy Economics, Volume I</u>. Amsterdam: North-Holland, 1985.

_____. <u>Handbook of Natural Resource and Energy Economics, Volume II</u>. Amsterdam: North-Holland, 1985.

Kramer, Randall A. and Leonard A. Shabman. <u>Development of Bottomland Hardwood Tracts for Agricultural Use: The Influence of Public Policies and Programs</u>. Prepared for the U.S. Department of the Interior, Fish and Wildlife Service, Washington, D.C., 1986.

Kusler, Jon A. <u>Our National Wetland Heritage: A Protection Guidebook</u>. Washington, D.C.: Environmental Law Institute, 1983.

Langsford, E.L. and B.H. Thibodeaux. <u>Plantation Organization and Operation in the Yazoo-Mississippi Delta Area</u>. Washington, D.C.: U.S. Department of Agriculture Technical Bulletin 682, May 1939.

Lavergne, David R., and Paxton, Kenneth W. <u>Projected Costs and Returns Cotton, Soybeans, Corn, Milo, and Wheat, Red River and Central Areas, Louisiana, 1984</u>. Department of Agricultural Economics and Agribusiness Research Report No. 623, Louisiana State University, January 1984.

214

_____. <u>Projected Costs and Returns, Cotton, Soybeans, Corn, Red River and Central Areas, Louisiana, 1985</u>. Department of Agricultural Economics and Agribusiness Research Report No. 633, Louisiana State University, January 1985.

Lea, Dallas M. and C. Dudley Mattson. <u>Evolution of the Small Watershed Program</u>. Washington, D.C.: U.S. Department of Agriculture, Economic Research Service, AER-262, 1974.

Leitch, Jay A. and William C. Nelson. <u>Review of the Effect of Selected Federal programs on Wetlands in the Prairie Pothole Region</u>. Barton-Aschman Associates, Inc., Minneapolis, Minnesota. Prepared for the U.S. Department of the Interior, Fish and Wildlife Service, Washington, D.C., 1986.

Lewis, Douglas. <u>Land Drainage Investment Survey, 1975-79: A Report on a Landownership Follow-on Survey</u>. U.S. Department of Agriculture, Economic Research Service, Staff Report AGES-820728, August 1982a.

_____. <u>Land Drainage Investment Survey, 1975-77: A Report on a Landownership Follow-on Survey</u>. U.S. Department of Agriculture, Economic Research Service, Staff Report AGES-820525, June 1982b.

Liles, James Pat. <u>Mississippi Agricultural Statistics 1954 - 73</u>. Jackson: Mississippi Crop and Livestock Reporting Service Supplement Number 9, 1975.

Lind, Robert C. <u>Discounting for Time and Risk in Energy Policy</u>. Washington, D.C.: Resources for the Future, Inc., 1982.

Louisiana Forestry Commission. "Annual Timber Stumpage Valuations, 1944- 1983," Baton Rouge, Louisiana, unpublished statistics.

Louisiana Crop and Livestock Reporting Service. <u>Louisiana Crop Production</u>. Department of Agricultural Economics, Louisiana State University, February 8, 1985.

MacDonald, Purificacion O., Warren E. Frayer and Jerome K. Clauser. <u>Documentation, Chronology, and Future Projections of Bottomland Hardwood Habitat Loss in the Lower Mississippi Alluvial Plain</u>. Volumes I (Basic Report). Ecological Services, Fish and Wildlife Service, U.S. Department of the Interior, November 1979a.

_____. <u>Documentation, Chronology, and Future Projections of Bottomland Hardwood Habitat Loss in the Lower Mississippi Alluvial Plain</u>. Volume II (Appendices). Ecological Services, Fish and Wildlife Service, U.S. Department of the Interior, November 1979b.

Maler, Karl-Goran. "Welfare Economics and the Environment." <u>Handbook of Natural Resource and Energy Economics, Volume I</u>, eds. Allen V. Kneese and James L. Sweeney, pp. 3-60. Amsterdam: North Holland, 1985.

Martin, John H., Warren H. Leonard and David L. Stamp. Principles of Field Crop Production. New York: Macmillan Publishing Company, Inc., 1976.

Mattson, C. Dudley. Effect of the Small Watershed Program on Major Uses of Land: Examination of 60 Projects in the Southeast, Mississippi Delta, and Missouri River Tributaries Regions. Washington, D.C.: U.S. Department of Agriculture, Economic Research Service, Natural Resources Economics Division, AER-279, February 1975.

May, Ralph D., and W. Charles Walden. Arkansas Soybean Budgets, 1979 Production Cost Estimates. Agricultural Experiment Station Special Report No. 69, University of Arkansas, January 1979.

_____. Arkansas Soybean Budgets, 1980 Production Cost Estimates. Agricultural Experiment Station Special report No. 80, University of Arkansas, March 1980.

May, Ralph D., W. Charles Walden, Donnie A. Smith, Robert W. Hale, and Clyde A. Stuart, Jr. Arkansas Cotton Budgets, 1981 Production Cost Estimates. Agricultural Experiment Station Special Report No. 90, University of Arkansas, March 1981a.

May, Ralph D., W. Charles Walden, Donnie A. Smith, Robert W. Hale, and Clyde A. Stuart, Jr. Arkansas Soybean Budgets, 1981 Production Cost Estimates. Agricultural Experiment Station Special Report No. 92, University of Arkansas, March 1981b.

_____. Arkansas Feed Grain Budgets, 1981 Production Cost Estimates. Agricultural Experiment Station Special Report No. 94, University of Arkansas, March 1981.

May, Ralph D., Charles Walden, and Ewell R. Welch. Arkansas Soybean Budgets, 1978 Production Cost Estimates. Agriculture Experiment Station Special Report No. 59, University of Arkansas, March 1978.

McCandliss, D.A. Base Book of Mississippi Agriculture 1866 - 1953. Jackson: Mississippi Crop and Livestock Reporting Service Number 1, 1955.

McColloch, Patrick R. and Donald J. Wissman. Analysis of the Impact of Federal Programs on Wetlands in the Prairie Pothole Region. Development Planning and Research Associates, Inc., Manhattan, Kansas. Prepared for the U.S. Department of the Interior, Fish and Wildlife Service, Washington, D.C., 1986.

McConnell, Kenneth E. "The Economics of Outdoor Recreation." Handbook of Natural Resource and Energy Economics, Volume II, ed. Allen V. Kneese and James L. Sweeney, pp. 677-722. Amsterdam: North Holland, 1985.

McElroy, Robert G., and Coleg Gustafson. Costs of Producing Major Crops, 1975-1981. Washington, D.C.: U.S. Department of Agriculture, Economic Research Service, April 1985.

Mississippi Agricultural and Forestry Experiment Station. Estimated Costs and Returns, Crops, Black Belt Area of Northeast Mississippi, 1984. Agricultural Economics Report No. 15, Mississippi State University January 1984a.

_____. Estimated Costs and Returns, Cotton, All Areas of Mississippi, 1985. Mississippi State University, January 1985a.

_____. Estimated Costs and Returns, Crops, Brown Loam Area of Mississippi, 1984. Agricultural Economics Report No. 13, Mississippi State University January 1984b.

_____. Estimated Costs and Returns, Crops, Delta Area of Mississippi, 1982. Agricultural Economics Report No. 3, Mississippi State University, February 1982.

_____. Estimated Costs and Returns, Crops, Delta Area of Mississippi, 1983. Agricultural Economics Report No. 8, Mississippi State University, January 1983.

_____. Estimated Costs and Returns, Crops, Delta Area of Mississippi, 1984. Agricultural Economics Report No. 14, Mississippi State University, January 1984c.

_____. Estimated Costs and Returns, Crops, Delta Area of Mississippi, 1985. Mississippi State University, January 1985b.

_____. Estimated Costs and Returns, Rice, Delta Area of Mississippi, 1982. Mississippi State University, January 1985c.

_____. Estimated Costs and Returns, Rice, Delta Area of Mississippi, 1985. Mississippi State University, January 1985d.

_____. Estimated Costs and Returns, Soybeans, All Areas of Mississippi, 1985. Mississippi State University, January 1985e.

Mississippi Crop and Livestock Reporting Service. Mississippi Agricultural Statistics 1974 - 80. Jackson: U.S. Department of Agriculture Statistical Reporting Service Supplement Number 15, 1981.

_____. Mississippi Agricultural Statistics 1980 - 1981. Jackson: U.S. Department of Agriculture Statistical Reporting Service Supplement Number 16, 1982.

_____. Mississippi Agricultural Statistics 1981 -1982. Jackson: U.S. Department of Agriculture Statistical Reporting Service Supplement Number 17, 1983.

Mississippi State Forestry Commission. _Timber Marketing News_. Jackson, Mississippi, selected quarterly issues.

Murphy, Paul A. _Louisiana Forests: Status & Outlook_. New Orleans, Louisiana: U.S. Department of Agriculture, Forest Service, Southern Forest Experiment Station, Resource Bulletin SO-53, 1975.

_____. _Mississippi Forests: Trends and Outlook_. U.S. Department of Agriculture Forest Service Resource Bulletin SO-67, 1978.

Musick, Joseph A. _Projected Costs and Returns, Rice and Soybeans Southwest Louisiana, 1982_. Department of Agricultural Economics and Agribusiness Research Report No. 587, Louisiana State University, January 1982.

Musick, Joseph A., and Michael E. Salassi. _Projected Costs and Returns, Rice and Soybeans Southwest Louisiana, 1983_. Department of Agricultural Economics and Agribusiness Research Report No. 607, Louisiana State University, January 1983.

National Research Council. _Impacts of Emerging Agricultural Trends on Fish and Wildlife Habitat_. Washington, D.C.: National Academy Press, 1982.

Neiring, William A. _Wetlands_. New York: Alfred A. Knopf, Inc., 1985.

Nelson, Aaron G., Warren F. Lee, and William G. Murray. _Agricultural Finance_, Sixth Edition. Ames: Iowa State University Press, 1973.

Nelson, Bergen A., and Abby P. Adenji. _Louisiana Wheat: Acreage, Yield and Production, 1982 Preliminary_. Department of Agricultural Economics, Louisiana State University, April 6, 1983.

Nelson, Bergen A., and Chris L. Cadwallader. _Acreage Yield and Production, 1982 Preliminary_. Department of Agricultural Economics, Louisiana State University, 1983/84, various months.

_____. _Acreage, Yield and Production, 1984 Preliminary_. Department of Agricultural Economics, Louisiana State University, 1985, various months.

Nerlove, Mark, and K. L. Bachman. "The Analysis of Changes in Agricultural Supply: Problems and Approaches." _Journal of Farm Economics_ 42(1960):531-554.

Nomsen, David E., Kenneth F. Higgins, Howard W. Browers, and Brian J. Smith. _Wetland Drainage in Association with Federal Highway Projects in the Prairie Pothole Region_. Cooperative Fish and Wildlife Research Unit, Department of Wildlife and Fisheries Sciences, South Dakota State University, Brookings, South Dakota. Prepared for the U.S. Department of the Interior, Fish and Wildlife Service, Washington, D.C., 1986.

Ogawa, H. "Evaluation Methodologies for the Flood Mitigation Potential of Inland Wetlands." Ph.D. thesis, University of Massachusetts, Amherst, 1982.

Pakes, Aerial. "Patents as Options: Some Estimates of the Value of Holding European Patent Stocks." Econometrica 54(1986):755-784.

Parvin, David W., Jr., et al. Budgets for Major Crops, Delta of Mississippi, 1981. Mississippi Agricultural and Forest Experiment Station AECM.R. No. 115, Mississippi State University, January 1981.

Parvin, David W., Jr., J.M. Anderson, F.T. Cooke, Jr., A.M. Heagler and S.M. Toney. Specific Inputs and Prices Associated with Cotton Production Costs for the Mississippi Delta, 1975. Mississippi Agricultural and Forest Experiment Station, Mississippi State University, 1975.

Parvin, David W., Jr., J.M. Anderson, Fred T. Cooke, Jr., S.H. Holder, Jr., and J.G. Hamill. Specific Inputs and Prices Associated with Soybean Production Costs for the Mississippi Delta, 1975. Mississippi Agricultural and Forest Experiment Station Bulletin, selected monthly issues.

Parvin, David W., Jr., J.M. Anderson, Shelby H. Holder, Jr., and Fred T. Cooke, Jr. Costs of Production Estimates for Major Crops, Mississippi Delta, 1976. Mississippi Agricultural and Forestry Experiment Station Bulletin 843, Mississippi State University, February 1976.

Parvin, David W., Jr., James G. Hammill, and Fred T. Cooke, Jr. Budgets for Major Crops, Delta of Mississippi, 1980. Mississippi Agricultural and Forestry Experiment Station AECM.R. No. 95, Mississippi State University, February 1980.

Parvin, David W., Jr., Fred T. Cooke, Jr., S.H. Holder, Jr., and J.G. Hamill. Budgets for Major Crops, Mississippi Delta, 1977. Mississippi Agricultural and Forest Experiment Station Bulletin No. 850, Mississippi State University, February 1977.

Parvin, D.W., Jr., J.G. Hamill, J.M. Anderson, and F.T. Cooke, Jr. Specific Inputs and Prices for Food Grains, Feed Grains and Silage Crops, Mississippi Delta, 1975. Mississippi Agricultural and Forestry Experiment Station, Mississippi State University, 1975.

Parvin, David W., Jr., James G. Hammill, Fred T. Cooke, Jr., Shelby H. Holder, Jr., and David M. Cameron. Budgets for Major Crops, Delta of Mississippi, 1978. Mississippi Agricultural and Forest Experiment Station Information Bulletin 2, February 1978.

219

_____. <u>Budgets for Major Crops, Delta of Mississippi, 1979</u>.
Mississippi Agricultural and Forest Experiment Station Special
Edition, Mississippi State University, April 1979.

Paxton, Kenneth W. <u>Cotton and Soybean Production Cost Estimates for
Louisiana, 1974</u>. Department of Agricultural Economics and
Agribusiness Research Report No. 511, Louisiana State University
and Agricultural and Mechanical College, October 1976.

_____. <u>Cotton and Soybean Production Costs and Returns, 1977</u>.
Department of Agricultural Economics and Agribusiness Research
Report No. 515, Louisiana State University and Agriculture and
Mechanical College, March 1977.

_____. <u>Cotton and Soybean Production Costs and Returns, 1978</u>.
Department of Agricultural Economics and Agribusiness Research
Report No. 528, Louisiana State University and Agriculture and
Mechanical College, January 1978.

Paxton, Kenneth W., and Donald Huffman. <u>Projected Costs and Returns,
Cotton, Soybean, Corn, Red River and Central Areas</u>. Louisiana
Department of Agricultural Economics and Agribusiness Research
Report 547, Louisiana State University, January 1979.

Paxton Kenneth W., Donald Huffman, and Robert Boucher. <u>Projected Costs
and Returns, Cotton, Soybean, Corn, Red River and Central Areas</u>.
Louisiana Department of Agricultural Economics and Agribusiness
Research Report No. 565, Louisiana State University, January 1980.

Paxton, Kenneth W., and David R. Lavergne. <u>Projected Costs and Returns,
Cotton, Soybean, Corn, Red River and Central Areas, Louisiana,
1982</u>. Department of Agricultural Economics and Agribusiness
Research Report No. 589, Louisiana State University, January 1982.

_____. <u>Projected Cost and Returns, Cotton, Soybeans, Corn, Red River
and Central Areas, Louisiana, 1983</u>. Department of Agricultural
Economics and Agribusiness. Research Report No. 606, Louisiana
State University, January 1983.

_____. <u>Projected Costs and Returns Cotton, Soybeans, Rice, Corn,
Milo and Wheat Northeast Louisiana, 1984</u>. Department of
Agricultural Economics and Agribusiness Research Report No. 624,
Louisiana State University, January 1984.

_____. <u>Projected Costs and Returns Rice and Soybeans Southwest
Louisiana, 1984</u>. Department of Agricultural Economics and
Agribusiness Research Report No. 625, Louisiana State University,
January 1985.

Paxton, Kenneth W., David R. Lavergne, John Zacharias, and Brian McManus. Projected Costs and Returns, Cotton, Soybean, Rice, Corn, Milo, and Wheat, Northeast Louisiana, 1985. Department of Agricultural Economics and Agribusiness Research Report No. 634, Louisiana State University, January 1985.

Paxton, Kenneth W. and Joe Musick. Projected Cost and Returns Cotton-Soybeans-Corn-Rice Northeast Louisiana 1981. Department of Agricultural Economics and Agribusiness Research Report No. 575, Louisiana State University and Agricultural and Mechanical College, January 1981.

_____. Projected Costs and Returns, Cotton, Soybean, Corn, Rice, Northeast Louisiana, 1982. Department of Agricultural Economics and Agribusiness Research Report No. 588, Louisiana State University, January 1982.

Peters, D. S., D. W. Ahrenholz, and T. R. Rice. "Harvest and Value of Wetland Associated Fish and Shellfish." Wetland Functions and Values: The State of our Understanding, ed. P. E. Greeson, J. R. Clark, and J. E. Clark, pp. 606-617. Minneapolis: American Water Resources Association, 1979.

Peterson, Frederick M. and Anthony C. Fisher. "The Exploitation of Extractive Resources: A Survey." The Economic Journal 87(1977):681-721.

Phipps, Tim T. "Land Prices and Farm-Based Returns." American Journal of Agricultural Economics 66(1984):422-429.

Pindyck, Robert S. "The Optimal Exploration and Production of Nonrenewable Resources." Journal of Political Economy 86(1978):841-861.

_____. "Uncertainty in the Theory of Renewable Resource Markets." Review of Economic Studies 51(1984):289-303.

Pomfret, Richard. "The Mechanization of Reaping in Nineteenth-Century Ontario: A Case Study of the Pace and Causes of the Diffusion of Embodied Technological Change." Journal of Economic History 36(1976):399-411.

Pontryagin, L. S., V. G. Boltyanskii, R. V. Gamkrelidze, and E. F. Mischenko. The Mathematical Theory of Optimal Processes, translated by K. N. Trirogoff. New York: John Wiley & Sons, Inc., 1962.

Pope, Rulon D. "Supply Response and the Dispersion of Price Expectations." American Journal of Agricultural Economics 63(1981):161-163.

221

Prescott, David M. and Thanasis Stengos. "Bootstrapping Confidence Intervals: An Application to Forecasting the Supply of Pork." American Journal of Agricultural Economics 69(1987):266-273.

Putnam, John A., George M. Furnival, and J.S. McKnight. Management and Inventory of Southern Hardwoods. U.S. Department of Agriculture, Agriculture Handbook No. 181, November 1960.

Randall, Alan, and Emery N. Castle. "Land Resources and Land Markets." Handbook of Natural Resource and Energy Economics, Volume II, ed. Allen V. Kneese and James L. Sweeney, pp. 571-620. Amsterdam: North-Holland, 1985.

Rust, J. "Optimal Replacement of GMC Bus Engines: An Empirical Model of Harold Zurcher." Econometrica 55(1987):999-1033.

Sahal, D. Patterns of Technological Innovation. Reading, Massachusetts: Addison-Wesley, Inc., 1981.

Sargen, N. P. Tractorization in the United States. New York: Garland Press, 1979.

Shabman, Leonard. "Economic Incentives for Bottomland Conversion: The Role of Public Policy and Programs." Transactions of the Forty-fifth North American Wildlife and Natural Resources Conference, ed. Kenneth Sabol, pp. 402-412. Washington, D.C.: Wildlife Management Institute, 1980.

Shabman, Leonard A. and Sandra S. Batie. "Socioeconomic Functions and Values of Wetlands: A State-of-the-Art Review." Working draft for the U.S. Army Corps of Engineers, Vicksburg, Mississippi, November 1985.

Shaw, S. P., and C. G. Fredine. Wetlands of the United States: Their Extent and Their Value to Waterfowl and Other Wildlife. Washington, D.C.: U.S. Department of the Interior, Fish and Wildlife Service, Circular 39, 1956.

Shulstad, Robert N., Billy E. Herrington, Ralph D. May, and E. Moye Rutledge. "Estimating a Potential Cropland Supply Function for the Mississippi Delta Region." Land Economics 56(1980):457-464.

Shulstad, Robert N. and Ralph D. May. "Conversion of Noncropland to Cropland: The Prospects, Alternatives, and Implications." American Journal of Agricultural Economics 62(1980):1077-1083.

Shulstad, Robert N., Ralph D. May, and Billey E. Herrington, Jr. Cropland Conversion Study for the Mississippi Delta Region Final Report to Resources for the Future. Department of Agricultural Economics and Rural Sociology, University of Arkansas, Fayetteville, 1979.

Sickle, Charles C., and Duane D. Van Hooser. Forest Resources of Mississippi. U.S. Department of Agriculture Forest Service Resource Bulletin SO-17, 1969.

Smith, Owen E., Ralph D. May, W. Charles Walden, and Waymon A. Halbrook. Crop Budgets for Arkansas: Cost of Production Estimates for 1977. Agriculture Experiment Station Special Report No. 43, University of Arkansas, January 1977.

Smith, Vernon L. "Control Theory Applied to Natural and Environmental Resources: An Exposition." Journal of Environmental Economics and Management 4(1977):1-24.

Solow, Robert M. "The Economics of Resources or Resources of Economics." American Economic Review 64(1974):1-14.

Stavins, Robert. "Conversion of Forested Wetlands to Agricultural Uses: An Econometric Analysis of the Impact of Federal Programs on Wetland Depletion in the Lower Mississippi Alluvial Plain, 1935-1984." Final project report by the Environmental Defense Fund to the U.S. Department of the Interior, May 1986.

_____. "The Effects of Major Economic, Hydrologic, and Climatic Factors on Forested Wetland Depletion in the Lower Mississippi Alluvial Plain, 1935-1984." Report of project extension by the Environmental Defense Fund to the U.S. Department of the Interior, January 1987a.

_____. Conversion of Forested Wetlands to Agricultural Uses. Executive Summary. New York: Environmental Defense Fund, 1987b.

Sternitzke, Herbert S. Arkansas Forests. U.S. Department of Agriculture Forest Survey Release 84, 1960.

_____. "Impact of Changing Land Use on Delta Hardwood Forests." Journal of Forestry 74(1976):25-27.

_____. Louisiana Forests. U.S. Department of Agriculture Forest Service Resource Bulletin SO-7, 1965.

Sternitzke, Herbert S. and J. F. Christopher. "Land Clearing in the Lower Mississippi Valley." Southern Geographer 10(1970):63-66.

Sternitzke, Herbert S. and John A. Putnam. Forests of the Mississippi Delta. U.S. Department of Agriculture Forest Survey Release 78, October, 1956.

Stiglitz, Joseph E. "Monopoly and the Rate of Extraction of Exhaustible Resources." American Economic Review 66(1976):655-661.

Stoneman, Paul. The Economic Analysis of Technological Change. Oxford, England: Oxford University Press, 1983.

Takayama, T. and G. G. Judge. Spatial and Temporal Price and Allocation Models. Amsterdam: North-Holland Publishing Company, 1971.

Tchobanoglous, G. and G. L. Culp. Wetland Systems of Wastewater Treatment: An Engineering Assessment. University of California, Davis, 1980.

Theil, Henri. Economic Forecasts and Policy. Amsterdam: North-Holland Publishing Company, 1961.

Thibodeau, F. W. and Bart D. Ostro. "An Economic Analysis of Wetland Protection." Journal of Environmental Economics and Management 12(1981): 19-33.

Thomas, Charles E., and Carl V. Bylin. Louisiana Mid-cycle Survey Shows Change in Forest Resource Trends, U.S. Department of Agriculture Forest Service Resource Bulletin SO=86, Nov. 1982.

Thomas, Charles E., and William H. McWilliams. Midcycle Survey of Mississippi's Forest Resources. U.S. Department of Agriculture Forest Service. Unpublished report.

Tiner, Ralph W., Jr. Wetlands of the United States: Current Status and Recent Trends. Washington, D.C.: U.S. Department of the Interior, Fish and Wildlife Service, March 1984.

Toon, T. G. "Factors Affecting Land Use Change in the Lower Mississippi Alluvium." Unpublished manuscript, U.S. Department of Agriculture, Economic Research Service, 1976.

Turner, R. E. and N. J. Craig. "Recent Areal Changes in Louisiana's Forested Wetland Habitat." Louisiana Academy of Sciences 43(1980):61-68.

U.S. Army Corps of Engineers. Alchafalaya Basin Floodway System, Louisiana. New Orleans, Louisiana: Feasibility Study, prepared by the New Orleans District, January 1982.

_____. Aloha-Rigolette Area, Grant and Rapides Parishes, Louisiana Project Report. Vicksburg, Mississippi, 1944.

_____. Annual Report of the Chief Engineers on Civil Works Activities. Washington, D.C., 1940-1984.

_____. Below Red River, Louisiana General Design Memorandum. Vicksburg, Mississippi. Design Memorandum prepared by the Vicksburg District, 1980.

_____. Boeuf River and Tributaries, Louisiana Reevaluation Report. Vicksburg, Mississippi: Draft Main Report and Environmental Impact Statement prepared by the Vicksburg District, January 1984a.

_____. The Bushley Bayou Project. Vicksburg, Mississippi: General Design Memorandum No. 38, prepared by the Vicksburg District, December 1977.

_____. Charles River Watershed, Massachusetts Natural Valley Storage Project, Design Memorandum No. 1, Hydrologic Analysis. Waltham, Massachusetts: New England Division, 1976.

_____. Choctaw Bayou and Tributaries Detailed Project Report. New Orleans, Louisiana: Report prepared by the New orleans District, March 1968.

_____. Environmental Impact Statement for the Sicily Island Levee Project. Vicksburg, Mississippi: Vicksburg District, September 1981e.

_____. Flood Control, Mississippi River and Tributaries, Yazoo River Basin, Upper Auxiliary Channel Alternative. Vicksburg, Mississippi: General Design Memorandum No. 41, prepared by the Vicksburg District, September 1975.

_____. Mississippi River and Tributaries Comprehensive Review Report. Annex H: St. Francis and L'Anguille Basins, Missouri and Arkansas. Memphis, Tennessee: Report prepared by the Memphis District, 1959a.

_____. Mississippi River and Tributaries Comprehensive Review Report. Annex L: Yazoo Backwater Project. Vicksburg, Mississippi: Report prepared by the Vicksburg District, 1959b.

_____. Mississippi River and Tributaries Comprehensive Review Report. Annex M: Big Sunflower River Basin, Mississippi. Vicksburg, Mississippi, 1959c.

_____. Mississippi River and Tributaries Comprehensive Review Report. Annex N: Boeuf and Tensas Rivers and Bayou Macon. Vicksburg, Mississippi, November 1959d.

_____. Mississippi River and Tributaries Comprehensive Review Report. Annex O: North Bank Arkansas River Levees. Vicksburg, Mississippi: Report prepared by the Vicksburg District, 1959e.

_____. Mississippi River and Tributaries Comprehensive Review Report. Annex P: Grand Prairie Region and Bayou Meto Basin, Arkansas. Vicksburg, Mississippi: Report prepared by the Vicksburg District, 1959f.

_____. Mississippi River and Tributaries Comprehensive Review Report. Annex Q: Yazoo Headwater Project. Vicksburg, Mississippi: Report prepared by the Vicksburg District, 1959g.

_____. Mississippi River and Tributaries Comprehensive Review Report. Annex R: Red River Backwater Area. New Orleans, Louisiana: Report prepared by the New Orleans District, 1959h.

_____. Ouachita River Basin, Bayou Bartholomew and Tributaries, Arkansas and Louisiana. Vicksburg, Mississippi: Design Memorandum No. 1, Resume of Project prepared by the Vicksburg District, November 1969.

_____. Ouachita River Levees, Louisiana Letter Report. Vicksburg, Mississippi: Report Prepared by the Vicksburg District for the Chief of Engineers, May 1966a.

_____. Ouachita River Basin, Ouachita River Levees Interim Study, Louisiana. Vicksburg, Mississippi: Draft Feasibility Report and Environmental Impact Statement prepared by the Vicksburg District, May 1984b.

_____. Pilot Study Performed under the Planning Assistance to States Program by the New Orleans District. Unpublished.

_____. Project Maps and Completion Schedule for the St. Francis Basin Project. Unpublished data from the Memphis District.

_____. Project Maps, U.S. Corps of Engineers, Little Rock District, Little Rock, Arkansas, 1984c.

_____. Project Maps, U.S. Army Corps of Engineers, Memphis District, Memphis, Tennessee.

_____. 1983 Project Maps, U.S. Army Corps of Engineers, New Orleans District, New Orleans, Louisiana, 1983a.

_____. 1983 Project Maps, U.S. Army Corps of Engineers Vicksburg District, Vicksburg, Mississippi, 1983b.

_____. Review Report Bayou Bartholomew and Tributaries, Arkansas and Louisiana. Vicksburg, Mississippi: Report prepared by the Vicksburg District, November 15, 1962.

_____. Review Report East Bank Warren to Wilkinson Counties, Mississippi. Vicksburg, Mississippi: Report prepared by the Vicksburg District, March 1971.

_____. Review Report Lake Chicot, Arkansas. Vicksburg, Mississippi: Report prepared by the Vicksburg District, May 2, 1966b.

_____. The Sicily Island Area Levee Project. Vicksburg, Mississippi: General Design Memorandum No. 15, prepared by the Vicksburg District, October 1978.

226

_____. Tensas River Basin Excluding Bayou Macon, Louisiana, Project, Phase I -- General Design Memorandum No. 25, Appendix 9, Land Use Analysis. Vicksburg, Mississippi: Vicksburg District Office, October, 1981a.

_____. Tensas River Basin Excluding Bayou Macon, Louisiana. Reevaluation Report. Final Main Report and Final Environmental Impact Statement. Vicksburg, Mississippi: Vicksburg District Office, March 1984d.

_____. Water Resources Development by the U.S. Army Corps of Engineers in Arkansas. Dallas, Texas, January 1981b.

_____. Water Resources Development by the U.S. Army Corps of Engineers in Louisiana, 1981. New Orleans, Louisiana, 1981c.

_____. Water Resources Development by the U.S. Army Corps of Engineers in Mississippi. Vicksburg, Mississippi, January 1981d.

_____. Yazoo Headwater Flood Control Project Report. Vicksburg, Mississippi: Report prepared by the Vicksburg District, June 1949.

U.S. Coast and Geodetic Survey. Map of Mississippi Flood of 1927 Showing Flooded Areas and Field of Operations. Washington, D.C.: Map prepared from data furnished by the U.S. Army Corps of Engineers, 1927.

U.S. Congress. Wetlands: Their Use and Regulation. Office of Technology Assessment, OTA-O-206, March 1984.

U.S. Congress, House of Representatives. Amite River and Tributaries. House Document No. 419, 84th Congress, 2nd Session, June 6, 1956.

U.S. Congress, House of Representatives, Committee on Flood Control. Flood Control on the Lower Mississippi River. House Document No. 259, 77th Congress, 1st Session, 1941.

U.S. Congress, House of Representatives, Committee on Public Works. Mississippi River and Tributaries, Vicksburg-Yazoo Area, Mississippi. House Document 85, 83rd Congress, 1st Session, 1953.

U.S. Congress, Senate, Committee on Public Works. Ouachita River and Tributaries, Arkansas and Louisiana. Senate Document No. 117, 81st Congress, 1st Session, 1950.

_____. Steele Bayou, Yazoo River (Lower Tributaries). Mississippi Senate Document No. 91-74, 91st Congress, 2nd Session, 1970.

U.S. Council of Economic Advisers. Economic Report of the President. Washington, D.C.: U.S. Government Printing Office, 1978.

U.S. Council of Economic Advisers. Economic Report of the President. Washington, D.C.: U.S. Government Printing Office, 1985.

U.S. Department of Agriculture. Agricultural Statistics. Washington, D.C.: U.S. Government Printing Office, various years.

_____. Arkansas Cotton Statistics. Washington, D.C.: Bureau of Agricultural Economics, July 1951.

_____. Arkansas Crop Statistics, 1960-1979. Arkansas Crop and Livestock Reporting Service, Report Series 261, February 1981.

_____. Arkansas County Estimates: Annual Statistics on Average Yield and Production for Selected Crops. Arkansas Crop and Livestock Reporting Service, selected years.

_____. Basic Statistics of the National Inventory of Soil and Water Conservation Needs. SB-317. Washington, D.C., August 1962.

_____. Basic Statistics, 1977 National Resources Inventory. SB-686. Washington, D.C., December 1982.

_____. Corn: Background for 1985 Farm Legislation. Economic Research Service, Agriculture Information Bulletin No. 471, September 1984a.

_____. Cotton: Background for 1985 Farm Legislation. Economic Research Service, Agriculture Information Bulletin No. 476, September 1984b.

_____. Evolution of the Small Watershed Program: Changes in Public Law 566 Watershed Protection and Flood Prevention Program, 1954-1972. Agricultural Economic Report No. 262, prepared by the Economic Research Service of the Natural Economics Division of the U.S. Department of Agriculture, June 1974a.

_____. Forest Statistics for Arkansas Counties. New Orleans, Louisiana: Forest Service Resource Bulletin SO-76, 1980.

_____. Forest Statistics for Mississippi Counties. New Orleans, Louisiana: U.S. Department of Agriculture Forest Service Resource Bulletin.

_____. Forests of Louisiana, 1953-54. New Orleans, Louisiana: Forest Service Forest Survey Release No. 75, April 1955.

_____. List of Soil Conservation Service Public Law 566 and 534 Projects in Arkansas, Louisiana, and Mississippi. Washington, D.C.: Unpublished data prepared by O.P. Lee.

_____. Mississippi Agriculture Report. Mississippi Crop and Livestock Reporting Service, Vol. 84-12, June 1984c.

_____. Mississippi Forests. New Orleans, Louisiana: Forest Service Forest Survey Release 81, 1958.

_____. Multiple-Purpose Watershed Projects under Public Law 566. Program Aid No. 575, prepared by the Soil Conservation Service, 1984d.

_____. National Inventory of Soil and Water Conservation Needs. Washington, D.C.: Soil Conservation Service, Statistical Bulletin 461, 1967.

_____. National Resources Inventory: A Guide for Users of the 1982 NRI Data Files. Washington, D.C.: Soil Conservation Service and Statistical Laboratory of Iowa State University, October 1984h.

_____. 1982 Agricultural Statistics for Arkansas. Arkansas Crop and Livestock Reporting Service, Report Series 280, August 1983.

_____. Project Maps for Selected Projects in Arkansas, Louisiana and Mississippi. Maps furnished by the State Offices of the Soil Conservation Service.

_____. Rice: Background for 1985 Farm Legislation. Economic Research Service, Agriculture Information Bulletin No. 470, September 1984e.

_____. Small Watershed Projects. Program Aid No. 1354, prepared by the Soil Conservation Service, 1984f.

_____. Soybeans: Background for 1985 Farm Legislation. Economic Research Service, Agriculture Information Bulletin No. 472, September 1984g.

_____. St. Francis River and Tributaries (Arkansas) Mississippi River and Tributaries Project Study Report on Present and Anticipated Agricultural Conditions. Little Rock, Arkansas: Report prepared by the Public Affairs Office of the Lower Mississippi Valley Division, March 1973.

_____. Stumpage and Log Prices for 1938. Washington, D.C.: Statistical Bulletin 71, February 1940.

_____. Stumpage and Log Prices. Washington, D.C.: Statistical Bulletin 74, 1941.

_____. Stumpage and Log Prices, 1940. Washington, D.C.: Statistical Bulletin 76, 1942.

_____. Stumpage and Log Prices, 1943. Washington, D.C.: Statistical Bulletin 80, 1945.

_____. What is a Watershed? Program Aid No. 420, prepared by the Soil Conservation Service, 1974b.

U.S. Department of Agriculture and Iowa State University Statistical Laboratory. "National Resources Inventory -- A Guide for Users of the 1982 NRI Data Files." Unpublished manuscript, October 1984.

U.S. Department of Agriculture, Mississippi Agricultural and Forestry Experiment Station and Mississippi Cooperative Extension Service. U.S. Department of Agriculture Estimated Costs and Returns, Crops, Lower Coastal Area of Mississippi, 1984. Agricultural Economics Report No. 16, 1984.

U.S. Department of Agriculture and Mississippi Department of Agriculture and Commerce. Mississippi Agricultural Statistics 1954-1973. Mississippi Crop and Livestock Reporting Service Supplement No. 9, 1975.

_____. Mississippi Agricultural Statistics 1969-1977. Mississippi Crop and Livestock Reporting Service Supplement No. 12, 1978.

_____. Mississippi Agricultural Statistics 1974-1980. Mississippi Crop and Livestock Reporting Service Supplement No. 15, 1981.

_____. Mississippi Agricultural Statistics 1980-1981. Mississippi Crop and Livestock Reporting Service Supplement No. 16, 1982.

U.S. Department of Agriculture and Commerce. Base Book of Mississippi Agriculture, 1866-1953. Mississippi Crop and Livestock Reporting Service, 1955.

_____. Mississippi Agricultural Statistics 1981-1982. Mississippi Crop and Livestock Reporting Service Supplement No. 17, 1983.

U.S. Department of Agriculture, Economic Research Service. Sodbusting: Land Use Change and Farm Programs. Agricultural Economic Report No. 536. Washington, D.C., June 1985.

_____. Cropland Use and Supply: Outlook and Situation Report. CUS-2. Washington, D.C., September 1985.

U.S. Department of Agriculture, Economics, Statistics and Cooperative Service. Costs of Producing Selected Crops in the United States, 1976, 1977, and Projections for 1978. Washington, D.C., March 1978.

_____. Oklahoma State University. Various photocopies of corn, soybeans, and cotton budgets.

U.S. Department of Agriculture, Economics and Statistics Service. Costs of Producing Selected Crops in the Unites States, 1978, 1979, 1980, and Projections for 1981. Washington, D.C., August 1981.

U.S. Department of Agriculture, Office of Information. Federal Crop Insurance Corporation. Office of Governmental and Public Affairs, December 1983.

U.S. Department of Commerce, Bureau of the Census. Census of Agriculture. Washington, D.C., 1924 - 1982a.

_____. Census of Manufacturers. Washington, D.C., 1937 - 1982b.

_____. Census of Population. Washington, D.C., 1930 - 1982c.

_____. County Business Patterns. Washington, D.C., 1956, 1959, 1962, 1964-1981d.

_____. Local Population Estimates. Washington, D.C.: Current Population Reports Series P-26, No. 84-52-C, March 1985e.

U.S. Department of the Interior. Classification of Wetlands and Deepwater Habitats of the United States. Fish and Wildlife Service, FWS/OBS-79/31, Washington, D.C., 1979.

Utz, Keith A., William E. Balmer, Henry D. Hammond, and Frank Shropshire. Investment Analysis of Bottomland Hardwoods. Washington, D.C.: U.S. Department of Agriculture, Forest Service, April 1977.

Van Sickle, Charles C. Arkansas Forests Resource Patterns. U.S. Department of Agriculture Resource Bulletin SO-24, 1970.

Varian, Hal R. Microeconomic Analysis. Second edition. New York: W. W. Norton & Company, 1984.

Walden, W. Charles, and Ralph D. May. Arkansas Cotton Budgets, 1979 Production Cost Estimates. Agricultural Experiment Station Special Report No. 68, University of Arkansas, January 1979a.

_____. Arkansas Cotton Budgets, 1980 Production Cost Estimates. Agricultural Experiment Station Special Report No. 79, University of Arkansas, March 1980a.

_____. Arkansas Feed Grain Budgets, 1979 Production Cost Estimates. Agricultural Experiment Station Special Report No. 70, University of Arkansas, February 1979b.

_____. Arkansas Feed Grain Budgets, 1980 Production Cost Estimates. Agricultural Experiment Station Special Report No. 83, University of Arkansas, April 1980b.

Walden, W. Charles, Ralph D. May, and Ewell R. Welch. Arkansas Cotton Budgets, 1978 Production Cost Estimates. Agriculture Experiment Station Special Report No. 58, University of Arkansas, January 1978a.

_____. Arkansas Feed Grain Budgets, 1978 Production Cost Estimates. Agricultural Experiment Station Special Report No. 60, University of Arkansas, April 1978b.

_____. Arkansas Feed Grain Budgets, 1980 Production Cost Estimates. Agricultural Experiment Station Special Report No. 83, University of Arkansas, April 1980.

Weisbrod, Burton A. "Collective-Consumption Services of Individual-Consumption Goods." Quarterly Journal of Economics 78(1964):471-477.

Wharton, C. H. and W. M. Kitchens. The Ecology of Bottomland Hardwood Swamps of the Southeast: A Community Profile. U.S. Fish and Wildlife Service, Biological Services Program, FWS/OBS-81/37. Washington, D.C., 1982.

Whatley, W. C. "Institutional Change and Mechanization in the Cotton South." Unpublished Ph.D. thesis, Stanford University, 1983.

Wheeler, Philip R. Forest Statistics for Arkansas. U.S. Department of Agriculture Forest Survey Release 71, March, 1953.

White, Halbert. "A Heteroscedasticity-Consistent Covariance Matrix and a Direct Test for Heteroscedasticity." Econometrica 48(1980a):721-746.

Wilson, W.T., and Stuart L. Bryan. Index Numbers of Prices Received for Arkansas Farm Products, 1910-1937. Agricultural Experiment Station Bulletin No. 353, University of Arkansas, June 1938.

Wolf, Scott Allen. "The Sport Fishing Conservation Stamp: A Proposal for Wetland Protection." Unpublished B.A. thesis, Harvard College, 1988.

Woolf, Williard F., and William L. Brugman. Effects of Production Practices on Soybean Yields, Costs and Returns Southwest Louisiana Rice Area. Department of Agricultural Economics and Agribusiness Research Report 454, Louisiana State University and Agricultural and Mechanical College, June 1973.

Woolf, Williard F., and Patrick D. Leary. Effects of Production Practices on Soybean Yields, Costs and Returns Macon Ridge Area, Louisiana. Department of Agricultural Economics and Agribusiness Research Report No. 497, Louisiana State University and Agricultural and Mechanical College, December 1975.

Woolf, Williard F., and Blake J. Vidrine. Costs and Returns for Soybeans Southwest Louisiana Rice Area 1978, Projected. Department of Agricultural Economics and Agribusiness Research Report No. 526 Louisiana State University and Agricultural and Mechanical College January 1978.

_____. Costs and Returns for Soybeans Southwest Louisiana Rice Area 1979, Projected. Department of Agricultural Economics and Agribusiness Research Report No. 545, Louisiana State University and Agricultural and Mechanical College, January 1979.

Woolf, Williard F., Blake J. Vidrine, and Adolf Martinez. <u>Costs and Returns for Soybeans Southwest Louisiana Rice Area Projections for 1977</u>. Department of Agricultural Economics and Agribusiness Research Report No. 512, Louisiana State University and Agricultural and Mechanical College, December 1976.

Wright, J. O. <u>Swamp and Overflowed Land in the United States</u>. Washington, D.C.: U.S. Department of Agriculture, Circular 76, 1907.

Young, Douglas L. "Risk Preferences of Agricultural Producers: Their Use in Extension and Research." <u>American Journal of Agricultural Economics</u> 61(1979):1063-1070.

Young, Robert A., and Robert H. Haveman. "Economics of Water Resources: A Survey." <u>Handbook of Natural Resource and Energy Economics, Volume II</u>, ed. Allen V. Kneese and James L. Sweeney, pp. 465-529. Amsterdam: North-Holland, 1985.

Zacharias, Tom, and Brian McManus. <u>Projected Cost and Returns, Rice and Soybeans, Southwest Louisiana, 1985</u>. Department of Agricultural Economics and Agribusiness Research Report No. 635, Louisiana State University, January 1985.

Zeckhauser, Richard J. "Resource Allocation with Probabilistic Individual Preferences." <u>American Economic Review</u> 59(1969):546-552.

Zellner, Arnold. "An Efficient Method of Estimating Seemingly Unrelated Regressions and Tests of Aggregation Bias." <u>Journal of the American Statistical Association</u> 57(1962):348-368.

_____. "Estimators for Seemingly Unrelated Regression Equations: Some Exact Finite Sample Results." <u>Journal of the American Statistical Association</u> 58(1963):977-992.